The Works Of The Earls Of Rochester, Roscomon And Dorset V1: The Dukes Of Devonshire, Buckinghamshire, Etc.

John Wilmot

THE
WORKS

Of the EARLS of

ROCHESTER,
ROSCOMON,

AND

DORSET;

The DUKES of

DEVONSHIRE,
BUCKINGHAMSHIRE, &c.

WITH

MEMOIRS of their LIVES.

In Two VOLUMES.

With ADDITIONS, and Adorned with CUTS.

LONDON:
Printed in the Year M.DCC.LII.

THE

CONTENTS

OF THE

Firſt VOLUME.

A 2   His

❀❀❀❀❀❀❀❀❀❀❀❀❀❀❀❀

The WORKS of the Earl of ROCHESTER, *viz.*

On

The CONTENTS. v

A

vi The CONTENTS.

SOME

SOME
MEMOIRS
OF THE
Earl of ROCHESTER.

To the Duchefs of MAZARIN.

MONG the Wonders your GRACE
every Day performs, it is not, perhaps,
the leaft, Madam, of making me fhake
off that habitual Lazinefs I have contracted, which has almoft begot an Averfion to Writing, efpecially on fuch a
Subject, and to fuch a Reader; both fufficient Checks to a
Man who could confider any Thing but your GRACE's
Commands. No, Madam, your Defires are never to be
difobeyed by me, however difficult the Tafk may prove
which you impofe; efpecially, when I remember, that
though you have the moft piercing Wit, as well as the
moft piercing Eyes in the World, yet you have too much
Juftice to be fevere on this Effay of my Obedince, not

B   Prefumption,

Prefumption, becaufe I chofe rather to forfeit your good Opinion of my Underftanding, than Refpect. I am fenfible that I take on me a Province far beyond my Capacity to execute; but I can venture at any Thing rather than your GRACE's Difpleafure.

PERHAPS your GRACE does not expect that I fhould carry you back beyond thofe fprightly Hours of Lord ROCHESTER's Life, when he fired the Breafts of Ladies with Love, and wounded thofe of Men with Envy. But, Madam, fince you have fet me a Tafk, I muft perform it in all its Parts, according to the Methods of thofe Gentlemen that have prefented the World with the Lives of Heroes; who always begin with their Parentage and Birth, and thence lead you by Degrees into a thorough Acquaintance of their Spirit, Temper, and Manners. This muft I do, Madam, with our Noble Lord, from his Birth to his early Death.

HIS Father was *Henry* Lord *Wilmot,* afterwards Earl of *Rochefter,* a Gentleman very eminent and renown'd in the *English* Hiftories of the Civil Wars, for his Valour and Fidelity both to the Father and Son. This gained him the chief Confidence of King CHARLES II. who entrufted his Perfon to him after the unfortunate Battle of *Worcefter;* which Truft he difcharged with fo much Conduct, as well as Faith, that the King was conveyed out of *England* into *France* chiefly by his Care, Application, and Vigilance. Such was his Father. And for the Mother of our Hero, fhe was of the ancient Family of the *Saint Johns,* of *Wiltfhire;* a Lady of equal Parts and Beauty, as I have been informed, and which I am induced to believe, Madam, becaufe the more charming the Object of Love is, the more fierce are our Defires, and the greater Energy is there in our Embraces. I

may

may, fay of him, with more Juftice and Reafon, what Mr. *Dryden* faid of *David* and *Abfalom.*

> *Whether, infpir'd by fome diviner Luft,*
> *His Father got him with a greater Guft.*

But leaving an Enquiry fo nice, I return to my Subject, by informing your GRACE, that the Son, *John Wilmot,* Earl of *Rochefter,* (Vifcount *Athlone* in *Ireland,* and Baron *Adderbury* in *Oxfordfhire,*) was born at *Ditchly* near *Woodftock,* in the fame County, (the Scene of many of his Pleafures, and of his Death,) in the Year 1648, diftinguifhed from other Years by two extraordinary Events, the Martyrdom of King CHARLES I, by a prevailing Party of his Subjects, at his own Palace-Window, and the Birth of my Lord *Rochefter,* as eminent for Wit and Gallantry, as that unfortunate Prince was for Piety and Religion. I will not here, Madam, enter into a Comparifon of their feveral Merits, or of the Preference of what each excelled in ; for, notwithftanding the Opinion fome have entertained of the Latitude of my religious Principles, I muft affure your GRACE, I think there is no Comparifon between them: All I fhall fay, is, the *King* was fitter for the *World* to which he went from the *Scaffold;* and his *Lordfhip* for *that* he entered into from his Mother's *Womb.*

My Lord's Father had the ill Fortune to reap none of the Rewards and Advantages of his Sufferings and Loyalty, becaufe he died before the RESTORATION, leaving his Son, as the principal Part of his Inheritance, his Titles of Honour, and the Merit of thofe extraordinary Services which he had done the Crown. But the prudent Conduct of the Mother fupplied the dotal Eftate left by the Father; for fhe managed it with fuch Addrefs, that his Education was ftill preferved fuitable to his Quality.

HERE,

HERE, Madam, were I to follow thofe famous Authors, who have given us the Lives of the ancient Heroes and Poets, I fhould entertain your GRACE with the Scene of all the extraordinary Accidents and pretty Events of his Childhood, not forgetting any of thofe little pert Sayings or Actions, which might be the Forerunners of that eminent Excellence he difcovered when he came to Man's Eftate. Nay, if all thefe important Affairs, by the Negligence of thofe who fhould have conveyed them to us, were loft, I fhould, to raife the Character of our Hero, give fo neceffary an Indulgence to Invention, as by that to form fome wonderful and early Promifes of his future Greatnefs: But not being fo fond of my own Fancy, as to write fictitious Wonders of his Childhood, and all thofe that were real, being not to be found in the authentick Records of Time, I fhall not prefume to amufe your GRACE with infipid Fables, which can neither entertain nor inftruct; but only let you know, that he was fo extremely docile, and made fuch an eafy Progrefs in Learning, on his firft Application to Letters at School, as difcovered the Seeds of that great Genius which afterwards appeared more confpicuoufly in his riper Years: For there, among Boys, firft fhone thofe fprightly Parts which afterwards dazzled the Eyes, and drew the Admiration of Men, and the Hearts of the Ladies.

WE may venture to fay, that it was at School he laid fuch a Foundation of the *Latin* Tongue, and obtained fo great a Maftery of it, that he never loft a true Tafte of any peculiar Beauty of thofe great Authors in that Language in its moft flourifhing Age; I mean that of *Horace*, *Virgil*, *Ovid*, and the like; in which he found thofe tranfporting Pleafures, Madam, which cannot be conveyed to your GRACE thro' any of the Tranflations we have;

tho'

tho' the *French* have made greater Progress in that Art, and have applied themselves more to it than any other Nation whatever, that I know of : Whether it be that the Moderns want Genius to come up to the Energy and Excellence of the Antients ; or that great Part of the Charm of the ancient Poets be in the Expression, which it is impossible to preserve in any less perfect Language ; and in spite of our Vanity, we must allow, that even the *French* cannot come up to the *Latin,* either in Strength, Harmony, or Copiousness. In short, Madam, no Pleasure can be so great to a Man of Sense, except it be your GRACE's Conversation ; which receives *from,* and gives fresh Force *to* the inevitable Charms of your Person.

If he began to lay the Foundation of Learning at School, he finished the Building on his Removal to the University of *Oxford* ; where, in *Wadham College,* under the Tuition of Dr. *Blanford,* (afterwards successively Bishop of *Oxford* and *Worcester,*) and the more immediate Care of Mr. *Phineas Berry,* Fellow of that College, he gained all the Knowledge, the Gaiety of the Times, and that universal Spirit of Joy and Pleasure which spread over all these fortunate Islands at the *Restoration,* would permit. For my Lord here, in the Arms of the Muses, and even under the Restriction of a Tutor, formed the first Accesses of Pleasure, so tempting and engaging to his Soul ; a Soul so adapted to them, that his Application to Study soon grew slack, and was, in a little Time, so totally lost in the Pursuit of Joys more agreeable to his Inclination, that he never entertained any Thoughts of returning to his Studies ; till, in his Travels, the fine Address of his Governor, Dr. *Balfour,* by engaging him with Books suitable to his Inclinations, won him to those Charms which he had by a youthful Levity forsaken :

B 3 Which

Which being backed by Reason more strong in him now, and a riper Taste of the Pleasures of Learning, which must gain the Heart of a sensible Man; and these his Governor always took care to place in so good a Light, that by Degrees he made him perfectly in Love with Knowledge; in the Pursuit of which he always spent those Hours which he sometimes stole from the *Witty* and the *Fair.*

I do not at all doubt, Madam, but your Grace is quite tired with this Part of his Lordship's Life, wherein Love and Beauty had so little Share; you must, Madam, think these so many tedious Impertinencies; yet, since you have obliged me to write a Life, you must undergo the Penance of those Modes and Forms which the Task, your own Authority imposed, requires. He has all this while been cultivating those fine Parts, and nourishing that great Genius, which is now to appear in the *Drawing-Room* among the Ladies, with Force not inferior to their Eyes, in their gayest Dawn, but of larger Extent in Duration and Power. Till now, he has been laying up a Fund for all that Spirit and Wit, which afterwards was the Terror of Knaves, Fools, and little Pretenders of all Sorts, and the Delight of the Witty, Honest, and Meritorious.

He now, Madam, comes from Travel, at the early Age of Eighteen, when other more backward Gentlemen are scarce fit to set out. But my Lord was not to take Measures from the common Race of Men; he was distinguished sufficiently by Nature from most Persons, who could therefore be no Rule to him. His Quality, Spirit, and Inclination, soon led him to Court, with the Advantage of such Endowments as few brought thither: For his Person was graceful, tho' tall and slender; his Mien and Shape having something extremely agreeable; and for his Mind, it discovered Charms not to be withstood:

ftood : His Wit was ftrong, fubtle, fublime, and fprightly : He was perfectly well bred, and adorned with a natural Modefty, which wonderfully became him : He was Mafter both of the ancient and modern Authors, well as of all thofe in the modern *French* and *Italian,* to fay nothing of the *Englijh,* which were worthy the Perufal of a Man of fine Senfe. From all which he drew a Converfation fo engaging, that none could enjoy without Admiration and Delight, and few without Love.

HE had not been long at Court, when infpired with a Defire of fhewing his Courage, he chofe the Sea for the Scene of Action, and under the Earl of *Sandwich* and Sir *Edward Sprogge,* he gave uncommon Proofs of an intrepid Soul ; however, he afterwards loft that Character in private Broils. But tho' there may very eafily be a Reafon affigned for fo great a Contrariety of Temper in the fame Man at different Times, on different Occafions, and in different Circumftances, yet the Difquifition is too philofophical and jejune to entertain your GRACE with : Let it fuffice to fay, that we differ not from *one another,* more than from *ourfelves,* at different Times.

HAVING fignalized himfelf in War, he returns to Court, where Pleafure and Love kept their perpetual Rendezvous, under the aufpicious Smiles of a Monarch made by Nature for all Enjoyments of the moft elegant Defires. Since his Travels, he had contracted a Temperance, which, being in itfelf extraordinary in an Age fo diffolute, was foon, tho' by infenfible Degrees, laid afide, and a Loofe given to all the Pleafures of the Court and Town, of Love and Wine ; for both which he was qualified by Nature, having a ftrong Conftitution, tho', by too frequent, and too continual Exceffes, he broke it, and died a young Man. As a Beauty owes her Ruin to her own Charms, fo did my Lord ; for as Beau-

ty

ty draws a Crowd of Adorers, and makes every one press for a Joy that so few can grant; Importunity, Opportunity, Affiduity, and Variety of Objects, win the Fair to surrender a Jewel that cannot be restored. Thus the uncommon Charms of my Lord's Conversation drew every Man of Taste to engage him with a Bottle; his pleasing Extravagance increasing with his Liquor, the Frolicks which that inspired affording Talk for the Town, as well as the Adventures in them for some Time after. It was not, indeed, Madam, for every Man to venture a Debauch with him; because, for a Jest, and Diversion, he would often hazard his Life; and that many would think paying too dear for his Conversation.

But he often mingled his Amours with his Frolicks, and covered the Extravagance of his Appetite under that of his Fancy. I will not detain your GRACE long with any of these Adventures, nor shall I give you many of them, tho' I might a thousand, because I would not swell my Account beyond the Bounds of a Letter.

His Talent of Satire was admirable; and in it he spared no Body, not even the King himself, whose Weakness for some of his Mistresses he endeavoured to cure by several Methods, that is, either by seducing them from him, in spite of the Indulgence and Liberality they felt from a Royal Gallant, or by severely lampooning them, or him, on various Occasions; which generally the King (who was a Man of Wit and Pleasure, as well as my Lord) took for the natural Sallies of his Genius, and meant as Sports of Fancy, more than the Efforts of Malice. Yet, either by a too frequent Repetition, or a too close and poignant Violence, he banished him the Court, for a *Satire* made directly on him.

THE

THE Duke of *Buckingham* * being at the same Time under Difgrace for Things of another Nature, they refolved to go in Search of Adventures; among many of which, this was one: There happens an Inn on *Newmarket* Road to be lett; they difguife themfelves fit for the Perfons they were to affume, and jointly take this Inn, in which, each in his Turn, officiates as Mafter. But this being not done either for abfconding from the Anger of their Sovereign, or the Sake of felling Ale, they foon fet themfelves to purfue the more pleafing Aim of their Rambles. They having obferved fuch of the pretty Girls of the Country as they fancied moft, (they confidered not whether Maids, Wives, or Widows,) to gain Opportunities, they invited the Country round, at leaft thofe Neighbours that had thefe Wives or Daughters, to frequent Feafts; where the Men were plied hard with good Liquor, and the Women fufficiently warmed, to make but as little Refiftance as would be agreeable to their Inclinations: Doubly qualifying both Sexes, the Men with Wine and ftrong Liquors, and the Women with Love.

YOUR GRACE muft not imagine, that this Sort of Life could be of any long Duration, becaufe Feafts fo common, and that without any Thing to pay, muft give a fhrewd Sufpicion that the Hofts muft foon break, or that they were of Circumftances much fuperior to the Pofts they were in. This they were fenfible of, nor much concerned about it, fince they were feldom fond of long continuing the fame Sort of Adventures; *Variety* being the Life of their Enjoyments. It was, befides, near the Time of his Majefty's going to *Newmarket*; when they defigned that a Difcovery of their real Plots

---

* *The Right Honourable* George Villers.

B 5

fhould clear them from the Imputation of being concerned in any more pernicious to his Majefty and his eafy
Government. Thefe two Conjunctures meeting, they
thought themfelves obliged to difpatch two important
Adventures, which they had not yet been able to com-
pafs. There was an old covetous Hunks in the Neighbourhood, who had, notwithftanding his Age, got a very
pretty young Wife: In the Poetical Age, fhe would have
been taken for one of the Wood-Nymphs: SALMACIS
was not more charming, nor more fit for the Joy. Her
Hufband was as watchful of her as of his Money, nor
ever trufted her out of his Sight, but under the Cuftody
of an old ill-natur'd, ugly, hypocritical Sifter, who having never experienced the Joys of Love herfelf, had the
true Envy of an old Maid to all that were young and
handfome. Our noble Hofts had no Manner of Doubt
of his accepting a Treat, (for he had done many) loving a Debauch with all his Heart, when it coft him nothing, elfe the moft temperate and abftemious Man
alive; but then they could never prevail on him
to bring his Wife along with him, notwithftanding
they urged the Prefence of fo many good Wives of the
Neighbourhood to keep her Company. All their Study
was then, how to charm the *Dragon* that he left behind
to guard the delicious *Hefperian* Fruit, which he could
neither eat himfelf, nor would fuffer any one elfe.

SUCH Difficulties as thefe did not ufe to puzzle their
Invehtions: It was therefore agreed, that my Lord *Rochefter* fhould be dreft in Women's Cloaths; and while
the Hufband was engaged by my Lord Duke, and the
good Liquor, he fhould go and try his Luck with the old
Beldam at Home. He knew that fhe was a mighty Lover
of a Dram at the Bottle, when fhe could come by it.
With that *Viaticum* he marches, equipp'd like a *Country*
Lafs,

Lass, to the old Mifer's Houfe. It was with much ado he found Means to get Sight or Speech of the old Woman; but at laft he obtained that Favour; when, perfect in all the Cant of thofe People, he began to tell the Occafion of his coming, and bantering her, in Hopes fhe would invite him in; but all in vain; he was admitted no farther than the Porch, with the Houfe-Door juft a-jar: At laft, my Lord takes this Method; rifing up as going away, pretends himfelf in a Fit, and falls againft the Door: The Noife brings the young Wife to them, who with much Intreaty, perfuades her Keeper to help the poor Girl into the Houfe, in refpect to the Decorum of the Sex, and the unhappy Condition fhe was in. The Door had not been long fhut, but by Degrees my Lord comes to himfelf, and being fet on a Chair, cants a very religious Thankfgiving, thro' the Nofe, for the Humanity of the good old Gentlewoman; and begins to tell how deplorable her hard Fortune was by fuch Fits, which often took her in the Street, and fo made her liable to many Accidents; but every now and then, as a Relief, took a Sip of the Bottle, and recommended it to the old Women, who was fure to drink a hearty Dram; and when offered the young Lafs fhe would ftop the Bottle, and fay, *It was nought for young People,* and the like, in order to fave a larger Share for herfelf.

My Lord had another Bottle qualified with a little *Opium,* which would fooner accomplifh his Defires, and lay the *Dragon* afleep. His Lordfhip made an End of the firft Bottle, and gave the old Beldam the fomni'erous Liquor, which drinking, with Greedinefs enough, fhe fell faft afleep. My Lord, now fired with the Prefence of the lovely Creature, to whom he had made fuch near Approaches, was full of eager Defires, which caufed him often to change Colour, and made her imagine fome Return

turn

turn of his Fits; and asking the Question, my Lord re-
plied, That, *if she would be so charitable to let him lie
down on the Bed, he should soon recover.* The good-
natured Creature conducted him to her Chamber, where
being laid down, and she staying by him at his Request,
his Lordship soon put her in Mind of her Condition,
asking about her Husband, whom the young Woman
painted in his true Colours both *up,* and *a-bed,* supposing
she had only a *Woman* with her. By her Story, my Lord
found that a little Love would not be disagreeable; Opportunity, Revenge, and various Pleasures concurring.
So soon as she had laid herself down by my Lord, pleased
with his Conversation, his Lordship began to kiss her,
embrace her, and to proceed farther. She was wonderfully surprized at such Addresses from a *Woman,* but was
soon made sensible by his Lordship, that he did not *provoke* without a Power of *appeasing.* In short, Madam,
my Lord was as happy as he could desire, and as long as
he durst stay, for fear of the Husband's *Return,* and the
Keeper's *awaking.*

But *Phillis* was unwilling to part with him, and resolved to escape from her Prison, where she had neither
Pleasure nor Ease, to a Place where she promised herself
abundance of both. My Lord was glad of the Opportunity of gratifying likewise his Friend the Duke of *Buckingham.* Besides, she took Care of some Money, having
long since resolved on a Flight; and being acquainted with
the old Gentleman's Hoards, supplied herself with one
hundred and fifty Broad Pieces, and marched off with my
Lord to the Inn about Midnight. They were to pass over
three or four Fields before they reached it; and, in the
last, they were very near falling into the Enemy's Hands:
The old Fellow calling out to the Servant who was lighting him home, and his Voice discovering him, our Ad-
venturers

venturers ſtruck down the Field, out of the Path, and, to be the more ſecure, lay down in the Graſs. The Place, the Occaſion, and the Perſon that was ſo near, put his Lordſhip in mind of renewing the Pleaſure in Sight of his Cuckold. The Nymph was no longer nice, and eaſily complied with any of his Deſires. But not to detain your GRACE any longer with this Story, my Lord got the Damſel home, conveyed her up Stairs, to the Duke's Bed, and there having laid her, retired, with a Promiſe of returning as ſoon as he could change his Cloaths, look after the Family, and the like. But he having had his Ends already, ſent up my Lord Duke in his Place, whom the ignorant and paſſive Nymph bore with equal Satisfaction.

WHEN the old Miſer came Home, finding his Doors open, his Siſter aſleep, his Wife fled, and his Money gone, after raving like a Mad-man, he hanged himſelf. This News was ſoon ſpread about the Neighbourhood, and reached the Inn; where both Lovers *now,* as weary of their Purchaſe, as deſirous of it *before,* doubling her Caſh, adviſed her to retire to *London,* where, this Diſgrace not being known, ſhe might get another Huſband; and told her they intended ſoon to be there themſelves. She followed their Advice, and ſo this Adventure ended. His Majeſty, ſoon after, coming that Way, found them both in their Poſts, and took them into Favour, and with him to *Newmarket.*

HIS Amours at Court are too well known to your GRACE, to need my repeating of them. Beſides, they are mingled too much with the Reputation of Ladies of Quality, to revive them. I cannot omit that Affair which my Lord had with the fine Miſs *Roberts,* Miſtreſs to the King, whom ſhe left and refuſed, for the Poſſeſſion of my Lord's Perſon and Heart, as ſhe imagined: But he was ſoon cloyed with the Enjoyment of any one Woman,

tho'

tho' the faireſt in the World, and forſook her. The Lady, after the firſt Emotion of her Paſſion was over, grew as indifferent, and confidered how ſhe ſhould retrieve the King's Heart. For this Purpoſe, a lucky Occaſion preſented it ſelf: One Morning, as ſhe was dreſſing her Head at her Window, ſhe ſaw the King coming by; down Stairs ſhe ran, with her Hair about her Ears, threw herſelf at his Majeſty's Feet, implored his Pardon, and vowed Conſtancy for the Future. The good King, vanquiſhed with the Sight, took her up, and proteſted *no Man could ſee her and not love*, waited on her up to her Lodging, and there compleated the Reconciliation.

The Story of his Lordſhip's turning Mountebank, is in every Body's Mouth, therefore it would be ſuperfluous to mention it here. And now, judging my Diſcourſe ſwelled to a larger Bulk than I deſigned it, having given your G R A C E a Specimen of his Humour in the Purſuit of odd Adventures, I ſhall draw to a Concluſion.

His continual Courſe of Drinking, and a perpetual Expence of Spirits, in Love and Writing, had broken his Conſtitution, and brought him into a Conſumption; of which, after a lingering Sickneſs, he died at the Lodge in *Woodſtock Park*, on the 26th of *July*, 1680, at Two in the Morning, without any Pangs at all, Nature being worn out, and all the Food of Life exhauſted, in the 33d Year of his Age.

As for his Repentance, and thoſe Arguments produced by Dr. Burnet, I am apt to depend on his Veracity, notwithſtanding ſome Reports to the contrary, tho' aſſerted with the Boldneſs which only belongs to Truth: For my Lord was Maſter of too much Reaſon to be an Atheiſt, or, when he came calmly to conſider, not to be a Chriſtian, which muſt neceſſarily lead him to that Repentance the Doctor aſſures us of.

IT may be here expected, that I should give a Character of his Lordship's Writings, his Genius, his Temper,
and the like: But the former are so well defended already,
that there is nothing left for me to add; and it is so difficult a Matter to paint the latter, that I am afraid to attempt it. However, since it is a Part of the Task I have
undertaken, I shall venture to add a few Words on both.

HE had a Strength of Expression, and a Happiness of
Thought peculiar to himself, and seems to me, of all the
Moderns, to have come nearest the Antients in *Satire*,
not excepting our BOILEAU; for tho' he be very correct,
and has spared no Pains to dress the *Satires* of HORACE in
good *French*, yet it smells too much of the Lamp: Whereas, when any Thought of HORACE, JUVENAL, PER-
SIUS, or BOILEAU, occurs in my Lord's Verses, it is
plainly his own, without any Marks of borrowing it from
any other, the Spirit and Easiness of the Whole being of a
Piece. His looser Songs, and Pieces, too obscene for the
Ladies Eyes, having their peculiar Beauties, and are indeed too dangerous to peruse; for what would have ren-
dered them nauseous, if they had been written by a Genius less powerful, in him alarms the Fancy, and rouzes
the Blood and Appetite more than all the Medicaments
of CLEOPATRA. There are two Books in *Latin* that
seem to be written with my Lord's Spirit, *Petronius Ar-
biter*, and *Meursius's Dialogues*, where the Beauty of the
Expression, and the Strength of the Spirit and Fancy,
have given a Sort of Merit to Lewdness, which no other
Writers could ever obtain.

As for his Lordship's Temper, it was various, as it was
more or less inspired with Wine. He was an excellent
Mimic; and in all his frolicksome Disguises, he so truly
personated the Thing he would seem, that his most intimate Acquaintance could not discover the Impostor.

The

The Pleasure he gave in his Conversation was a Snare to him; for his Mirth increasing with his Liquor, many Persons of Quality, his Friends, promoted the Glass, to his Detriment, for their own Satisfaction. It is certain, that in his natural Temper, when sober, he was a good-natured Man, and had not that Allay of Malice, which in many Things he discovered, when heated by a Debauch. He had a particular Pique to Mr. DRYDEN, after his mighty Success in the Town; either, because he was sensible that he deserved not that Applause for his *Tragedies*, which the mad unthinking Audience gave them, (which Corruptness of Taste was afterwards somewhat corrected by the Duke of BUCKINGHAM's *Rehearsal*) or whether it was out of Indignation at being rivalled in Reputation; either as a Poet in general, or a Satirist in particular; *Satire*, indeed, being one of the chief Excellencies of Mr. DRYDEN, as well as of my Lord ROCHESTER. The Effect of this was discovered, by his Lordship's setting up Mr. CROWN in Opposition to Mr. DRYDEN. He recommended him to the King, ordering him to compose a *Masque* * for the Court, when it was the Business of the Poet-Laureat. But when Mr. CROWN's *Destruction of Jerusalem* † had met with as wild and unaccountable Success as Mr. DRYDEN's *Conquest of Granada*, his Lordship withdrew his Favours, as if he would be still in Contradiction to the Town; and, in that, perhaps, he was generally in the right; for of all Audiences, in polite Nations, perhaps there is not one that judges so very falsely of the *Drama* as the *English*, unless it be the *Spaniards*, who seem to have much the same wild, injudicious Taste. This the incomparable CERVANTES has shewn in his in-

---

* *It was entitled,* CALISTO: Or, The Chaste Nymph. *Perform'd in the Year* 1675.
            † 1677.

                                            imitable

imitable DON QUIXOT. My Lord was generally fickle
in his *Amours*, and made no great Scruple of his Oaths of
Fidelity. Sir GEORGE ETHEREGE wrote DORIMANT*
in Compliment to him, as drawing his Lordship's Character, and burnishing all the Foibles of it, to make
them shine like Perfections.

To conclude, his Lordship was a Man of Wit and
Pleasure, and spared nothing that would increase the
one, or promote the other.

THUs, Madam, I have complied with your GRACE's
Desire; and if I have not given you diverting Relations
enough of his Lordship, you must impute it to the Limits
of a Letter, to which I was confined; but I am ready at
any Time to write all I know, or that can with Decency
be conveyed to your GRACE's View. I am, Madam,

Your GRACE's

Most Obedient,

Humble Servant,

EVREMOND.

----

* DORIMANT *is the first Gentleman in* The Man of
Mode: Or, Sir Fopling Flutter. *A Comedy.*

A CHA-

A

CHARACTER

OF THE

Earl of ROCHESTER.

By Mr. WOLSLEY, *in the Preface to*
Valentinian, *a Tragedy, alter'd by his
Lordship.*

HERE has not lived in many Ages, if ever,
so extraordinary, and, I think I may add,
so useful a Person as most *Englishmen* know
my Lord *Rochester* to have been; whether
we consider the constant good Sense, and the
agreeable Mirth of his ordinary Conversation, or the vast
Reach and Compass of his Invention, and the wonderful
Depth of his retired Thoughts; the uncommon Graces of
his Fashion, or the inimitable Turns of his Wit; the be-
coming Genteelness, the bewitching Softness of his Civility, or the Force and Fitness of his *Satire*; for, as he was
both the Delight and the Wonder of Men, the Love and
the Dotage of Women, so was he a continual Curb to Impertinence, and the publick Censor of Folly. Never did
Man

Man stay in his Company unentertained, or leave it unin-
structed; never was his Understanding biassed, or his Pleasantness forced; never did he laugh in the wrong Place, or
prostitute his Sense to serve his Luxury; never did he stab
into the Wounds of falling Virtue with a base and cow-
ardly Insult, or smooth the Face of prosperous Villainy
with the Paint and Washes of a mercenary Wit; never
did he spare a Fop for being rich, or flatter a Knave for
being great. As most Men had an Ambition (thinking
it an indisputable Title to Wit) to be in the Number of
his Friends, so few were his Enemies, but such as did not
know him, or such as hated him for what others loved
him; and never did he go among Strangers, but he gained
Admirers, if not Friends; and commonly of such who
had been before prejudiced against him. Never was his
Talk thought too much, or his Visit too long; Enjoyment
did but increase Appetite; and the more Men had of his
Company, the less willing they were to part with it. He
had a Wit that could make even his Spleen and his ill Humour pleasant to his Friends, and the public chiding of his
Servants, which would have been ill Breeding, and in-
tolerable in any other Man, became not only civil and
inoffensive, but agreeable and entertaining in him: A
Wit that could please the most morose, persuade the most
obstinate, and soften the most obdurate; a Wit, whose
Edge could ease by cutting, and whose Point could tickle
while it probed; a Wit, that used to nip in the very Bud
the growing Fopperies of the Times, and keep down those
Weeds and Suckers of Humanity; nor was it an Enemy
to such only as are troublesome to Men of Sense in Conversation, but to those also of a far worse Nature, that
are destructive of publick Good, and pernicious to the
common Interest of Mankind.

H 2

HE had a Wit that was accompanied with an unaffected Greatness of Mind, and a natural Love to Justice
and Truth; a Wit that was in perpetual War with Knavery, and ever attacking those Kind of Vices most, whose
Malignity was like to be most diffusive, such as tended
more immediately to the Prejudice of publick Bodies, and
were of a common Nusance to the Happiness of human
Kind.   Never was his Pen drawn but on the Side of good
Sense, and usually employed, like the Arms of the ancient Heroes, to stop the Progress of arbitrary Oppression,
to beat down the Brutishness of strong Will, and to do his
King and Country Justice upon such public *State-Thieves*,
as would beggar a Kingdom to enrich themselves.   These
were the Vermin whom (to his eternal Honour) his Pen
was continually pricking and goading ; a Pen, if not so
happy in the Success, yet as generous in the Aim, as
either the Sword of THESEUS, or the Club of HERCU-
LES ; nor was it less sharp than *That*, or less weighty than
This.   If he did not take so much Care of himself as he
ought, he had the Humanity, however, to wish well to
others ; and I think I may truly affirm, he did the World
as much Good by a right Application of *Satire*, as he
hurt himself by a wrong Pursuit of Pleasure.

I MUST not here forget, that a considerable Time before his last Sickness, his Wit began to take a more serious Bent, and to frame and fashion itself to public Business.   He began to inform himself of the Wisdom of
our Laws, and the excellent Constitution of the *English*
Government, and to speak in the *House of Peers* with general Approbation.   He was inquisitive after all Kind of
Histories that concerned *England*, both antient and modern, and set himself to read the *Journals* of *Parliament Proceedings*. In Effect, he seemed to study nothing
more, than which Way to make that great Understanding

ing *God* had given him, moft ufeful to his Country; and
I am confident, had he lived, his riper Age would have
ferved it, as much as his Youth had diverted it. Add to
this, the Generofity of his Temper, and the Affability
of his good Senfe; the Willingnefs he ftill fhewed to
raife the Oppreffed, and the Pleafure he took to humble
the Proud; the conftant Readinefs of his Parts, and that
great Prefence of Mind, which never let him want a fit
and pertinent Anfwer to the moft fudden and unexpected
Queftion; a Talent as ufeful as it is rare. The admirable Skill he was Mafter of, to countermine the Plots of
his Enemies, and break thro' the Traps that were laid
for him; to work himfelf out of the Entanglement of
unlucky Accidents, and repair the Indifcretions of his
Youth, by the Quicknefs and Finenefs of his Wit; the
ftrange Facility he had to talk to all Capacities in their
own Dialect, and make himfelf good Company to all
Kind of People at all Times; fo that if we would find
a Soul to refemble that beautiful Portraiture of Man
with which LUCRETIUS (according to his fublime
Manner of Defcription) compliments his Friend MEM-
MIUS, when he fays, That VENUS, the Goddefs of Beauty, and fecond Caufe of all Things, had formed him to
excel (and that upon all Occafions) in every neceffary
Grace and Virtue; I fay, if we would juftify this charming Picture, and clear it from Flattery, even to human
Nature, we muft fet it by my Lord ROCHESTER, Of
him it may be truly faid in the fulleft Senfe of the Words,

> —— *Quem tu, Dea, Tempore in omni,*
> *Omnibus ornatum voluifti excellere rebus.*

WHAT laft and moft of all deferves Admiration in
my Lord, was his POETRY, which alone is Subject
enough for perpetual Panegyric. But the Character of
it

it is so generally known; it has so eminently distinguished itself from that of other Men, by a thousand irresist-
ible Beauties; every Body is so well acquainted with it,
by the Effect it has had upon them; that to trace and
single out the several Graces, may seem a Task as super-
fluous, as to describe to a Lover the Lines and Features
of his Mistress's Face. It is sufficient to observe, that his
Poetry, like himself, was all Original; and has a Stamp
so particular, so unlike any Thing that has been wrote
before, that as it disdained all servile Imitation, and co-
pying from others, so neither is it capable (in my Opinion) of being copied, any more than the Manner of his
Discourse could be copied; the Excellencies are too many and too masterly. On the other Side, the Faults are
few, and those inconsiderable: Their Eyes must be better than ordinary, who can see the minute Spots with
which so bright a Jewel is stained, or rather set off; for
those it has, are of the Kind which, HORACE says, can
never offend.

───── *Quas aut incuria fudit;*
    Aut humana parum cavit Natura.

Such little Negligences as Humanity cannot be exempt from;
and such, as perhaps were necessary to make his Lines
run natural and easy; for as nothing is more disagreeable,
either in Verse or Prose, than a slovenly Looseness of
Style, so, on the other hand, too nice a Correctness will
be apt to deaden the Life, and make the Piece too stiff.
Between these two Extremes, is the just Character of
my Lord ROCHESTER's *Poetry* to be found; it has every where a Tincture of that unaccountable Charm in his
Fashion and Conversation, that peculiar Becomingness

in

in all he said or did, that drew the Eyes and won the Hearts of all who came near him.

To conclude. The Applause of his *Wit* was so *universal*, and the Manner so *agreeable*, none ever *disliked* it, but those who *feared* it; none ever *decried* it, but those who *envied* it.

A

CHARACTER

OF THE

Earl of ROCHESTER.

By Mr. WOOD, *in his* Athen. Oxon.

HE was a Person of most rare Parts; and his natural Talent was excellent, much improved by Learning and Industry, being thoroughly acquainted with all *Classic Authors*, both *Greek* and *Latin*; a Thing very rare, if not peculiar to him, among those of his Quality. He knew also how to use them; not as other Poets have done, to translate or steal from, but rather to better and improve them by his natural Fancy. But the eager Tendency and violent Impulses of his natural Temper, unhappily inclining him to the Excesses of Pleasure and Mirth, which, with the wonderful Pleasantness of his inimitable Humour, did so far engage the Affections of the Dissolute towards him, that, to make

him

him delightfully venturous and frolickfome, to the utmoft Degrees of riotous Extravagancy, they for fome
Years heightened his Spirits (inflamed with Wine) into
one almoft uninterrupted Fit of Wantonnefs and Intem-
perance.

ANDREW MARVELL, who was a good Judge of
Wit, did ufe to fay, That ROCHESTER *was the only
Man in* England *that had the true Vein of Satire.* At
length, after a fhort, but pleafant Life, this noble and beau-
tiful Earl paid his laft Debt to Nature, on the 26th of
July, 1680, and was buried the 17th of *Auguft,* in a
Vault under the North Ifle joining to *Spelfbury* Church in
Oxfordfhire, by the Body of his Father HENRY, the
Generous, Loyal, and Valiant Earl of ROCHESTER.

HE left behind him a Son named CHARLES, who
dying upon the 12th of *November,* was buried by his
Father on the 7th of *December* following. He alfo
left behind him three Daughters, named ANNE, ELI-
ZABETH, and MALET; fo that the Male Line ceaf-
ing. His Majefty King CHARLES II. conferred the
Title of ROCHESTER on LAURENCE, Vifcount KIL-
LINGWORTH, a younger Son of EDWARD Earl of
CLARENDON.

A CHA-

✼✼✼✼✼✼✼✼✼✼✼✼✼✼✼✼✼✼

A

CHARACTER

OF THE

Earl of ROCHESTER.

By the Rev. Mr. PARSONS, *in the Sermon he preach'd at his Lordship's Funeral.*

HIS Quality I shall take no Notice of, there being so much of what was excellent and extraordinary in this Great Person, that I have no Room for any Thing that is common to him with others.

A WIT he had, so rare and fruitful in its Invention, and withal so choice and delicate in its Judgment, that there is nothing wanting in his Compofures to give a full Anfwer to that Queftion, *What and where Wit is ?* Except the Purity and Choice of Subject. Whoever reads his Compofures, will find all Things in them fo peculiarly great, new, and excellent, that he will eafily pronounce, That tho' he has lent to many others, yet he has borrowed of none; and that he has been as far from a fordid Imitation of thofe before him, as he will be from being reached by thofe that follow him.

In his other Perfonal Accomplifhments, in all the Perfections of a Gentleman, for the Court or the Country, he was known by all Men to be a very great

C
Mafter.

Mafter. He declared, That *that abfurd and Foolifh Philofophy, which the World fo much admired, propagated by the late Mr.* HOBBES, *and others, had undone him, and many more, of the beft Parts in the Nation.*

FROM the Breafts of his Mother, the Univerfity, he firft fucked thofe Perfections of Wit, Eloquence, and Poetry, which afterward:, by his own corrupt Stomach, or fome ill Juices after, were turned into Poifon to himfelf and others ; which certainly can be no more a Blemifh to thofe illuftrious Seminaries of Piety and good Learning, than a difobedient Child is to a wife and virtuous Father, or the Fall of Man to the Excellency of *Paradife.*

A

CHARACTER

OF THE

Earl of ROCHESTER.

By Dr. BURNET, *in fome Paffages of his Life and Death,* &c.

THIS Noble Lord appeared at Court with as great Advantages as moft ever had. He was a graceful and well-fhaped Perfon, tall and well made, if not a little too flender : He was exactly well-bred, and, what by a modeft Behaviour natural to him, what by a
Civility

Civility become almoſt as natural, his Converſation was eaſy and obliging.

HE had a ſtrange Vivacity of Thought, and Vigour of Expreſſion : His Wit had a Subtilty and Sublimity both, that were ſcarce imitable. His Style was clear and ſtrong : When he uſed Figures, they were very lively, and yet far enough out of the common Road. He had made himſelf Maſter of the ancient and modern Wit, and of the modern *French* and *Italian*, as well as the *Engliſh*. He loved to talk and write of *Speculative Matters* ; and did it with ſo fine a Thread, that even thoſe who hated the Subjects that his Fancy ran upon, yet could not but be charmed with his Way of treating them. BOILEAU among the *French*, and COWLEY among the *Engliſh* Wits, were thoſe he admired moſt. Sometimes other Men's Thoughts mixed with his Compoſures ; but that flowed rather from the Impreſſions they made on him when he read them, by which they came to return upon him as his own Thoughts, than that he ſervilely copied from any : For few Men ever had a bolder Height of Fancy, more ſteadily governed by Judgment, than he had. No Wonder a young Man ſo made, and ſo improved, was very acceptable in a Court.

HE laid out his Wit very freely in *Libels* and *Satire*, in which he had a peculiar Talent of mixing his Wit with his Malice, and fitting both with ſuch apt Words, that Men were tempted to be pleaſed with them. From thence his *Compoſures* came to be eaſily known ; for few had ſuch a Way of tempering theſe together as he had : So that when any Thing extraordinary that Way came out, as a Child is fathered ſometimes by its Reſemblance, ſo was it laid at his Door, as its Parent and Author. C 2 HE

HE would often go into the Country, and be for some Months wholly employed in Study, or the Sallies of his Wit, which he came to direct chiefly to *Satire*. And this he often defended to me, by saying, *" There " were some People that could not be kept in Order, or " admonished, but in this Way."*.

FOR his other Studies, they were divided between the comical and witty Writings of the Antients and Moderns, the *Roman* Authors, and Books of Physick, which the ill State of Health he was fallen into, made more necessary to himself.

IN his latter Years, he read Books of History more. He took Pleasure to disguise himself as a Porter, or as a Beggar; sometimes to follow some mean Amours, which, for the Variety of them, he affected: At other Times, meerly for Diversion, he would go about in odd Shapes, in which he acted his Part so naturally, that even those who were in the Secret, and saw him in these Shapes, could perceive nothing by which he might be discovered.

HE died in the 33d Year of his Age. Nature had fitted him for great Things, and his Knowledge and Observation qualified him to have been one of the most extraordinary Men, not only of this Nation, but of the Age he lived in. And I do verily believe, that if God had thought fit to have continued him longer in the World, he had been the Wonder and Delight of all that knew him.

The following is a true Copy of his Lordship's SPEECH, *when he set up for an* Italian *Mountebank on* Tower-Hill, *under the feigned Name of* ALEXANDER BENDO.

To

C   R

To all Gentlemen, Ladies, and Others,
whether of City, Town, or Country,
ALEXANDER BENDO wisheth all
Health and Prosperity.

WHEREAS this famous *Metropolis* of *England*,
(and were the Endeavours of its worthy Inhabitants equal to their Power, Merit, and Virtue, I
should not stick to denounce it, in a short Time, the
Metropolis of the whole World;) Whereas, I say, this
City (as most great ones are) has ever been infested with
a numerous Company of such, whose arrogant Confidence, backed with their Ignorance, has enabled them
to impose upon the People, either by premeditated
Cheats, or, at best, the palpable, dull, and empty
Mistakes of their self-deluded Imagination in Physic,
Chymical and Galenic; in Astrology, Physiognomy,
Palmestry, Mathematicks, Alchymy, and even in Government itself, the last of which, I will not propose to
discourse of or meddle at all in, since it no Way belongs
to my Trade or Vocation, as the rest do; which (Thanks
to my God) I find much more safe, I think equally
honest, and therefore more profitable.

But as to all the former, they have been so erroneously practised by many unlearned Wretches, whom Poverty and Neediness, for the most Part, (if not the restless Itch of deceiving) has forced to straggle and wander in unknown Paths, that even the Professions themselves, tho' originally the Products of the most learned and wise Men's laborious Studies and Experience, and by them left a wealthy and glorious Inheritance for Ages to come, seem, by this Bastard Race of Quacks and Cheats, to have been run out of all Wisdom, Learning, Perspicuousness, and Truth, with which they were so plentifully stocked; and now run into a Repute of meer Mists, Imaginations, Errors, and Deceits, such as, in the Management of these idle Professors, indeed they were.

You will therefore, (I hope) Gentlemen, Ladies and others, deem it but just, that I, who for some Years have with all Faithfulness and Assiduity courted these Arts, and received such signal Favours from them, that they have admitted me to the happy and full Enjoyment of themselves, and trusted me with their greatest Secrets, should, with an Earnestness and Concern more than ordinary, take their Parts against those impudent Fops, whose saucy impertinent Addresses and Pretensions, have brought such a Scandal upon their most immaculate Honours and Reputations.

Besides, I hope you will not think I could be so impudent, that if I had intended any such foul Play myself, I would have given you so fair Warning, by my severe Observations upon others. *Qui alterum incusant Probri, ipsum se intueri oportet,* says *Plautus.* However, *Gentlemen,* in a World like this, where Virtue is so exactly counterfeited, and Hypocrisy so generally taken Notice of, that every one (armed with Suspicion) stands upon his Guard against it, it will be very hard, for a Stranger especially,

especially, to escape Censure. All I shall say for myself on this Score, is this: If I appear to any one like *a Counterfeit*, even for the Sake of that, chiefly, ought I to be construed *a true Man.* Who is the Counterfeit's Example? His Original, and that which he employs his Industry and Pains to imitate and copy. Is it therefore my Fault, if the Cheat, by his Wits and Endeavours, makes himself so like me, that consequently I cannot avoid resembling him? Consider, pray, the Valiant, and the Coward; the wealthy Merchant, and the Bankrupt; the Politician, and the Fool; they are the same in many Things, and differ but in *one* alone.

THE valiant Man holds up his Head, looks confidently round about him, wears a Sword, courts a Lord's Wife, and owns it; so does the Coward: *One* only Point of Honour excepted, and that is Courage, which (like false Metal, *one* only Trial can discover) makes the Distinction.

THE Bankrupt walks the *Exchange,* buys Bargains, draws Bills, and accepts them with the Richest, whilst Paper and Credit are current Coin: That which makes the Difference is real Cash; a great Defect indeed, and yet but *one,* and *that* the last found out, and still, 'till then, the least perceived.

Now for the Politician; he is a grave, deliberating, close, prying Man: Pray, are they not grave, deliberating, close, prying Fools?

IF then the Difference betwixt all these (tho' infinite in Effect) be so nice in all Appearance, will you expect it should be otherwise betwixt the false Physician, Astrologer, &c. and the true? The first calls himself learned Doctor, sends forth his Bills, gives Physic and Counsel, tells and foretells; the other is bound to do just as much: It is only your Experience must distinguish betwixt them; to which I willingly submit myself. I will only say something to the Honour of the MOUNTEBANK, in case you discover me to be one.

REFLECT a little what Kind of Creature it is: He is one then, who is fain to supply some higher Ability he pretends to, with Craft; he draws great Companies to him by undertaking strange Things, which can never be effected. The *Politician*, (by his Example, no doubt) finding how the People are taken with specious miraculous Impossibilities, plays the same Game; protests, declares, promises I know not what Things, which he is sure can never be brought about. The People believe, are deluded, and pleased; the Expectation of a future Good, which shall never befal them, draws their Eyes off a present Evil. Thus are they kept and established in Subjection, Peace, and Obedience; he in Greatness, Wealth, and Power. So you see the Politician is, and must be a *Mountebank* in State Affairs; and the *Mountebank*, no doubt, if he thrives, is an errant *Politician* in Physic. But that I may not prove too tedious, I will proceed faithfully to inform you, what are the Things in which I pretend chiefly, at this Time, to serve my Country.

FIRST, I will (by the Leave of God) perfectly cure that *Labes Britannica*, or *Grand English Disease*, the *Scurvy*; and that with such Ease to my *Patient*, that he shall not be sensible of the least Inconvenience, whilst I steal his Distemper from him. I know there are many who treat this Disease with *Mercury, Antimony, Spirits,* and *Salts*; being dangerous Remedies, in which, I shall meddle very little, and with great Caution; but by more secure, gentle, and less fallible Medicines, together with the Observation of some few Rules in Diet, perfectly cure the *Patient*, having freed him from all the Symptoms, as Looseness of the Teeth, Scorbutick Spots, Want of Appetite, Pains and Lassitude in the Limbs and Joints, especially the Legs.

And

And to fay true, there are few Diftempers in this Nation that are not, or at leaft proceed not originally from the *Scurvy*; which, were it well rooted out, (as I make no queftion to do it from all thofe who fhall come into my Hands) there would not be heard of fo many Gouts, Aches, Dropfies, and Confumptions; nay, even thofe thick and flimy Humours, which generate Stones in the Kidneys and Bladder, are for the moft Part Offsprings of the *Scurvy*. It would prove tedious to fet down all its malignant Race; but thofe who addrefs themfelves here, fhall be ftill informed by me of the Nature of their Diftempers, and the Grounds I proceed upon to their Cure. So will all reafonable People be fatisfied that I treat them with Care, Honefty, and Underftanding; for I am not of their Opinion, who endeavours to render their Vocations rather myfterious than ufeful and fatisfactory.

I will not here make a Catalogue of Difeafes and Diftempers; it behoves a *Phyfician*, I am fure, to underftand them all; but if any one come to me, (as I think there are very few that have efcaped my *Practice*) I fhall not be afhamed to own to my *Patient* where I find myfelf to feek; and, at leaft, he fhall be fecure with me from having Experiments tried upon him; a Privilege he can never hope to enjoy, either in the Hands of the grand Doctors of the Court and Town, or in thofe of the leffer Quacks and Mountebanks.

It is thought fit, that I affure you of great Secrecy, as well as Care, in Difeafes, where it is requifite; whether Venereal, or others; as fome peculiar to Women, the Green-Sicknefs, Weakneffes, Inflamations, or Obftructions in the Stomach, Reins, Liver, Spleen, &c. for I would put no Word in my Bill that bears any unclean Sound; it is enough that I make myfelf underftood. I have feen Phyficians Bills as bawdy as *Aretine's Dialogues*,

whicn

which no Man, that walks warily before *God*, can approve of; but I cure all Suffocations in those Parts, producing Fits of the Mother, Convulsions, nocturnal Inquietudes, and other strange Accidents, not fit to be set down here; persuading young Women very often, that their Hearts are like to break for Love, when, God knows, the Distemper lies far enough from that Place.

I HAVE likewise got the Knowledge of a great Secret to cure Barrenness, (proceeding from any accidental Cause, as it often falls out, and no natural Defect; for Nature is easily assisted, difficultly restored, but impossible to be made more perfect by Man, than God himself had at first created and bestowed it) which I have made use of for many Years with great Success, especially this last Year, wherein I have cured *one* Woman that had been married twenty Years, and *another* that had been married one and twenty Years, and *two* Women that had been *three Times* married; as I can make appear by the Testimonies of several Persons in *London*, *West-minster*, and other Places thereabouts. The Medicines I use, cleanse and strengthen the Womb, and are all to be taken in the Space of seven Days. And because I do not intend to deceive any Person, upon Discourse with them, I will tell them whether I am like to do them any Good. My usual Contract is, to receive one Half of what is agreed upon, when the Party shall be quick with Child, the other Half when she is brought to bed.

CURES of this Kind I have done signal, and many; for the which, I doubt not but I have the good Wishes and hearty Prayers of many Families, who had else pined out their Days under the deplorable and reproachful Misfortune of barren Wombs, leaving plentiful Estates and Possessions to be inherited by Strangers. -

As

As to _Astrological Predictions, Physiognomy, Divina-tion_ by _Dreams_, and otherwise, (_Palmistry_ I have no Faith in, becaufe there can be no Reafon alledged for it) my own Experience has convinced me more of their con-fiderable Effects, and marvellous Operations, chiefly in the Directions of future Proceedings, to the avoiding of Dangers that threaten, and laying hold of Advantages that might offer themfelves; I fay, my own Practice has convinced me, more than all the fage and wife Writings extant, of thofe Matters; for I might fay this of myfelf, (did it not look like Oftentation) that I have very feldom failed in my Predictions, and often been very ferviceable in my Advice. How far I am capable in this Way, I am fure is not fit to be delivered in Print: Thofe who have no Opinion of the Truth of this _Art_, will not, I fuppofe, come to me about it; fuch as have, I make no queftion of giving them ample Satisfaction.

Nor will I be afhamed to fet down here my Willing-nefs to practife _Rare Secrets_, (tho' fomewhat collateral to my Profeffion) for the Help, Confervation, and Aug-mentation of _Beauty_ and _Comelinefs_; a Thing created at firft by _God_, chiefly for the _Glory of his own Name_, and then for the better Eftablifhment of mutual Love between Man and Woman; for when _God_ had beftowed on _Man_ the Power of Strength and Wifdom, and thereby ren-dered _Woman_ liable to the Subjection of his abfolute Will, it feemed but requifite that fhe fhould be endued likewife, in Recompence, with fome Quality that might beget in him Admiration of her, and fo enforce his Tendernefs and Love.

The Knowledge of thefe Secrets I gathered in my Travels abroad (where I have fpent my Time ever fince I was fifteen Years old, to this my nine and twentieth Year) in _France_ and _Italy_. Thofe that have travelled in _Italy_, will

will tell you to what a Miracle *Art* does there affift *Nature* in the Prefervation of *Beauty*; how Women of Forty bear the fame Countenance with thofe of Fifteen: Ages are no ways diftinguifhed by Faces; whereas here in *England*, look a *Horfe* in the *Mouth*, and a *Woman* in the *Face*, you prefently know both their Ages to a Year. I will therefore give you fuch Remedies, that, without deftroying your Complexion, (as moft of your Paints and Daubings do) fhall render them purely fair; clearing and preferving them from all Spots, Freckles, Heats, Pimples, and Marks of the Small-Pox, or any other accidental ones, fo the Face be not feamed or fcarred.

I WILL alfo cleanfe and preferve your *Teeth* white and round as Pearls, faftening them that are loofe: Your Gums fhall be kept entire, as red as Coral; your Lips of the fame Colour, and foft as you could wifh your lawful Kiffes.

I WILL likewife adminifter that which fhall cure the worft of Breaths, provided the Lungs be not totally perifhed and impofthumated; as alfo certain and infallible Remedies for thofe whofe Breaths are yet untainted; fo that nothing but either a very long Sicknefs, or Old-Age itfelf, fhall ever be able to fpoil them.

I WILL befides (if it be defired) *take away* from their Fatnefs who have *over-much*, and *add* Flefh to thofe that *want it*, without the leaft Detriment to their Conftitutions.

Now fhould *Galen* himfelf look out of his Grave, and tell me thefe were Baubles, below the Profeffion of a Phyfician, I would boldly anfwer him, That I take more Glory in preferving *God's* Image, in its unblemifhed Beauty, upon one good Face, than I fhould do in patching up all the decayed Carcaffes in the World.

THEY

THEY that will do me the Favour to come to me, ſhall be ſure, from Three of the Clock in the Afternoon, 'till Eight at Night, (at my Lodgings in *Tower-Street,* next Door to the Sign of the *Black-Swan,* at a Gold-ſmith's Houſe) to find

Their Humble Servant,

ALEXANDER BENDO.

P. S. In ſome Meaſure to illuſtrate his Lordſhip's Life, as well as his Works, we thought it would be neither improper, nor unacceptable to the Readers, to inſert the Character of King CHARLES II. as it was moſt excellently drawn by the Right Honourable *John Sheffield,* late Duke of *Buckinghamſhire.*

A SHORT

CHARACTER

OF

King CHARLES II.

I Have pitched upon this Character of King CHARLES II. not for his being a *King,* nor my having had the Honour to ſerve him : The *firſt* of theſe would be too vulgar a Conſideration ; and the *other* too particular. But I think it a Theme of great Variety ; and whatever is wanting in the Writer, may, I hope, be recompenced

in

in the Agreeablenefs of the Subject; which is fometimes enough to recommend a Picture, tho' ill drawn; and to make a Face one likes, oftner looked on, than the beft Piece of *Raphael*.

To begin then, according to Cuftom, with his *Religion*, which (fince his Death) hath made fo much Noife in the World: I yet dare confidently affirm it to have been only that which is vulgarly, tho' unjuftly, counted *none at all*, I mean Deism. And this uncommon Opinion he owed more to the Livelinefs of his Parts, and Carelefnefs of his Temper, than either to Reading, or much Confideration; for his Quicknefs of Apprehenfion, at firft View, could difcern thro' the feveral Cheats of pious Pretences; and his natural Lazinefs confirmed him in an equal Miftruft of all, for fear he fhould be troubled with examining which was beft.

If in his early Travels, and late Defigns, he feemed a little biaffed to *one Sort of Religion*, the *firft* is to be imputed to a certain Eafinefs of Temper, and a Complaifance for that Company he was then forced to keep; and the *laft* was no more than his being tired (which he foon was in any Difficulty) with thofe bold Oppofitions in Parliament; which made him almoft throw himfelf into the Arms of a *Roman* Catholick Party, fo remarkable of late for their Loyalty; who embrac'd him gladly, and lull'd him to Sleep with thofe enchanting Songs of Sovereignty and Prerogative, which the beft and wifeft Princes are often unable to refift.

And tho' he engaged himfelf on that Side more fully, at a Seafon when it was in vain, and too late, to diffemble; we ought lefs to wonder at it, than to confider that our very Judgments are apt to grow, in Time, as partial as our Affections: And thus, by Accident only, he became of their Opinion in his Weaknefles, who

had

had so much endeavoured always to contribute to his Power.

HE loved Ease and Quiet, to which his unnecessary Wars are so far from being a Contradiction, that they are rather a Proof of it, since they were made only to comply with those Persons whose Dissatisfaction would have proved more uneasy to one of his Humour, than all the distant Noise of Cannon, which he would often listen to with a great deal of Tranquility. Besides, the great and almost only Pleasure of Mind he seemed addicted to, was Shipping, and Sea-Affairs; which seemed to be so much his Talent for Knowledge, as well as Inclination, that a War of that kind was rather an Entertainment, than any Disturbance to his Thoughts.

IF he did not go himself at the Head of so magnificent a Fleet, it is only to be imputed to that Eagerness of Military Glory in his *Brother*; which, under Shew of decent Care for preserving the *Royal Person* from Danger, engrossed all that Sort of Honour to himself, with as much Jealousy of any other's interposing in it, as a *King* of another Temper would have had of his. It is certain no Prince was ever more fitted by Nature for his Country's Interest, than he was, in all his Maritime Inclinations; which might have proved of sufficient Advantage to this Nation, if he had been as careful of depressing all such Improvements in *France*, as of advancing and encouraging our Town; but it seems he wanted Jealousy in all his Inclinations, which leads us to consider him in his Pleasures.

IN these he was rather abandoned, than luxurious; and, like our Female Libertines, apter to be persuaded into Debauches for the Satisfaction of others, than to seek, with Choice, where most to please himself. I am of Opinion also, that in his latter Times, there was as

much

much of Lazinefs as-of Love, in all thofe Hours he
paffed among his Miftreffes ; who, after all, only ferved
to fill up his Seraglio, while a betwitching kind of Pleafure, called Sauntering, and talking without any Con-
ftraint, was the true *Sultana* QUEEN he delighted in.

HE was furely inclined to Juftice ; for nothing elfe
would have retained him fo faft in the Succeffion of a
Brother, againft a *Son* he was fo fond of, and the Humour of a Party which he fo much feared. I am willing
alfo to impute to his Juftice, whatever feems, in fome
Meafure, to contradict the general Opinion of his Cle-
mency ; as his fuffering always the Rigour of the Law
to proceed, not only againft all Highwaymen, but alfo
feveral others ; in whofe Cafes the Lawyers, according
to their wonted Cuftom, had fometimes ufed a great deal
of Hardfhip and Severity.

HIS Underftanding was quick and lively in little
Things, and fometimes would foar high enough in great
ones ; but unable to keep it up with any long Attention
or Application. Witty in all Sorts of Converfation ;
and telling a Story fo well, that, not out of Flattery,
but the Pleafure of hearing it, we feemed ignorant of
what he had repeated to us ten times before, as a good
Comedy will bear the being often feen.

OF a wonderful Mixture ; lofing all his Time, and
fetting his whole Heart upon the Fair Sex, yet, neither
angry with Rivals, nor in the leaft nice as to their being
beloved ; and while he facrificed all his Cafh to his Miftreffes, he would ufe to grudge and be uneafy at their
lofing a little of it again at Play, tho' ever fo neceffary for their Diverfion ; nor would he venture five Pounds
at Tennis to thofe Servants, who might obtain as many
Thou-

Thoufands, either before he came thither, or as foon as he left off.

FULL of Diffimulation, and very *adroit* at it; yet no Man eafier to be impofed on; for his great Dexterity was in cozening himfelf, by gaining a little one Way, while he loft ten times as much another; and by careffing thofe Perfons moft, who had deluded him the ofteneft; and yet the quickeft in the World at fpying fuch a Ridicule in another.

EASY and good-natured to all People in Trifles; but in great Affairs fevere and inflexible. In one Week's Abfence quite forgetting thofe Servants, to whofe Faces he could hardly deny any Thing, in the Midft of all his Remiffnefs; fo induftrious and indefatigable upon fome particular Occafions, that no Man would either toil longer, or be able to manage better.

HE was fo liberal, as to ruin his Affairs by it; for *Want* in a KING of *England*, turns Things juft upfide down, and expofes a Prince to his People's Mercy. It did yet worfe in him; for it forced him alfo to depend on his *Great Neighbour* in *France*, who played the *Broker* with him fufficiently in all thofe Times of Extremity. Yet this Profufenefs of his, did not fo much proceed from his overvaluing thofe he favoured, as from his undervaluing any Sums of Money which he did not fee; tho' he found his Error in this, but, I confefs, a little of the lateft.

HE had fo natural an Averfion to all Formality, that with as much Wit as moft Men ever had, and as Majeftic a Mien, yet he could not, on Premeditation, aft the Part of a KING for a Moment, either in Parliament or in Council, either in Words or Gefture; which carried him into the other Extream, (more in-

con-

convenient of the two for a *Prince*,) of letting all Diftinction and Ceremony fall to the Ground, as ufelefs and foppifh.

His Temper, both of Body and Mind, was admirable; which made him an eafy generous Lover, a civil obliging Hufband, a friendly Brother, an indulgent Father, and a good-natur'd Mafter. If he had been as folicitous about improving the Faculties of his *Mind*, as he was in the Management of his *bodily Health*, tho', alas! this proved unable to make his Life *long*, that had not failed to make it *famous*.

He was an illuftrious Exception to all the common Rules of Phyfiognomy; for, with a moft *Saturnine*, harfh Sort of Countenance, he was both of a merry and merciful Difpofition; and in the laft Thirty Years of his Life, as fortunate as thofe of his Father had been difmal and tumultuous. If his Death had fome Appearance of being untimely, it may be partly imputed to his extream healthy Conftitution, which made the World as much furprized at his dying before Threefcore, as if nothing but an ill Accident could have killed him.

I would not fay any Thing on fo fad a Subject, if I did not think that Silence itfelf would in fuch a Cafe fignify too much; and therefore, as an impartial Writer, I am obliged to obferve, that the *moft knowing*, and the *moft deferving* of all his *Phyficians*, did not only believe him poifoned, but thought *himfelf fo too*, not long after, for having declared his *Opinion* a little *too boldly*.

But here I muft needs take Notice of an unufual Piece of Juftice, which yet all the World has almoft unanimoufly agreed in; I mean, in not fufpecting his *Succeffor* of the leaft Connivance at fo horrid a Villany;

and

and perhaps there is hardly a more remarkable Inſtance of that invincible Power of Truth and Innocence : For it is next to a Miracle, that ſo *unfortunate a Prince*, in the Midſt of all thoſe Diſadvantages he lies under, ſhould be yet cleared of this, even by his greateſt Enemies, notwithſtanding all thoſe Circumſtances that uſed to give a Suſpicion, and that extream Malice, which has of late attended him in all his other Actions.

A

PASTORAL

ON THE

DEATH

OF THE

Earl of Rochester.

By Mr. FLATMAN.

I.

AS on his Death-bed gaſping STREPHON lay.
STREPHON, the Wonder of the Plains,
The nobleſt of th' *Arcadian* Swains,
STREPHON the Bold, the Witty, and the Gay.

With

With many a Sigh, and many a Tear, he said,
Remember me, ye Shepherds, when I'm dead.

II.

Ye trifling Glories of this World, adieu,
And vain Applauses of the Age:
For when we quit this Earthly Stage,
   Believe me, Shepherds, for I tell you true,
Those Pleasures which from virtuous Deeds we have,
Procure the sweetest Slumbers in the Grave.

III.

Then since your fatal Hour must surely come,
Surely your Heads lie low as mine.
Your bright Meridian Sun decline,
   Beseech the mighty *P A N* to guard you Home:
If to *Elysium* you would happy fly,
Live not like STREPHON, but like STREPHON die.

O N

✿❀✿❀✿❀✿❀✿❀✿❀✿❀✿❀✿❀✿❀✿❀✿

ON THE

D E A T H

OF THE

Earl of ROCHESTER.

By Mrs. BEHN.

MOurn, mourn, ye Mufes all; your Lofs deplore,
The young, the noble STREPHON is no more.
Yes, yes, he's fled quick as departing Light,
And ne'er fhall rife from Death's eternal Night ;
So rich a Prize the *Stygian* Gods ne'er bore,
Such Wit, fuch Beauty, never grac'd their Shore:
He was but *lent* this duller World t'im'prove,
In all the Charms of *Poetry* and *Love :*
Both were his *Gifts,* which freely he beftow'd,
And, like a *God,* dealt to the wond'ring Crowd,
Scorning the little Vanity of Fame,
Spite of himfelf, attain'd a glorious Name.
But, O ! in vain was all his peevifh Pride ;
The *Sun* as foon might his vaft Luftre hide,
As piercing, pointed, and more lafting bright,
As fuff'ring no Viciffitudes of Night.

Mourn, mourn, ye Mufes All; your Lofs deplore,
The young, the noble STREPHON is no more.

Now

Now uninfpir'd upon your Banks we lie,
Unlefs when we would mourn his Elegy ;
His Name's a Genius that wou'd Wit difpenfe,
And give the Theme a Soul, the Words a Senfe.
But all fine Thoughts, that ravifh'd when he fpoke,
With the foft Youth eternal Leave has took :
Uncommon Wit, that did the Soul o'ercome,
Is bury'd all in STREPHON's worfhipp'd Tomb.
SATIRE has loft his Art, its Sting is gone,
The Fop and Cully now may be undone ;
That dear inftructing Rage is now allay'd,
And no fharp Pen dares tell 'em how they've ftray'd :
Bold as a God was ev'ry Lafh,he took,
But kind and gentle the chaftifing Stroke.
   Mourn, mourn, ye Youths, whom Fortune has betray'd,
   The laft Reproacher of your Vice is dead.

   MOURN, all ye Beauties, put your *Cyprefs* on,
The trueft Swain that e'er ador'd you's gone.
Think how he lov'd, and wrote, and figh'd and fpoke ;
Recal his Mien, his Fafhion, and his Look.
By what dear Arts the Soul he did furprize,
Soft as his Voice, and charming as his Eyes.
Bring Garlands, all, of never-dying Flow'rs,
Bedew'd with everlafting fallen Show'rs ;
Fix your fair Eyes upon your victim'd Slave,
Sent gay and young to his untimely Grave.
See where the noble Swain extended lies,
Too fad a Triumph of your Victories ;
Adorn'd with all the Graces Heav'n e'er lent ;   ⎫
All that was great, foft, lovely, excellent,   ⎬
You've laid into his early Monument.   ⎭
   Mourn, mourn, ye Beauties ; your fad Lofs deplore,
   The young, the charming STREPHON is no more.
                         MOURN

MOURN, all ye little Gods of Love, whofe Darts
Have loft their wanted Pow'r of piercing Hearts;
Lay by the Gilded Quiver and the Bow,
The ufelefs Toys can do no Mifchief now.
Thofe Eyes, that all your Arrows-Points infpir'd,
Thofe Lights that gave you Fire, are now retir'd;
Cold as his Tomb, Pale as your Mother's *Doves:*
Bewail him then, O! all ye little Loves!
For you the humbleft Votary have loft,
That ever your Divinities could boaft.
Upon your Hands your weeping Heads recline,
And let your Wings encompafs round his Shrine;
Inftead of Flow'rs, your broken Arrows ftrow,
And at his Feet lay the neglected Pow.
   Mourn, all ye little Gods, your Lofs deplore;
   The foft, the charming STREPHON is no more.

   LARGE was his Fame, but fhort his glorious Race;
Like young LUCRETIUS, liv'd and dy'd apace:
So early Rofes fade, fo over all
They caft their fragrant Scents, then foftly fall;
While all the fcatter'd perfum'd Leaves declare,
How lovely 'twas when whole; how fweet, how fair.
Had he been to the *Roman* Empire known,
When Great AUGUSTUS fill'd the peaceful Throne;
Had he that noble wond'rous *Poet* feen,
And known his Genius, and furvey'd his Mien,
(When *Wits* and *Heroes* grac'd divine Abodes)
He had increas'd the Number of their *Gods*;
The Royal Judge had Temples rear'd t' his Name,
And made him as Immortal as his Fame.
In Love and Verfe his OVID he'd outdone,
And all his Laurels, and his JULIA won.
   Mourn, mourn, unhappy World, his Lofs deplore,
   The great, the charming STREPHON is no more.

                   O N

✿✿✿✿✿✿✿✿!✿!✿!✿!✿✿✿✿✿✿✿

ON THE

DEATH

OF THE

Earl of ROCHESTER.

By an Unknown Hand.

WHAT Words, what Senſe, what Night-piece
        can expreſs
The World's Obſcurity and Emptineſs!
Since ROCHESTER withdrew his vital Beams
From the great *Chaos*, fam'd for high Extreams:
The Hero's Talent, or in Good or Ill,
Dull Mediocrity misjudging ſtill.
Seraphic Lord! whom Heaven for Wonders meant,
The earlieſt Wit, and the moſt ſudden Saint.
What tho' the Vulgar may traduce thy Ways,
And ſtrive to rob thee of thy Moral Praiſe!
If, with thy Rival *Solomon*'s Intent,
Thou ſinn'd'ſt a little for Experiment;
Or to maintain a Parodox, which none
Had Wit to anſwer, but thy ſelf alone:
Thy Soul flew higher; that ſtrict ſacred Tie
With thy Creator *Time* was to deſcry.

                       Thus

Thus pregnant *Prophets* us'd uncommon Ways,
Play'd their wild Pranks, and made the Vulgar gaze,
Till their great Meſſage came to be declar'd :
They ſin in Types, that ſin ſo unprepar'd :
An unexpected Change attracts all Eyes;
They needs muſt conquer, that can well ſurprize.
Now, Lechers, whom the Pox could ne'er convert,
Know where to fix a reſtleſs rambling Heart.
Drunkards, whoſe Souls, not their ſick Maws, love
    Drink,
Confound their Glaſſes, and begin to think.
The Atheiſt now has nothing elſe to ſay;
His Arguments were lent for Sport, not Prey :
Like Guns to Clowns, or Weapons to raſh Boys,
Reſum'd again for Miſchief or for Noiſe.
The Spark cries out, now, e'er he is aware,
(Making an Oath a Prologue to a Pray'r)
ROCHESTER ſaid 'twas true! It muſt be ſo!
He had no Diſpenſation from below.
Thy Dying Words (than Thouſands of Harangues,
Urg'd with Grimaces, fortify'd with Bangs
On dreadful Pulpit) have made more recant,
Than Plague, or War, or penitential Want,
A Declaration ſo well tim'd, has gain'd
More Proſélites than e'er thy Wildneſs feign'd :
Mad Debauchees, whom thou didſt but allure
With pleaſant Baits, and tempt 'em to their Cure.
Satan rejoic'd to ſee thee take his Part,
His Malice not ſo proſp'rous as thy Art :
He took thee for his Pilot, to convey
Thoſe eaſy Souls he ſpirited away :
But to his great Confuſion ſaw thee ſhift
Thy ſwelling Sails, to take another Drift,

D   With

With an illustrious Train, imputed his,
To the bright Region of eternal Bliss.

So have I seen a prudent *Gen'ral* * act,
When Fate had forc'd with Rebels to contract
A hated League, fight, vote, adhere, obey,
Own the vile Cause as zealously as they ;
Suppress the *Loyal* Side, and pull all down,
With unresisted Force, that propt the *Crown* :
But when he found out the propitious Hour
To quit his *Mask*, and own his *Prince*'s Pow'r ;
Boldly asserted his great *Sov'reign*'s Cause,
And brought *Three* Kingdoms to his *Master*'s Laws:

---

* MONCK.

THE

THE
WORKS
OF THE
Earl of ROCHESTER.

SATIRE againſt MAN.

WERE I (who to my Coſt already am
One of thoſe ſtrange, prodigious Creatures,
Man)
A Spirit free to chuſe, for my own Share
What Caſe of Fleſh and Blood I'd pleaſe to wear,
I'd be a *Dog*, a *Monkey*, or a *Bear :*
Or any Thing, but that vain Animal,
Who is ſo proud of being *rational.*
His Senſes are too groſs, and he'll contrive
A *ſixth* to contradict the other five.
And before certain Inſtinct will prefer
Reaſon, which fifty Times for one does err.
Reaſon, an *Ignis fatuus* in the Mind,
Which leaving Light of Nature (Senſe) behind,
Pathleſs and dang'rous wand'ring Ways it takes,
Thro' *Error's* fenny Bogs, and thorny Brakes ;

D 2

What

Whilst the misguided Follower climbs with Pain,
Mountains of Whimsies, heap'd in his own Brain;
Stumbling from Thought to Thought, falls head-long
    down
Into *Doubt's* boundless *Sea*; where, like to drown,
Books bear him up a-while, and make him try
To swim with *Bladders of Philosophy*;
In Hopes still to o'ertake the skipping Light,
The Vapour dances in his dazzling Sight,
'Till spent, it leaves him to eternal Night.
Then old Age and Experience, Hand-in-hand,
Lead him to Death, and make him understand,
After a Search so painful and so long,
That, all his Life, he has been in the wrong.
Huddled in Dirt, the *Reas'ning* Engine lies,
Who was so proud, so witty, and so wise.
Pride drew him in, as Cheats their Bubbles catch,
And made him venture to be made a Wretch.
His Wisdom did his Happiness destroy,
Aiming to know what World he should enjoy;
And *Wit* was his vain frivolous Pretence,
Of pleasing others at his own Expence:
For *Wits* are treated just like common *Whores,*
First they're *enjoy'd*, and then *kick'd out of Doors.*
The Pleasure past, a threat'ning Doubt remains,
That frights th'Enjoyer with succeeding Pains.
Women and Men of Wit are dang'rous Tools,
And ever fatal to admiring Fools.
Pleasure allures; and when the Fops escape,
'Tis not that they're belov'd, but fortunate;
And therefore what they fear, at least they hate.

    But now, methinks, some formal Band and Beard
Takes me to Task: Come on, Sir, I'm prepar'd.

                                Then,

Then, by your Favour, any Thing that's writ
Against this gibing, jingling Knack, call'd Wit,
Likes me abundantly ; but take you Care,
Upon this Point, not to be too severe.
Perhaps my Muse were fitter for this Part ;
For I profess I can be very smart
On Wit, which I abhor with all my Heart.
I long to lash it in some sharp Essay ;
But your grand Indiscretion bids me stay,
And turns my Tide of Ink another Way.
What Rage ferments in your degen'rate Mind,
To make you rail at Reason *and* Mankind *?*
Bless'd, glorious Man, *to whom alone kind Heav'n*
An everlasting Soul has freely giv'n ;
Whom his great Maker *took such Care to make,*
That from himself he did the Image take,
And this fair Frame in shining Reason *drest,*
To dignify his Nature above Beast.
Reason, *by whose aspiring Influence,*
We take a Flight beyond material *Sense ;*
Dive into Mysteries *; then, soaring, pierce*
The flaming Limits of the Universe ;
Search Heav'n *and* Hell, *find out what's acted there,*
And give the World true Grounds of Hope *and* Fear.

HOLD; mighty Man, I cry, all this we know
From the pathetic Pen of *Ingelo* * ;

---

* Dr. Ingelo *wrote a religious Romance, called* Benti-
voglio *and* Urania.

D 3 From

* From *Patrick's* Pilgrim, *Stillingfleet's* Replies;
And 'tis this very Reason I despise ;
This supernat'ral Gift, that makes a *Mite*
Think he's the Image of the *Infinite* ;
Comparing his short Life, void of all Rest,
To the *Eternal,* and the *Ever-blest.*
This busy puzzling Stirrer up of Doubt,
That frames deep Mysteries, then finds 'em out ;
Filling with frantick Crowds of thinking *Fools,*
Those rev'rend *Bedlams, Colleges* and *Schools* ;
Borne on whose Wings, each heavy Sot can pierce
The Limits of the boundless Universe ;
So charming Ointments make an old *Witch* fly,
And bear a crippled Carcass thro' the Sky.
'Tis this exalted Pow'r, whose Bus'ness lies
In *Nonsense* and *Impossibilities,*
This made a whimsical *Philosopher*
Before the spacious *World* his *Tub* prefer ;
And we have modern *cloister'd Coxcombs,* who
Retire to think, 'cause they have Nought to do :
But Thoughts are giv'n for Action's Government ;
Where Action ceases, Thought's impertinent.
Our Sphere of Action is Life's Happiness ;
And he who thinks beyond, thinks like an *Ass.*
Thus whilst against *false Reas'ning* I inveigh,
I own *right Reason,* which I would obey ;
That *Reason* which distinguishes by *Sense,*
And gives us Rules of *Good* and *Ill* from thence :
That bounds *Desires* with a reforming Will,
To keep 'em more in *Vigour,* not to kill.

---

* *Bishop* Patrick, *after* Bunyan's Pilgrim's Progress,
wrote, *The* Parable *of the* Pilgrim : *A much inferior Per-*
formance.

Your

Your *Reason* hinders, mine helps to enjoy ;
Yours would renewing Appetites deftroy :
My *Reason* is my Friend, yours is a Cheat ;
Hunger calls out, my *Reason* bids me eat ;
Perverfely yours your Appetite does mock,
This *asks for Food*, that anfwers, *What's a Clock ?*
This plain *Diftinction* , Sir, your *Doubt* fecures ;
'Tis not *true Reason* I defpife, but *yours.*
Thus I think *Reason* righted ; but for *Man,*
I'll ne'er recant, defend *him* if you can ;
For all his Pride, and his Philofophy,
'Tis evident, *Beafts* are, in their Degree,
As wife at leaft, and better far than *be.*
Thofe Creatures are the wifeft who attain,
By fureft Means, the Ends at which they aim.
If therefore JOWLER finds and kills his Hare,
Better than MEERS fupplies Committee Chair ;
Tho' one's a *Statefman,* t'other but a *Hound,*
JOWLER, in Juftice, will be wifer found.
You fee how far *Man's* Wifdom here extends ;
Look next, if *human Nature* makes Amends,
Whofe Principles moft gen'rous are, and juft,
And to whofe Morals you will fooner truft.
Be Judge yourfelf, I'll bring it to the Teft,
Which is the bafeft Creature, *Man* or *Beaft :*
Birds feed on Birds, Beafts on each other prey ;
But favage Man alone does Man betray.
Prefs'd by Neceffity, they kill for Food ;
Man undoes Man, to do himfelf no Good.
With Teeth and Claws by Nature arm'd, they hunt
Nature's Allowance, to fupply their Want :
But Man with Smiles, Embraces, Friendfhip's Praife,
Inhumanly his Fellow's Life betrays ;

With voluntary Pains works his Diſtreſs,
Not thro' Neceſſity, but Wantonneſs.
For Hunger, or for Love, they bite or tear,
Whilſt wretched Man is ſtill in Arms for Fear ;
For Fear he arms, and is of Arms afraid ;
From Fear to Fear ſucceſſively betray'd.
Baſe Fear, the Source whence his beſt Paſſions came,
His boaſted Honour, and his dear-bought Fame ;
That Luſt of Pow'r, to which he's ſuch a Slave,
And for the which alone he durſt be brave ;
To which his various Projects are deſign'd,
Which make him gen'rous, affable, and Kind ;
For which he takes ſuch Pains to be thought wiſe,
And ſcrews his Actions in a forc'd Diſguiſe,
Leading a tedious Life in Miſery,
Under laborious mean Hypocriſy.
Look to the Bottom of this vaſt Deſign,
Wherein Man's Wiſdom, Pow'r and Glory join ;
The Good he acts, the Ill he does endure,
'Tis all for Fear, to make himſelf ſecure.
Merely for Safety after Fame we thirſt ;
For all Men would be Cowards if they durſt ;
And Honeſty's againſt all Common-Senſe ;
Men muſt be Knaves, 'tis in their own Defence.
Mankind's diſhoneſt ; if you think it fair
Amongſt known Cheats to play upon the Square,
You'll be undone ———
Nor can weak Truth your Reputation ſave,
The Knaves will all agree to call you Knave :
Wrong'd ſhall he live, inſulted o'er, oppreſt,
Who durſt be leſs a Villain than the reſt.
Thus, Sir, you ſee what human Nature craves ;
Moſt Men are *Cowards,* all Men ſhould be *Knaves.*

The

The Diff'rence lies (as far as I can see)
Not in the Thing itself, but the Degree ;
And all the Subject-Matter of Debate,
Is only, Who's *a Knave of the first Rate ?*

ALL this with Indignation have I hurl'd
At the pretending Part of the proud World,
Who, swoln with selfish Vanity, devise
False Freedoms, holy Cheats, and formal Lies,
Over their Fellow-Slaves to tyrannize.

BUT if in Court so just a Man there be,
(In Court a just Man ! yet unknown to me)
Who does his needful Flattery direct,
Not to oppose and ruin, but protect ;
Since Flattery, which Way soever laid,
Is still a Tax on that unhappy Trade ;
If so upright a Statesman you can find,
Whose Passions bend to his unbyas'd Mind ;
Who does his Arts and Policies apply
To raise his Country, not his Family ;
Nor while his Pride known Avarice withstands,
Receives *Aureal* Bribes from Friends corrupted Hands.

Is there a *Churchman* who on *God* relies,
Whose Life his Faith and Doctrine justifies ?
Not one; blown up with vain Prelatic Pride,
Who, for Reproof of Sins, does Man deride ;
Whose envious Heart makes Preaching a Pretence,
With his obstrep'rous saucy Eloquence,
To chide at Kings, and rail at Men of Sense ;
Who from his Pulpit vents more peevish Lies,
More bitter Railings, Scandals, Calumnies,
Than at a Gossiping are thrown about,
When the good Wives get drunk, and then fall out ;

None

None of the fenfual Tribe, whofe Talents lie
In Avarice, Pride, Sloth, and Gluttony;
Who hunt good Livings, but abhor good Lives;
Whofe Luft exalted, to that Height arrives,
They act Adultery with their own Wives;
And e'er a Score of Years compleated be,
Can from the lofty Pulpit proudly fee
Half a large Parifh their own Progeny.
Nor doating BISHOP, who would be ador'd
For domineering at the Council-Board;
A greater Fop in Bufinefs at Fourfcore,
Fonder of ferious Toys, affected more
Than the gay glitt'ring Fool at *Twenty* proves,
With all his Noife, his taudry Cloaths, and Gloves.

   BUT a meek humble Man, of honeft Senfe,
Who, preaching Peace, does practife Continence;
Whofe pious Life's a Proof he does believe
Myfterious Truths which no Man can *conceive*.

   IF upon Earth there dwell fuch Godlike Men,
I'll here recant my Paradox to them,
Adore thofe Shrines of Virtue, Homage pay,
And with the Rabble World their Laws obey:
If fuch there are, yet grant me *this at leaft*,
Man differs more from *Man*, than *Man* from *Beaft*.

HORACE'S

✿✿✿✿✿ ✿✿✿✿✿✿✿✿✿ ✿✿✿✿✿

HORACE'S *Tenth Satire of the Firſt Book imitated.*

Nempe incompoſito dixi pede currere verſus. Lucil.

WELL, Sir, 'tis granted, I ſaid DRYDEN's Rhimes
 Were ſtol'n, unequal, nay, dull many Times.
  What fooliſh Patron is there found of his,
So blindly partial, to deny me this?
But that his Plays, embroider'd up and down,
With *Wit* and *Learning*, juſtly pleaſe the *Town*, ⎫
In the ſame Paper I as freely own: ⎬
Yet, having this allow'd, the heavy Maſs,   ⎭
That ſtuffs up his looſe Volumes, muſt not paſs;
For, by that Rule, I might as well admit,
CROWN's tedious Scenes for *Poetry* and *Wit*.
'Tis therefore not enough, when your *falſe Senſe*
Hits the *falſe Judgment* of an Audience
Of clapping Fools aſſembling, a vaſt Croud,
'Till the throng'd Play-Houſe cracks with the dull Load.
Tho' ev'n that Talent merits in ſome Sort,
That can divert the *Rabble* and the *Court*;
Which *blund'ring* SETTLE never could attain,
And *puzzling* OTWAY labours at *in vain* *.
But within due Proportion circumſcribe
Whate'er you write, that with a flowing Tide
The Stile may riſe; yet in its Riſe forbear
With uſeleſs Words t'oppreſs the weary'd Ear.
Here be your Language lofty; there more light,
Your *Rhet'ric* with your *Poetry* unite;

---

* *His Lordſhip here alludes only to* Mr. Otway's *Comedies.*

For Elegance fake, fometimes allay the Force
Of Epithet; 'twill foften the Difcourfe:
A *Jeft* in *Scorn* points out, and hits the Thing
More home, than the morofeft Satire's Sting.
SHAKESPEARE and JOHNSON did in *this* excel,
And might herein be imitated well;
Whom refin'd ETHEREGE copies not at all,
But is himfelf a mere *Original:*
Nor that *flow Drudge* in *fwift Pindaric* Strains,
FLATMAN, who COWLEY imitates-with Pains,
And rides a *jaded Mufe* whipt with *loofe Reins.*
When LEE makes *temp'rate* SCIPIO fret and rave,
And HANNIBAL a *whining am'rous Slave,*
I laugh, and wifh the hot-brain'd Fuftian Fool
In BUSBY's Hands, to be well lafh'd at School.
Of all our Modern Wits, none feem to me
Once to have touch'd upon true COMEDY,
But hafty SHADWELL and flow WYCHERLY.
SHADWELL's unfinifh'd Works do yet impart
Great Proofs of Force of *Nature,* none of *Art;*
With juft bold Strokes he dafhes here and there,
Shewing *Great Maftery* with *Little Care;*
Scorning to *varnifh* his *Good Touches* o'er,
To make the *Fools* and *Women* praife him more.
But WYCHERLY earns hard whate'er he gains;
He wants no *Judgment,* and he fpares no *Pains;*
He frequently excels; and, at the leaft,
Makes fewer Faults, than any of the reft.
WALLER, by Nature for the Bays defign'd,
With *Force,* and *Fire,* and *Fancy,* unconfin'd,
In *Panegyric* does excel Mankind.
He beft can turn, inforce, and foften Thing,
To praife great *Conquerors,* and flatter Kings,

For *pointed Satire* I would BUCKHURST chuse,
The *Beſt good Man*, with the *Worſt natur'd* Muſe.
For *Songs* and *Verſes* mannerly obſcene,
That can ſtir *Nature* up by Springs unſeen,
And, without forcing Bluſhes, warm the Queen;
SEDLEY has that prevailing gentle Art,
That can with a *Reſiſtleſs Pow'r* impart
The *Looſeſt* Wiſhes to the *Chaſteſt* Heart;
Raiſe ſuch a Conflict, kindle ſuch a Fire,
Betwixt declining Virtue and Deſire,
Till the poor vanquiſh'd Maid diſſolves away
In Dreams all Night, in Sighs and Tears all Day.
DRYDEN in vain try'd this nice Way of Wit,
For he to be a Tearing Blade thought fit;
But when he would be ſharp, he ſtill was *blunt*,
To friſk and frolick *Fancy* he'd cry ⸺ .
Would give the *Ladies* a Dry-bawdy Bob,
And thus he got the Name of *Poet-Squab.*
But, to be juſt, 'twill to his Praiſe be found,
His *Excellencies* more than *Faults* abound;
Nor dare I from his ſacred Temple tear.
The *Laurel*, which he beſt deſerves to wear.
But does not DRYDEN find ev'n JOHNSON dull,
BEAUMONT and FLETCHER incorrect, and full
Of *Lewd Lines*, as he calls them? SHAKESPEARE's Stile,
Stiff and affected? To *his own*, the while,
Allowing all the *Juſtice*, that his *Pride*
So arrogantly had to theſe deny'd?
And may not I have Leave impartially
To ſearch and cenſure DRYDEN's Works, and try,
If thoſe groſs Faults his *Choice Pen* does commit,
Proceed from Want of *Judgment*, or of *Wit*?
Or, if his lumpiſh Fancy does refuſe
Spirit and Grace to his looſe ſlattern Muſe?

Five

Five Hundred Verſes ev'ry Morning writ,
Prove him no more a *Poet* than a *Wit*.
Such *ſcribbling Authors* have been ſent before;
Muſtapha, the *Iſland Princeſs*, forty more,
Were Things, perhaps, compos'd in Half an Hour.
To write what may ſecurely ſtand the Teſt,
Of being well read over, thrice at leaſt ;
Compare each *Phraſe*, examine ev'ry *Line*,
Weigh ev'ry *Word*, and ev'ry *Thought* refine:
Scorn all *Applauſe* the *vile Rout* can beſtow,
And be content to *pleaſe thoſe few* who *know*.
Can'ſt thou be ſuch a vain miſtaken Thing,
To wiſh thy Works may make a *Play-houſe* ring.
With the *unthinking Laughter* and *poor Praiſe*
Of *Fops* and *Ladies*, faƐious for thy *Plays ?*
Then ſend a cunning Friend to learn thy Doom,
From the ſhrew'd Judges in the *Drawing-Room*.
I've no Ambition on that idle Score,
But ſay with BETTY MORRICE heretofore,
When a *Court-Lady* call'd her BUCKHURST's Whore:
I pleaſe one Man of Wit, am proud on't too ;
Let all the Coxcombs dance to Bed to you.
Should I be troubled with the PURBLIND KNIGHT*,
Who ſquints more in his *Judgment*, than his *Sight*,
Picks *ſilly Faults*, and cenſures what I write ?'
Or when the *Poor-fed Poets* of the Town,
For *Scraps* and *Coach-Room* cry my Verſes down ?
I loath the Rabble, 'tis enough for me,
If SEDLEY, SHADWELL, SHEPHARD, WYCHERLY,
GODOLPHIN, BUTLER, BUCKHURST, BUCKINGHAM,
Or ſome few more, whom I omit to name,
Approve my Senſe, I count their *Cenſure* Fame.

---

* *Sir* Carr Scrope.

* * * * * * * * * * * * * * * * * * * *

An Imitation of the First Satire of JUVENAL.

Semper ego Auditor tantum? ————

MUST I with Patience ever silent sit,
Perplex'd with *Fools*, who still believe they've Wit?
Must I find ev'ry Place by *Coxcombs* seiz'd,
Hear this affected Nonsense, and seem pleas'd?
Must I meet HENNINGHAM where'er I go,
ARP, ARRAN, Villain FRANK, nay, POULT'NEY too?
Shall HEWET pertly crawl from Place to Place,
And scabby VILLERS for a Beauty pass?
Shall HOWE and BRANDON Politicians prove,
And SUTHERLAND presume to be in Love?
Shall pimping DENCOURT patient Cuckolds blame,
LUMLEY and SAVAGE 'gainst the Pope disclaim?
Who can abstain from *Satire* in this Age?
What Nature wants, I find supply'd by Rage.
Some do for Pimping, some for Treach'ry rise;
But none's made Great for being Good or Wise.
Deserve a Dungeon, if you would be *Great*;
Rogues always are our *Ministers of State*;
Mean prostrate Bitches, for a *Bridewell* fit,
With *England's* wretched *Queen* must equal sit:
Ranelagh and fearful MULGRAVE are preferr'd;
Virtue's commended, but ne'er meets Reward.
May I ne'er be like these, I'll ask no more;
I would not be the Men, to have their Pow'r.
Who'd be a *Monarch*, to endure the prating
Of NELL and sawcy OGLETHORP, in Waiting?
Who

Who would Southampton's driv'ling Cuckold be?
Who would be York, and bear his *Infamy*?
What Wretch would be Green's base-begotten Son?
Who wou'd be James, out-witted and undone?
Who'd be like Sunderland, a cringing Knave?
Like *Hall'fax* wise, like boorish Pembroke brave?
Who'd be that patient Bardish Shrewsbury?
Or who would Frazier's chatt'ring Mordaunt be?
Who'd be a *Wit*, in Dryden's *cudgell'd Skin*?
Or who'd be *safe*, and *senseless*, like Tom-Thynne?

⚖⚖⚖⚖ ⚖⚖⚖⚖⚖⚖⚖⚖ ⚖⚖⚖⚖

SATIRE on the TIMES.

Nobilitas sola atque unica Virtus *est.*	Juv. Sat. viii.
Virtue *alone is true* Nobility.	Dryd.

NOT *Rome*, in all her Splendor, could compare
   With those great Blessings happy *Britons* share;
Vainly they boast their *Kings* of heav'nly Race;
A *King* incarnate *England*'s Throne does grace?
Chaste in his Pleasures, in Devotion grave,
To his Friends constant, to his Foes he's brave:
His Justice is thro' all the World admir'd,
His Word held sacred, and his Scepter fear'd.
No Tumults do about his Palace move,
Freed from Rebellion by his People's Love.
Nor do we less in Councils wise prevail,
As all our late Transactions loudly tell.
Not only *Prorogations* Good create,
But th' adjourn'd *Play-House* is a *Coup d' Eclat*:

So learned *Chymifts*, when they long have try'd,
For Secrets thrifty *Nature* fain would hide,
In bafeft Matter often *Spirits* find,
Which Providence for greater Ufe defign'd.
But who can wonder at fuch vaft Succefs ?
Our CATO, SUNDERLAND, ne'er promis'd lefs.
Abroad in Embaffay he firft was fam'd,
Where he fo ftrictly *England's* Rights maintain'd ;
At Home an humble Creature to her Grace,
And Mrs. WARD preferr'd him to the Place.

THEN, for *Commanders*, both by Sea and Land;
(New ones we *make*, and Old ones we *difband*,)
YORK, who thrice chang'd his Ship; thro' warlike Rage,
And MONMOUTH, who's the SCIPIO of the Age,.
The firft, Lord Admiral, but more renown'd,
For Pox and Popery than public Wound.
This is the Man, whofe Vice each *Satire* feeds,
And for whom no one Virtue intercedes ;
Deftin'd for *England's* Plague, from infant Time,.
Curs'd with a Perfon fouler than his Crime.
But mightier Things than thefe do ftill remain :
PLYMOUTH, who lately fhew'd upon the Plain,
And did by HEWIT's Fall, immortal Honour gain. }

So, *Moufe* and *Frog* came gravely to the Field,
Both fear'd to fight, and yet both fcorn'd to yield;
Their famous *Billet-Doux* and Duel, prove
Them both as fit for Combat, as for Love.
Amongft all thefe, 'twere not amifs to name
POULTNEY, to whom *St. Omers* Siege gave Fame.

NoR do Wits lefs our polifh'd Court adorn,
Than Men of Prowefs, for Atchievements born.
Romantic MORDAUNT, who in *empty* Lines
His happier Rival tedioufly defines ;
That well knew how to value painted Toys,
And left the *Tartar* to be catch'd by *Boys :*
But his chief Talent is in *Hiftories,*
Which of *himfelf* he tells, and always lies.
DAINCOURT would fain be thought both Wit and Bully,.
But Punk-rid RADCLIFFE's not a greater Cully,
Nor taudry ISHAM, intimately known
To all pox'd Whores, and famous Rooks in Town.

No *Ladies* my refpectful Mufe will name ;
She thinks it Blafphemy to touch their Fame.
Safe may they live, who faithful are, and kind ;
But may lewd Scowrers no Redemption find.
May Young and.Old inceffantly give Thanks
For that blefs'd Nurs'ry of Intrigue, *Mill-Banks.*
May *Leic'fter-Fields* repair their *Matron's* Fall ;
But ftill fubfcribe in *Feafts* of *Love* to th' *Mall,*
And Mrs. STAFFORD yield to BETTY HALL.

A SATIRE *which the* KING *took out of his Pocket.*

PReferv'd by Wonder in the *Oak,* O CHARLES !
And then brought in by Trick of ALBEMARLE's :
The firft by *Providence,* the next all *Devil,*
Shews thou'rt a Compound both of *Good* and *Evil ;*

The

The *Bad* we've too-long known, the *Good*'s to come,
But not expected 'till the *Day* of *Doom*.
Was ever *Prince*'s Soul so meanly poor,
To be a Slave to ev'ry little *Whore*?
The Seamen's Needle nimbly points the Pole,
But thine still turns to ev'ry craving Hole;
Which, *Wolf*-like, in that Breast raw Flesh devours,
And must be fed all Seasons, and all Hours.
—— is the Mansion-House where thou dost dwell;
But thou art fix'd as *Tortoise* to her Shell,
Whose Head peeps out a little now and then,
To take the Air, and then creeps in again.
Strong is thy Lust; in —— thou'rt always diving,
And I dare say thou pray'st to die a f——

How poorly squander'st thou thy S—— away,
Who should'st get Kings for Nations to obey.
But thou, poor *Prince*, so uselesly hast sown it,
That the *Creation* is asham'd to own it.
Witness the Royal Heirs, sprung from the Belly
Of thy anointed *Princess*, Madam NELLY,
Whose first Employment was, with open Throat,
To cry *Fresh-Herrings*, even *Ten a Groat*.
Then was by Madam Ross expos'd to Town;
I mean to those who would give *Half-a-Crown*:
Next in the *Play-House* she took her Degree,
As *Men* commence at *University*,
No *Doctors*, 'till they've *Masters* been before;
So she no *Player* was, 'till first a *Whore*.
Look back, and see the *People* mad with Rage,
To see the Bitch in such an Equipage;
And ev'ry Day that *they* the Monster see,
They let ten thousand Curses fly at thee:

Aloud

Aloud in public Streets they ufe thee thus,
And none dare check 'em, they're fo numerous.
Stopping the *Bank* in thee was only great,
But in a Subject it had been a Cheat.
To pay thy Debts, what Sum can'ft thou advance,
Now thy *Exchequer* is remov'd to *France*;
T'enrich a Harlot all made up of *French*,
Not worthy to be call'd a *Whore*, but *Wench* ?

CLEVELAND indeed deferves that NOBLE *Name*,
Whofe monft'rous Letchery exceeds all *Fame*;
The Emprefs MESSALINE was cloy'd with Luft at laft;
But you could never fatisfy this letch'rous Beaft :
CLEVELAND, I fay, is much to be admir'd,
Altho' fhe ne'er was fatisfy'd, or tir'd :
Full forty Men a Day provided for this Whore,
Yet, like a Bitch, fhe wags her Tail for more.
Where are the *Bifhops* now? Where is their *Bawdy-Court*?
Inftead of *Penance*, they indulge the Sport ;
For ftanding in *White Sheets* their Courage cools,
And's only fit for *Frenchmen*, and for Fools.
O Heav'ns ! wer't thou for this loofe Life preferv'd ?
Are there no *Gods* nor *Laws* to be obferv'd ?
Nineveh repented after *forty* Days ;
Be yet a KING, and wear the Royal Bays ·
But JONAH's Threats will ne'er awaken thee ;
Repentance is too *mean* for *Majefty*.
Go, practife HELIOGABALUS's Sin,
Forget to be a *Man*, and learn to *fpin*.
Go, dally with the *Women* at their *Wheels*,
'Till, NERO-like, they pull thee out by th' *Heels*.
Go, read what MAH'MET did, (that was a Thing
Did well become the Grandeur of a *King*,)

Who-

Who all tranfported with his *Miftrefs'* Charms,
And never p'eas'd, but in her *lovely* Arms,
Yet, when his *Janizaries* wifh'd her dead,
With his own Hand cut off IRENE's Head.
Make fuch a Practice with thyfelf as this,
Then thou may'ft once more tafte of Happinefs;
Each one will love thee, and the *Parliament*
Will their unkind and ftubborn *Votes* repent;
And at your Feet lay open all their Purfes,
And give you all their Prayers, unmix'd with Curfes.

ALL this I wifh, altho' I'm not your Friend,
'Till, like a Child, you promife to amend;
If not, you'll find your Subjects rugged Stuff;
But, now I think on't, *I have faid enough.*

❊❊❊❊❊❊❊❊❊❊❊❊❊

The DEBAUCHEE.

I Rife at Eleven, I dine about Two,
  I get drunk before Sev'n; and the next Thing I do,
I fend for my Whore, when, for fear of a *Clap*,
I —— in her Hand, and I fpew in her Lap;
Then we quarrel and fcold, 'till I fall faft afleep,
When the Bitch, growing bold, to my Pocket does creep;
Then flily fhe leaves me, and, to revenge the Affront,
At once fhe bereaves me of Money and ——.
If by Chance then I wake, hot headed and drunk,
What a Coil do I make for the Lofs of my Punk!
I ftorm, and I roar, and I fall in a Rage,
And miffing my Whore, I b——r my Page.
Then Crop fick all Morning, I rail at my Men,
And in Bed I lie yawning 'till Eleven again.

✳✳✳✳✳✳✳✳✳✳✳✳✳✳✳✳✳✳✳

A SATIRE *on the* KING, *for which he was banished the* COURT, *and turned* MOUNTEBANK.

IN the Isle of *Great-Britain*, long since famous
    known
For breeding the best ———— in *Christendom*,
There reigns, and there, long may he reign and
    thrive.
The easiest *Prince*, and best-bred *Man* alive;
Him no Ambition moves to seek Renown,
Like the *French* Fool, to wander up and down,
Starving his Subjects, hazarding his Crown.
Nor are his high Desires above his Strength,
His *Sceptre* and his ———— are of a Length;
And she that plays with *one*, may sway the *other*,
And make him little wiser than his *Brother*.
I hate all Monarchs, and the Thrones they sit on,
From the *Hector* of *France*, to the *Cully* of *Briton*.
Poor *Prince!* thy ———— like the Buffoons at Court,
It governs thee, because it makes thee Sport.
Tho' Safety, Law, Religion, Life, lies on't,
'Twill break thro' all, to make its Way to ————
Restless he rolls about from Whore to Whore,
A merry *Monarch*, scandalous, and poor.
To *Carewell*, the most dear of all thy Dears,
The sure Relief of thy declining Years;
Oft he bewails his Fortune, and her Fate,
To love so well, and to be lov'd so late.

For

For when in her he fettles well his T——,
Yet his dull gracelefs Buttocks hang an A——.
This you'd believe, had I but Time to tell ye,
The Pain it cofts to poor laborious *Nelly*,
While fhe employs Hands, Fingers, Lips and Thighs,
E'er fhe can raife the *Member* fhe enjoys.

The MAIDENHEAD.

HAVE you not in a Chimney feen
A fullen Faggot wet and green,
How coyly it receives the Heat,
And at both Ends does fume and fweat ?

So fares it with the harmlefs Maid,
When firft upon her Back fhe's laid ;
But the well-experienc'd Dame,
Cracks and rejoices in the Flame.

TUNBRIDGE-WELLS:

A SATIRE.

AT Five this Morn, when PHOEBUS rais'd his
Head
From THETIS' Lap, I rais'd myfelf from Bed ;
And mounting Steed, I trotted to the WATERS,
The Rendezvous of Fools, Buffoons, and Praters,
Cuckolds, Whores, Citizens, their Wives and Daugh-
ters,

My

My fqueamifh Stomach I with Wine had brib'd,
To undertake the Dofe that was prefcrib'd:
But turning Head, a fudden curfed Crew
That innocent Provifion overthrew,
Did, without drinking, make me purge and fpew.
From Coach and Six a THING unweildy roll'd,
Whom Lumber-Cart more decently would hold ;
As wife as Calf it look'd, as big as Bully,
But handled, prov'd a mere Sir NICH'LAS CULLY;
A bawling Fop, a *nat'ral* NOKES, and yet
He dar'd to *cenfure*, to be thought a *Wit*.
To make him more ridiculous, in fpight,
Nature contriv'd the Fool fhould be a Knight.
How wife is *Nature*, when fhe does difpenfe
A large Eftate, to cover Want of Senfe !
The Man's a Fool, 'tis true, but that's no Matter ;
For he's a mighty Wit with thofe that flatter ;
But a poor Blockhead is a wretched Creature.
Tho' he alone was difmal Sight enough,
His Train contributed to fet him off,
All of his Shape, all of the felf-fame Stuff ;
No Spleen or Malice cou'd on them be thrown,
Nature had done the Bus'nefs of Lampoon,
And in their Looks their Characters were fhown.
Endeavouring this irkfome Sight to baulk,
And a more irkfome Noife, their filly Talk,
I filently flunk down to th' lower Walk.
(But often, when we would *Charybdis* fhun,
Down upon *Scylla* 'tis our Fate to run :)
For there it was my curfed Luck to find
As great a Fop, tho' of another Kind.
A tall ftiff Fool, that walk'd in *Spanifh* Guife ;
The Buckram Puppet never ftirr'd his Eyes ;
But grave as Owl it look'd, as Woodcock wife.

He

He fcorns the empty Talk of this mad Age,
And fpeaks all Proverb, Sentence and Adage;
Can with as much Solemnity buy Eggs,
As a Cabal can Talk of their Intrigues;
Mafter of Ceremonies, yet can't difpenfe
With the Formality of talking Senfe.
From hence unto the upper Walk I ran,
Where a new Scene of Foppery began;
A Tribe of Curates, Priefts, Canonical Elves,
Fit Company for none befide themfelves,
Were got together; each his Diftemper told,
Scurvy, Stone, Strangury; fome were fo bold
To charge their Spleen to be their Mifery,
And on that wife Difeafe lay Infamy;
But none had Modefty enought t'explain
His Want of Learning, Honefty or Brain,
The general Difeafes of that Train.
Thefe call themfelves Ambaffadors of Heaven,
And faucily pretend Commiffions given;
But fhould an *Indian* King, whofe fmall Command
Seldom extends beyond ten Miles of Land,
Send forth fuch wretched Fools on an Embaffage,
He'd find but fmall Effects of fuch a Meffage.
Lift'ning, I found the Top of all this Rabble,
Pert * *Bayes,* with his *Importance* comfortable.
He being rais'd to an Arch-Deaconry,
By trampling on *Religion, Loyalty* †,
Was grown fo great, and look'd too fat and jolly
To be diflurb'd with Care and Melancholy;
Tho' *Marvell* had enough expos'd his Folly ‡.

---

* *Dr. Parker, afterwards Bifhop of* Oxford.
† *He writ a Book, entitled,* Religion and Loyalty.
‡ *In His* Rehearfal Tranfpros'd.

He drank to carry off some old Remains
His lazy dull Distemper left in's Veins ;
Let him drink on; it is not a whole Flood
Can give sufficient Sweetness to his Blood,
Or make his Nature or his Manners good.
* *Importance* drank too, tho' she'ad been no Sinner,
To wash away some Dregs he had spew'd in her.
Next after these, a fulsome *Irish* Crew
Of silly *Macks* were offer'd to my View ;
The Things did talk, but hearing what they said,
I hid myself the Kindness to evade.
Nature had plac'd these Wretches beneath Scorn,
They can't be call'd so vile as they are born.
Amidst the Crowd I next myself convey'd,
For now there comes, White-Wash and Paint being laid,
Mother and Daughter, Mistress and the Maid,
And 'Squire, with Wig and Pantaloons display'd.
But ne'er could Conventicle, Play or Fair,
For a true Medley, with this Herd compare.
Here Lords, Knights, 'Squires, Ladies and Countesses,
Chandlers, and barren Women, Sempstresses,
Were mix'd together ; nor did they agree
More in their Humours than their Quality.
Here, waiting for Gallant, young Damsel stood,
Leaning on Cane, and muffled up in Hood.
The Would-be-Wit, whose Bus'ness was to woe,
With Hat remov'd, and solemn Scrape of Shoe.

———————————————

* Parker *excused himself, for delaying to answer*
Marvell, *on Account of* Matters *of a more comfortable* Importance, *(which prov'd to be* Matrimony.*)* Marvell
is very witty upon that Word. *See the* Rehearsal Tranfpros'd, *Part II.*

*Advances

Advances bowing, then genteely fhrugs,
And ruffled Fore-Top into Order tugs;
And thus accofts her; *Madam, methinks the Weather*
Is grown much more ferene fince you came hither;
You influence the Heav'ns; but fhould the Sun
Withdraw himfelf, to fee his Rays out-done
By your bright Eyes, They could fupply the Morn,
And make a Day, before the Day be born.
With Mouth fcrew'd up, conceited winking Eyes,
And Breaft thruft forward, *Lord, Sir,* (fhe replies)
It is your Goodnefs, and not my Deferts,
Which makes you fhew this Learning, Wit and Parts.
He, puzzled, bites his Nails, both to difplay
The fparkling Ring, and think what next to fay,
And thus breaks forth afrefh; *Madam, Egad,*
Your Luck at Cards laft Night was very bad;
At Cribbidge fifty nine —— *and the next Shew.*
To make the Game, —— *and yet to want thofe two.*
G — d D ——, *Madam, I'm the Son of a Whore,*
If in my Life I faw the like before.
To Pedlar's Stall he drags her, and her Breaft,
With Hearts, and fuch like foolifh Toys, he dreft;
And then more fmartly to expound the Riddle
Of all this Prattle, gives her a *Scotch* Fiddle.
Tir'd with this difmal Stuff, away I ran,
Where were two Wives, with Girl juft fit for Man, }
Short-breath'd, with pallid Lips, and Vifage wan; }
Some Courtefies pafs'd, and the old Compliment,
Of being glad to fee each other, fpent,
With Hand in Hand they lovingly did walk,
And one began thus to renew the Talk:
I pray, good Madam, if it mayn't be thought
Rudenefs in me, what Caufe has hither brought

Your Ladyſhip? She, ſoon replying, ſmil'd,
We've got a good Eſtate, but have no Child;
And I'm inform'd, theſe Wells will make a barren
Woman as fruitful as a Coney-Warren.

  THE firſt return'd, *For this Cauſe I am come,*
For I can have no Quietneſs at Home;
My Huſband grumbles, tho' we have got one,
This poor young Girl, and mutters for a Son;
And ſhe is griev'd with Head-Ach, Pangs and Throws,
Is full Sixteen, and never yet had Thoſe.
She ſoon reply'd, *Get her a* Huſband, *Madam;*
I marry'd 'bout that Age, and ne'er 'ad had 'em;
Was juſt like her: Steel Waters *let alone,*
A Back of Steel will better bring them down;
And ten to one but they themſelves will try
The ſame Means to increaſe their Family.
Poor ſilly Fribble, who, by Subtilty
Of Midwife, trueſt Friend to Lechery,
Perſuaded art to be at Pains and Charge,
To give thy Wife Occaſion to enlarge
Thy ſilly Head; for here walks *Cuff* and *Kick*,
With brawny Back and Legs, and potent ——
Who more ſubſtantially can cure thy Wife,
And on her half-dead Womb beſtow new Life.
From theſe the Waters got their Reputation
Of good Aſſiſtants unto Propagation.
Some warlike Men were now got into th' Throng,
With Hair ty'd back, ſinging a bawdy Song.
Not much afraid, I got a nearer View,
And 'twas my Chance to know the dreadful Crew.
They were Cadets, that ſeldom can appear,
Damn'd to the Stint of Thirty Pounds a Year;
With Hawk or Fiſt, and Greyhound led in Hand,
The Dog and Foot-Boy ſometimes to command;

                                            Now

Now having trimm'd a caſt-off ſpavin Horſe,
With three Halfpence for Guineas in their Purſe,
Two ruſty Piſtols, Scarf about their Arſe,
Coat lin'd with Red, they here preſume to ſwell ;
This goes for *Captain*, that for *Colonel*.

So the *Bear-Garden* APE, on his Steed mounted,
No longer is *Jackanapes* accounted ;
But is, by Virtue of his Trumpery, then
Call'd by the Name of the *young Gentleman*.
Bleſs me ! thought I, what Thing is *Man*, that thus,
In all his Shapes, is ſo ridiculous !
Ourſelves with Noiſe of *Reaſon* we do pleaſe
In vain, Humanity's our worſt Diſeaſe ;
Thrice happy Beaſts are, who, becauſe they be
Of *Reaſon* void, are ſo of Foppery.
Faith, I was ſo aſham'd, that with Remorſe,
I us'd the Inſolence to mount my *Horſe* :
For *he*, doing only Things fit for his *Nature*,
Did ſeem to *me* by much the wiſer *Creature*.

To all Curious CRITICKS *and* ADMIRERS *of* Metre.

HAVE you not ſeen the raging ſtormy Main,
Toſs a Ship up, then caſt her down again ?
Sometimes ſhe ſeems to touch the very Skies,
And then again upon the Sand ſhe lies.
Or have you ſeen a Bull, when he is jealous,
How he does tear the Ground, and roars, and bellows ?

Or have you seen the pretty Turtle Dove,
When she laments the Absence of her Love?
Or have you seen the Fairies, when they sing,
And dance with Mirth together in a Ring?
Or have you seen our Gallants make a Puther,
With GRACE the Fair; and, fairer yet, *Ann Struther**?
Or have you seen the *Daughters* of APOLLO †
Pour down their rhiming Liquors in a hollow
Cane ——————
In spungy Brain congealing into Verse?
If you have seen all this, then kiss mine Arse.

The Happy NIGHT ‖.

SINCE now my SYLVIA is as kind as fair,
Let Wit and Joy succeed my dull Despair.
O what a Night of Pleasure was the last!
A full Reward for all my Troubles past;
And on my Head if future Mischiefs fall,
This happy Night shall make amends for all.
Nay, tho' my SYLVIA's Love should turn to Hate,
I'll think of this, and die contented with my Fate.

TWELVE was the lucky Minute when we met,
And on her Bed were close together set;
Tho' list'ning Spies might be perhaps too near,
Love fill'd our Hearts; there was no Room for Fear.
Now, whilst I strive her melting Heart to move,
With all the pow'rful Eloquence of Love,

---

* *Two Sisters.*   † *The* Nine *Muses.*
‖ *The late Duke of* Buckinghamshire *was pleased to own himself the Author of this Poem.*

In

In her fair Face I faw the Colour rife,
And an unufual Softnefs in her Eyes;
Gently they look, and I with Joy adore,
That only Charm they never had before.
The Wounds they made her Tongue was us'd to heal, ⎫
But now thefe gentle Enemies reveal   ⎬
A Secret, which that Friend would ftill conceal. ⎭
My Eyes tranfported too with am'rous Rage,
Seem fierce with Expectation to engage;
But faft fhe holds my Hands, and clofe her Thighs
And what fhe longs to do, with Frowns denies.
A ftrange Effect on foolifh Women wrought,
Bred in Difguifes, and by Cuftom taught:
Cuftom, that Prudence fometimes over-rules,
But ferves inftead of Reafon to the Fools!
Cuftom, which all the World to Slav'ry brings,
The dull Excufe for doing filly Things.
She, by this Method of her foolifh Sex,
Is forc'd a-while me and herfelf to vex:
But now, when thus we had been ftruggling long,
Her Limbs grow weak, and her Defires grow ftrong;
How can fhe hold to let the *Hero* in?
He ftorms without, and Love betrays within.
Her Hands at laft, to hide her Blufhes, leave
The Fort unguarded, willing to receive
My fierce Affault, made with a Lover's Hafte,
Like Lightning piercing, and as quickly paft.

Thus does fond Nature with her Children play;
Juft fhews us Joy, then fnatches it away.
'Tis not th'Excefs of Pleafure makes it fhort,
The Pain of Love's as raging as the Sport;
And yet, alas! that loft, we figh all Night
With Grief; but fcarce one Moment with Delight.

Some little Pain may check her kind Defire,
But not enough to make her once retire.
Maids Wounds for Pleafure bear, as Men for Praife ;
Here Honour heals, there Love the Smart allays.
The World, if juft, would harmful Courage blame,
And this more innocent reward with Fame.
Now fhe her well contented Thoughts employs
On her paft Fears, and on her future Joys:
Whofe Harbinger did roughly all remove,
To make fit Room for great, luxurious Love.
Fond of the welcome Gueft, her Arms embrace
My Body, and her Hands another Place ;
Which with one Touch fo pleas'd and proud doth grow,
It fwells beyond the Grafp that made it fo ;
Confinement fcorns, in any ftraiter Walls
Than thofe of Love, where it contented falls.

THO' twice o'erthrown, he more enflam'd does rife,
And will, to the laft Drop, fight out the Prize,
She like fome *Amazon* in Story proves,
That overcomes the *Hero* whom fhe loves.
In the clofe Strife fhe takes fo much Delight,
She then can think of nothing but the Fight :
With Joy fhe lays him panting at her Feet,
But with more Joy does his Recov'ry meet.
Her trembling Hands firft gently raife his Head ;
She almoft dies for fear that he is dead :
Then binds his Wounds up with a bufy Hand,
And with that Balm enables him to ftand ;
'Till by her Eyes fhe conquers him once more,
And wounds him deeper than fhe did before.
Tho' fallen from the Top of Pleafure's Hill,
With longing Eyes we look up thither ftill ;

Still

Still thither our unweary'd Wishes tend,
'Till we that Height of Happiness ascend
By gentle Steps ; th' Ascent itself exceeds
All Joys, but that alone to which it leads :
First then, so long and lovingly we kiss,
As if like Doves, we knew no dearer Bliss.
Still in one Mouth our Tongues together play,
While groping Hands are pleased no less than they.
Thus cling'd together, now a while we rest,
Breathing our Souls into each other's Breast ;
Then give a gen'ral Kiss of all our Parts,
While this best Way we make Exchange of Hearts.
Here would my Praise, as well as Pleasure, dwell ;
Enjoyment's self I scarcely like so well :
The little this comes short of Rage and Strength,
Is largely recompenc'd with endless Length.
This is a Joy would last, if we could stay ;
But Love's too eager to admit Delay,
And hurries us along so smooth a Way.
Now, wanton with Delight, we nimbly move
Our pliant Limbs, in all the Shapes of Love ;
Our Motion's not like those of gamesome Fools,
Whose active Bodies shew their heavy Souls ;
But Sports of Love, in which a willing Mind
Makes us as able, as our Hearts are kind:
At length, all languishing, and out of Breath,
Panting, as in the Agonies of Death,
We lie entranc'd, 'till one provoking Kiss
Transports our ravish'd Souls to Paradise.
O Heaven of Love ! thou Moment of Delight !
Wrong'd by my Words, my Fancy does thee Right.
Methinks I lie all melting in her Charms,
And fast lock'd up within her Legs and Arms ;

E 5. Bent

Bent are our Minds, and all our Thoughts on Fire,
Just lab'ring in the Pangs of fierce Defire.
At once, like Mifers, wallowing in their Stcre,
In full Poffeffion ; yet defiring more.

Thus with repeated Pleafures, while we wafte
Our happy Hours, that, like fhort Minutes paft,
To fuch a Sum of Blifs our Joys amount,
The Number now becomes too great to count.
Silent, as Night, are all fincereft Joys,
Like deepeft Waters running with leaft Noife.
But now at laft, for Want of farther Force,
From Deeds, alas ! we fall into Difcourfe :
A Fall which each of us in vain bemoans ;
A greater Fall than that of Kings from Thrones.
The Tide of Pleafure flowing now no more,
We lie like Fifh left gafping on the Shore ;
And now, as after fighting, Wounds appear,
Which we in Heat did neither feel, nor fear :
She, for her Sake, entreats me to give o'er,
And yet, for mine, would gladly fuffer more.
Her Words are coy, while all her Motions woo,
And, when fhe asks me, if it pleafe me too,
I rage to fhew how well, but 'twill not do.

Thus would hot Love run itself out of Breath,
And wanting Reft, find it too foon in Death ;
Did not wife Nature, with a gentle Force,
Reftrain its Rage, and ftop its headlong Courfe :
Indulgently fevere, fhe well does fpare
This Child of hers, that moft deferves her Care.

✿✿✿✿✿✿✿✿✿✿✿✿✿✿✿✿

The *Imperfect* ENJOYMENT.

FRUITION was the Queſtion in Debate,
  Which like ſo hot a Caſuiſt I ſtate,
That ſhe my Freedom urg'd as my Offence,
To teach my Reaſon to ſubdue my Senſe ;
But yet this angry Cloud, that did proclaim
Vollies of Thunder, melted into Rain ;
And this adult'rate Stamp of ſeeming nice,
Made feigned Virtue but a Bawd to Vice ;
For, by a Compliment that's ſeldom known,
She thruſts me out, and yet invites me Home ;
And theſe Denials but advance Delight,
As Prohibition ſharpens Appetite ;
For the kind Curtain raiſing my Eſteem,
To wonder at the Opening of the Scene,
When of her *Breaſt* her *Hands* the Guardians were,
Yet I ſalute each *ſullen* OFFICER ;
The', like the flaming Sword before my Eyes,
They block the Paſſage to my Paradiſe ;
Nor could thoſe Tyrant-Hands ſo guard the Coin,
But Love, where't cannot purchaſe, may purloin :
For tho' her Breaſts are hid, her Lips are Prize,
To make me rich beyond my Avarice ;
Yet my Ambition my Affection fed,
To conquer both the *White Roſe* and the *Red*.
Th' Event prov'd true ; for on the Bed ſhe ſate,
And ſeem'd to court what ſhe had ſeem'd to hate ;
Heat of Reſiſtance had increas'd her Fire,
And weak Defence is turn'd to ſtrong Deſire.

                                        What

What unkind Influence could interpose,
When two such Stars did in Conjunction close?
Only too hasty Zeal my Hopes did foil,
Pressing to feed her Lamp, I spilt my Oil;
And that which most Reproach upon me hurl'd,
Was dead to her, gives Life to all the World;
Nature's chief Prop, and Motion's primest Source,
In me lost both their Figure and their Force.
Sad Conquest! when it is the Victor's Fate,
To die at th' Entrance of the op'ning Gate:
Like prudent Corporations, had we laid
A common Stock by, we'ad improv'd our Trade;
But as a prodigal Heir, I spent by-th'-bye,
What, Home-directed, would serve her and I,
When next in such Assaults I chance to be,
Give me less Vigour, more Activity;
For Love turns impotent, when strain'd too high;
His very Cordials make him sooner die;
Evaporates in Fume the Fire too great;
Love's Chymistry thrives best in equal Heat.

A SATIRE *against* MARRIAGE.

HUSBAND, thou dull unpity'd Miscreant,
 Wedded to Noise, to Misery and Want;
Sold an eternal Vassal for thy Life,
Oblig'd to cherish and to hate thy Wife:
Drudge on 'till Fifty at thy own Expence,
Breathe out thy Life in one Impertinence:
Repeat thy loath'd Embraces ev'ry Night,
Prompted to act by Duty, not Delight:

Christen

Chriften thy forward Bantling once a Year,
And carefully thy fpurious Iffue rear :
Go once a Week to fee the Brat at Nurfe,
And let the young Impoftor drain thy Purfe :
Hedge-Sparrow like, what Cuckoos have begot,
Do thou maintain, incorrigible Sot !
Oh ! I could curfe the Pimp, (who could do lefs ?)
He's beneath Pity, and beyond Redrefs.
Pox on him, let him go, what can I fay ?
Anathemas on him are thrown away.
The Wretch is marry'd, and hath known the worft,
And his great Bleffing is, he can't be curft.
Marriage! O Hell and Furies ! name it not ;
Hence ! hence ! ye holy Cheats ; a Plot ! a Plot !
Marriage ! 'Tis but a licens'd Way to fin ;
A Noofe to catch religious Woodcocks in ;
Or the Nick-Name of Love's malicious Fiend,
Begot in Hell to perfecute Mankind.
'Tis the Deftroyer of our Peace and Health,
Mif-fpender of our Time, our Strength and Wealth ;
The Enemy of Valour, Wit, Mirth, all
That we can virtuous, good, or pleafant call.
By Day 'tis nothing but an endlefs Noife,
By Night the Eccho of forgotten Joys :
Abroad, the Sport, and Wonder of the Crowd,
At Home, the hourly Breach of what they vow'd :
In Youth, 'tis *Opium* to our luftful Rage,
Which fleeps a-while, but wakes again in Age ;
It heaps on all Men much, but ufelefs Care,
For with more Trouble they lefs happy are.
Ye GODS ! that Man, by his own flavifh Law,
Should on himfelf fuch Inconvenience draw ?
If he would wifer Nature's Laws obey,
Thofe chalk him out a far more pleafant Way.

When.

When lusty Youth and potent Wine confpire
To fan the Blood into a gen'rous Fire,
We muft not think the Gallant will endure
The puiffant Iffue of his Calenture
Nor always in his fingle Pleafures burn,
Tho' Nature's Hand-Maid fometimes ferves the Turn.
No, he muft have a fprightly youthful Wench,
In equal Floods of Love his Flames to quench ;
One that will hold him in her clafping Arms,
And in that Circle all his Spirits charms.
That with new Motion and unpractis'd Art,
Can raife the Soul, and re-infnare his Heart.
Hence fpring the Noble, Fortunate and Great,
Always begot in Paffion, and in Heat.
But the dull Offspring of the *Marriage-Bed,*
What is it ; but a human Piece of Lead ?
A fottifh Lump, engender'd of all Ills,
Begot, like Cats, againft their Fathers Wills ?
If it be baftardiz'd, 'tis doubly fpoil'd,
The Mother's Fear's entail'd upon the Child ;
Thus, whether ill'egitimate, or not,
Cowards and Fools in Wedlock are begot.
Let no enobled Soul himfelf debafe,
By lawful Means to baftardize his Race ;
But if he muft pay Nature's Debt in Kind,
To check his eager Paffion, let him find
Some willing Female out ; what tho' fhe be
The very Dregs and Scum of Infamy ;
Tho' fhe be Linfey-Woolfey, Bawd or Whore,
Clofe-Stool to VENUS, Nature's Common-Shore.
Impudent, foolifh, rotten with Difeafe,
The Sunday-Crack of Suburb 'Prentices :
What then ? She's better than a Wife by Half ;
And if thou'rt ftill unmarry'd, thou art fafe.

With

With Whores thou can't but venture ; what thou'st loft
May be redeem'd again with Care and Coft.
But a damn'd WIFE, b'inevitable Fate,
Deftroys Soul, Body, Credit and Eftate.

The RESTORATION: *Or, The Hiftory
of* Infipids. *A* Lampoon.

I.

CHASTE, pious, prudent *Charles* the Second,
The Miracle of thy Reftoration,
May like to that of Quails be reckon'd,
Rain'd on the *Ifraelitifh* Nation :
The wifh'd-for B'effing from Heaven fent,
Became their Curfe and Punifhment.

II.

The Virtues in Thee, *Charles*, inherent,
Altho' thy Count'nance be an odd Piece,
Prove thee as true a God's Vicegerent,
As e'er was *Harry* with his Cod-piece :
For Chaftity and pious Deeds,
His Grandfire *Harry*, *Charles* exceeds.

III.

Our *Romifh* Bondage-breaker *Harry*,
Efpoufed Half a Dozen Wives :
Charles only One refolv'd to marry,
And other Mens he never ——— ;
Yet has he Sons and Daughters more,
Than e'er had *Harry* by Threefcore.

IV.

IV.

Never was such a Faith's Defender;
 He, like a politick Prince, and pious,
Gives Liberty to Conscience tender,
 And does to no Religion tie us ;
Jews, Christians, Turks, Papists, he'll please us
With *Moses, Mahomet,* or *Jesus.*

V.

In all Affairs of Church or State
 He very zealous is, and able;
Devout at Pray'rs, and sits up late
 At the Cabal and Council-Table.
His very Dog, at Council-Board,
Sits grave and wife as any Lord.

VI.

Let *Charles's* Policy no Man flout,
 The wisest Kings have all some Folly ;
Nor let his Piety any doubt ;
 Charles, like a Sov'reign, wise and holy,
Makes young Men Judges of the Bench,
And Bishops, those that love a Wench,

VII.

His Father's Foes he does reward,
 Preserving those that cut off's Head ;
Old Cavaliers, the Crown's best Guard,
 He lets them starve for Want of Bread.
Never was any King endu'd
With so much Grace and Gratitude.

VIII.

Blood, that wears Treason in his Face,
 Villain compleat in Parson's Gown,
How much is he at Court in Grace,
 For stealing *Ormond* and the Crown !
Since Loyalty does no Man good,
Let's steal the King, and out-do *Blood.*

IX.

A Parliament of Knaves and Sots
  (Members, by Name you muſt not mention)
He keeps in Pay, and buys their Votes,
  Here with a Place, there with a Penſion :
When to give Money he can't collogue 'em,
He does with Scorn prorogue, prorogue 'em.

X.

But they long ſince, by too much giving,
  Undid, betray'd, and ſold the Nation,
Making their Memberſhips a Living,
  Better than e'er was Sequeſtration.
God give Thee, *Charles,* a Reſolution
To damn the Knaves by Diſſolution.

XI.

Fame is not grounded on Succeſs,
  Tho' Victories were *Cæſar*'s Glory :
Loſt Battles make not *Pompey* leſs,
  But left him ſtiled Great in Story.
Malicious Fate does oft deviſe
To beat the Brave, and fool the Wiſe.

XII.

Charles in the firſt *Dutch* War ſtood fair
  To have been Sov'reign of the Deep,
When *Opdam* blew up in the Air,
  Had not his Highneſs gone to ſleep :
Our Fleet ſlack'd Sails, fearing his Waking,
The *Dutch* had elſe been in ſad Taking.

XIII.

The *Bergen* Buſineſs was well laid,
  Tho' we paid dear for that Deſign ;
Had we not three Days parly'ng ſtaid,
  The *Dutch* Fleet there, *Charles,* had been Thine :
Tho' the falſe *Dane* agreed to ſell 'em,
He cheated us, and ſaved *Skellum.*

XIV.

XIV.

Had not *Charles* fweetly chous'd the *States*,
  By *Bergen* Baffle grown more wife ;
And made 'em fhit as fmall as Rats,
  By their rich *Smyrna* Fleet's Surprize :
Had haughty *Holmes* but call'd in *Spragg*,
Hans had been put into a Bag.

XV.

Mifts, Storms, fhort Victuals, adverfe Winds,
  And once, the Navy's wife Divifion,
Defeated *Charles*'s beft Defigns,
  'Till he became his Foes Derifion :
But he had fwing'd the *Dutch* at *Chatham*,
Had he had Ships but to come at 'em.

XVI.

Our *Black-Heath* Hoft, without Difpute,
  (Rai.'d, put on Board, why ! no Man knows,)
Muft *Charles* have render'd abfolute
  Over his Subjects, or his Foes :
Had not the *French* King made us Fools,
By taking *Maeftricht* with our Tools ?

XVII.

But, *Charles*, what could thy Policy be,
  To run fo many fad Difafters ?
To join thy Fleet with falfo *d'Eftrees* ?
  To make the *French* of *Holland* Mafters ?
Was't *Carwell*, Brother *James*, or *Teague*,
That made Thee break the *Triple League* ?

XVIII.

Could *Robin Viner* have forefeen
  The glorious Triumphs of his Mafter ;
The *Wooll-Church* Statue Gold had been,
  Which now is made of Alabafter.
But wife Men think, had it been Wood,
'Twere for a Bankrupt King too good.

XIX.

XIX.

Thofe that the Fabrick well confider,
 Do of it diverfly difcourfe ;
Some pafs their Cenfure on the Rider,
 Others their Judgment on the Horfe.
Moft fay, the Steed's a goodly Thing
But all agree, 'tis a lewd King.

XX.

By the Lord-Mayor and his grave Coxcombs,
 Freeman of--*London Charles* is made ;
Then to *Whitehall* a rich Gold Box comes,
 Which was beftow'd on the *French* Jade * ;
But wonder not it fhould be fo, Sirs,
When Monarchs rank themfelves with Grocers ?

XXI.

Cringe, fcrape no more, ye City-Fops,
 Leave off your Feafting and fine Speeches ;
Beat up your Drums, fhut up your Shops,
 The Courtiers then will kifs your Breeches.
Arm'd, tell the Popifh Duke that rules,
You're free-born Subjects, not *French* Mules.

XXII.

New Upftarts, Baftards, Pimps and Whores,
 That, Locufts-like, devour the Land,
By fhutting up th' Exchequer Doors,
 When there our Money was trepann'd,
Have render'd *Charles's* Reftoration
But a fmall Blefling to the Nation.

---

* *The Duchefs of* Portfmouth.

XXIII.

XXIII.

Then, *Charles*, beware of thy Brother *York*,
  Who to thy Government gives Law ;
If once we fall to the old Sport,
  You muſt again both to *Breda* ;
Where, ſpite of all that would reſtore you,
Grown wife by Wrongs, we ſhould-abhor you.

XXIV.

If, of all Chriſtian Blood, the Guilt
  Cries loud for Vengeance unto Heaven,
That Sea by treach'rous *Lewis* ſpilt,
  Can never be by God forgiven :
Worſe Scourge unto his Subjeſts, Lord !
Than Peſt'lence, Famine, Fire or Sword.

XXV.

That falſe rapacious Wolf of *France*,
  The Scourge of *Europe*, and its Curſe,
Who at his Subjeſts Cries does dance,
  And ſtudies how to make them worſe :
To ſay ſuch Kings, Lord, rule by thee,
Were moſt prodigious Blaſphemy.

XXVI.

Such know no Law, but their own Luſt ;
  Their Subjeſts Subſtance and their Blood,
They count it Tribute due and juſt,
  Still ſpent and ſpilt for Subjeſts Good.
If ſuch Kings are by God appointed,
The Devil may be the Lord's Anointed.

XXVII.

Such Kings ! curs'd be the Pow'r and Name,
  Let all the World henceforth abhor 'em;
Monſters, which Knaves ſacred proclaim,
  And then, like Slaves, fall down before 'em.

What

What can there be Kings Divine?
The moft are Wolves, Goats, Sheep or Swine.
XXVIII.
Then farewell, Sacred Majefty,
  Let's pull all brutifh Tyrants down;
Where Men are born, and ftill live free,
  There ev'ry Head doth wear a Crown:
Mankind, like miferable Frogs,
Prove wretched, King'd by Storks and Logs.

SONG.

I.
WHERE is he gone, whom I adore?
  The God-like Man I fee no more;
Yet, without Reft, his Tyrant Charms
Beat in my Heart ftill new Alarms.

II.
Affift, dear Honour, take my Part,
Or I am loft, with all my Art;
Tear his Idea from my Breaft,
Tho' with it I am more than bleft.

III.
My Reafon too, prepare your Arms,
Left he return with greater Charms;
Love's fatal and imprifon'd Dart,
Draw from my tender bleeding Heart.

✿✿✿✿✿✿✿✿✿✿✿✿✿✿✿✿✿✿

The YOUNG STATESMAN.

A SATIRE.

I.

CLARENDON had Law and Senfe,
  CLIFFORD was bold and brave;
BENNET's grave Looks was a Pretence,
And DANBY's matchlefs Impudence
  Help'd to fupport the Knave.

II.

But SUNDERLAND, GODOLPHIN, LORY,
Thefe will appear fuch Chits in Story,
  'Twill turn all Politicks to Jefts,
To be repeated like JOHN DORY,
  When Fidlers fing at Feafts.

III.

Protect us, mighty Providence!
  What would thefe mad Men have?
Firft they would bribe us without Pence,
Deceive us without common Senfe,
  And without Pow'r enflave.

IV.

Shall free-born Men, in humble Awe,
  Submit to fervile Shame?
Who, from Confent and Cuftom, draw
The fame Right to be rul'd by Law,
  Which Kings pretend to reign.

V.

V.

The Duke shall wield his conqu'ring Sword,
  The *Chancellor* * make his Speech;
The King shall pass his honest Word,
The *pawn'd Revenue* Sums afford,
  And then come kiss my Breech.

VI.

So have I seen a King at Chess,
  His Rooks and Knights withdrawn;
His Queen and Bishops in Distress,
Shifting about, grow less and less,
  With here and there a Pawn.

The ENCOURAGEMENT.

'TIS the *Arabian* Bird alone
  Lives chaste, because there is but *One*:
But had kind Nature made them *Two*,
They wou'd like Doves and Sparrows do.

On the Lord Chancellor HYDE.

PRIDE, Lust, Ambition, and the People's Hate,
  The Kingdom's Broker, Ruin of the State,
Dunkirk's sad Loss, Divider of the Fleet,
Tangier's Compounder for a barren Sheet.
This Shrub of Gentry, marry'd to the Crown,
His Daughter to the Heir is tumbled down;

---

* *Jefferies.*

The grand Defpifer of the Nobles lies
Grov'ling in Duſt, as a juſt Sacrifice,
T'appeaſe the injur'd King and Nation ;
Who would believe this ſudden Alteration ?
God will revenge too, for the Stones he took
From aged *Paul's*, to make a Neſt for *Rook*.
More Cormorants of State, as well as he,
We ſhortly hope in the ſame Plight to ſee.
Go on, Great Prince, thy People do rejoice ;
Methinks I hear the Nation's total Voice,
Applauding this Day's Action to be ſuch,
As roaſting *Rump*, or beating of the *Dutch*.
Now, look upon the wither'd Cavaliers,
Who, for Reward, have nothing had but Tears :
Thanks to the *Wiltſhire* Hog, Son of the *Spittle*,
Had they been look'd on, he had had but little.
Break up the Coffers of this hoarded Thief,
Three Millions will be found to make him Chief
Of Sacrilege, Ambition, Luſt and Pride,
All comprehended in the Name of *Hyde* ;
For which his due Reward (I'ad almoſt ſaid)
The Nation may moſt juſtly claim his Head.

Written under NELLY's Picture.

SHE was ſo exquiſite a Whore,
   That in the Belly of her Mother,
She plac'd her —— ſo right before,
   Her Father —— them both together.

The W I S H.

O That I now cou'd, by fome Chymic Art,
  To Sperm convert my Vitals and my Heart,
That at one Thruft I might my Soul tranflate,
And in the Womb myfelf regenerate:
There fteep'd in Luft, nine Months I wou'd remain;
Then boldly——my Paffage out again.

P R O L O G U E.

Againft the

Difturbers of the PIT.

GEntle Reproofs have long been try'd in vain,
  Men but defpife us, while we but complain;
Such Numbers are concern'd for the wrong Side;
A Weak Refiftance ftill provokes their Pride,
And cannot ftem the Fiercenefs of the Tide.
Laughers, Buffoons, with an unthinking Croud
Of gaudy Fools, impertinent and loud,
Infult in ev'ry Corner. Want of Senfe,
Confirm'd with an outlandifh Impudence,
Among the rude Difturbers of the Pit,
Have introduc'd ill Breeding and falfe Wit.
To boaft their Lewdnefs here, young Scow'rers meet,
And all the vile Companions of a Street,

F   Keep

Keep a perpetual Bawling at the Door,
Who beat the Bawd laſt Night? Who bilkt the Whore?
They ſnarl, but neither fight, nor pay a Farthing;
A Play-Houſe is become a meer Bear-Garden,
Where ev'ry one with Inſolence enjoys
His Liberty and Property of Noiſe.
Should true Senſe, with revengeful Fire, come down,
Our *Sodom* wants Ten Men to ſave the Town.
Each Pariſh is infected; to be clear,
We muſt loſe more, than when the Plague was here.
While ev'ry little Thing perks up ſo ſoon,
That at Fourteen it hectors up and down,
With the beſt Cheats and the worſt Whores in Town;
Swears at a Play, who ſhould be whipt at School,
The Foplings muſt in Time grow up to Rule;
The Faſhion muſt prevail to be a Fool.
Some pow'rful Muſe, inſpir'd by our Defence,
Ariſe, and ſave a little common Senſe.
In ſuch a Cauſe, let thy keen Satire bite,
Where Indignation bids thy Genius write;
Mark a bold leading Coxcomb of the Town,
First ſingle out the Beaſt, then hunt him down;
Hang up his mangled Carcaſs on the Stage,
To fright away the Vermin of the Age.

✻✻✻✻✻✻✻✻✻✻✻✻✻✻✻✻

ACROSTICK.

A Knight delights in hardy Deeds of Arms;
  Perhaps a Lady loves ſweet Muſick's Charms.
Rich Men in Store of Wealth delighted be;
Infants love dandling on the Mother's Knee.
Coy Maids love ſomething, nothing I'll expreſs;
Keep the firſt Letters of theſe Lines, and gueſs.

In

✿✿✿✿✿✿✿✿✿✿✿✿✿✿✿✿✿✿

In Defence of S A T I R E.

By Sir CARR SCROOPE.

WHen *Shakespear, Johnson, Fletcher,* rul'd the Stage,
They took so bold a Freedom with the Age,
That there was scarce a Knave or Fool in *Town,*
Of any Note, but had his Picture shown.
And (without doubt) tho' some it may offend,
Nothing helps more than *Satire* to amend }
Ill Manners, or is trulier Virtue's Friend. }
Princes may Laws ordain, Priests gravely *preach,*
But Poets more successively will teach:
For, as the Passing-Bell frights from his Meat
The greedy sick Man, that too much would eat;
So, when a Vice ridiculous is made,
Our Neighbour's Shame keeps us from growing bad:
But wholesome Remedies few *Palates* please,
Men rather love what flatters their Disease;
Pimps, Parasites, Buffoons, and all the Crew,
That under Friendship's Name weak Man undo,
Find their false Service kindlier understood,
Than such as tell bold Truths to do us Good;
Look where you will, and you shall hardly find
A Man without some Sickness of the Mind:
In vain we Wise would seem, while ev'ry Lust,
Whisks us about, as Whirlwinds do the Dust.

HERE, for some needless Gain, a Wretch is hurl'd
From Pole to Pole, and slav'd about the World;
While the Reward of all his Pains and Care
End in that despicable Thing, his *Heir.*

THER

THERE a vain Fop mortgages all his Land,
To buy that gaudy Thing, call'd *a Command*;
To ride a Cockhorse, wear a Scarf at's Arse,
And play *Jack-Pudding* in a *May-Day* Farce.
HERE one, whom God to make a *Fool* thought fit,
In spite of Providence will be a Wit;
But wanting Strength t'uphold his ill-made Choice,
Sets up with Lewdness, Blasphemy and Noise.
There at his Mistress' Feet a Lover lies,
And for a tawdry painted Baby dies;
Falls on his Knees, adores, and is afraid
Of the vain Idol he himself has made.
These, and a thousand Fools not mention'd here,
Hate Poets all, because they Poets fear.
Take heed, they cry, yonder mad Dog will bite,
He cares not whom he falls on in his Fit;
Come but in's Way, and strait a new *Lampoon*
Shall spread your mangled Fame about the Town.
　　BUT why am I this Bug-bear to you all?
My Pen is dipp'd in no such bitter Gall.
He that can rail at one he calls his Friend,
Or hear him absent wrong'd, and not defend;
Who, for the Sake of some ill-natur'd Jest,
Tells what he should conceal, invents the rest;
To fatal Midnight-Quarrels can betray
His brave * Companion, and then run away,
Leaving him to be murder'd in the Street,
Then put it off, with some Buffoon Conceit;
This, this is He, you should beware of all;
Yet him a pleasant witty Man you call!
To whet your dull Debauches, up and down
You seek him, as top *Fidler* of the Town.

_____

* *Downes.*

But

But if I laugh, when your Court-Coxcombs show,
To see the booty *Sotus* dance *Provoe*,
Or chatt'ring *Porus* from the Side-Box grin,
Trick'd like a Lady's Monkey new made clean,
To me the Name of *Railer* strait you give,
Call me a Man that knows not how to live.

But Wenches to their Keepers true shall turn;
Stale Maids of Honour proffer'd Husbands scorn;
Great Statesmen Flattery and Clinches hate,
And, long in Office, die without Estate;
Against a Bribe Court-Judges shall decide
The City Knavery, the Clergy Pride,
E'er that black Malice in my Rhimes you find,
Which wrongs an honest Man, or hurts a Friend.
But then, perhaps, you'll say, Why did you write?
What you call harmless Mirth, the World call Spite.
Why should your Fingers itch to have a Lash
At *Simius* the Buffoon, or Cully *Bash*?
What is't to you, if *Alidore's* fine Whore
Lies with some Fop, while he's shut out of Door?
Consider too, that dang'rous Weapon, Wit,
Frights a whole Million, when some Few you hit.
Whip but a Cur, as you ride through a Town,
And strait his Fellow-Curs his Quarrel own.
Each Knave, or Fool, that conscious of a Crime,
Tho' now he 'scapes, looks for't another Time.

Sir, I confess all you have said is true;
But who has not some Folly to pursue?
Milo turn'd *Quixot*, fancy'd Battles fights,
When the fifth Bottle had increas'd the Lights.

Warlike Dirt-Pies our Hero *Paris* forms,
Which desp'rate *Bessus* without Armour storms.

Cornus, the kindest Husband e'er was born,
Still courts the Spark that does his Brows adorn;

Invites

Invites him home to dine, and fills his Veins
With the hot Blood which his dear Doxy drains.

   Grandio too, thinks himself a *Beau Garçon*,
Goggles his Eyes, writes Letters up and down,
And with his faucy Love plagues all the Town ;
Whilft pleas'd to have his Vanity thus fed,
He's caught with *Goſwell*, that old Hag, a-bed.
But, ſhould I all the crying Follies tell,
That rouze the ſleeping *Satyr* from his Cell,
I to my Reader ſhould as tedious prove,
As that old Spark *Albanus* making Love ;
Or florid * *Roſcius*, when with ſome ſmooth Flam,
He gravely on the Publick ſtrives to ſham.

   Hold then, my Muſe, 'tis Time to make an End,
Leſt taxing others, thou thy ſelf offend.
The World's a Wood, in which all loſe their Way,
Tho' by a diff'rent Path each goes aſtray.

❀❀❀❀❀❀❀❀❀❀❀❀❀❀

The Earl *of* Rochester's *Anſwer to the foregoing* SATIRE.

TO rack and torture thy unmeaning Brain,
   In Satire's Praiſe, to a low untun'd Strain,
In thee was moſt impertinet and vain.
When in thy Perſon we moſt plainly ſee
Satires are of divine Authority ;
For God made one of Man, when he made Thee.
To ſhew there are ſome Men, as there are Apes,
Fram'd for meer Sport, who differ but in Shapes ;
In thee are all thoſe Contradictions join'd,
That make an Aſs prodigious and refin'd.

---

* *Mr.* Betterton.

                             A Lump

A Lump deform'd and shapeless wert thou born,
Begot in Love's Despite and Nature's Scorn,
And art grown up the most ungrateful Wight,
Harsh to the Ear, and hideous to the Sight;
Yet Love's thy Business, Beauty thy Delight.
Curse on that silly Hour that first inspir'd
Thy Madness, to pretend to be admir'd,
To paint thy grisly Face, to dance, to dress,
And all those aukward Follies that express
Thy loathsome Love, and filthy Daintiness;
Who needs will be an ugly *Beau-Garçon*,
Spit at, and shun'd by ev'ry Girl in Town;
Where dreadfully Love's Scare-Crow thou art plac'd,
To fright the tender Flock that long to taste;
While ev'ry coming Maid, when you appear,
Starts back for Shame, and strait turns chaste for Fear;
For none so poor or prostitute have prov'd,
Where you made Love, t'endure to be belov'd.
'Twere Labour lost, or else I would advise;
But thy *half* Wit will ne'er let thee be wise:
Half witty, and *half* mad, and scarce *half* brave,
Half honest, which is very much a Knave;
Made up of all these *Halves*, thou can'st not pass
For any Thing *entire*, but for an Ass.

Spoken Extempore *to a Country Clerk, after having heard him sing* PSALMS.

STernbold and *Hopkins* had great Qualms
When they translated *David's Psalms,*
  To make the Heart full glad;
But had it been poor *David's* Fate,
To hear Thee Sing, and Them translate,
  By G—d 't had made him mad.

A Pane-

✿✿✿✿✿✿✿✿✿✿✿✿✿✿✿✿✿

A Panegyrick upon NELLY.

OF a great Heroine I mean to tell,
   And by what juſt Degrees her Titles ſwell,
To Mrs. *Nelly* grown, from Cinder *Nell.*
Much did ſhe ſuffer firſt on Bulk and Stage,
From the Black-Guard and Bullies of the Age;
Much more her growing Virtue did ſuſtain,
While dear * *Charles Hart* and *Buckhurſt* ſu'd in vain.
In vain they ſu'd; curs'd be the envious Tongue,
That her undoubted Chaſtity would wrong.
For, ſhould we Fame believe, we then might ſay,
That Thouſands lay with her, as well as they:
But, Fame, thou ly'ſt; for her Prophetick Mind
Foreſaw her Greatneſs, Fate had well deſign'd;
And her Ambition choſe to be before
A virtuous Counteſs, an imperial Whore.
E'en in her native Dirt her Soul was high,
And did at Crowns and ſhining Monarchs fly;
E'en while ſhe Cinders rak'd, her ſwelling Breaſt
With Thoughts of glorious *Whoredom* was poſſeſs'd;
Still did ſhe dream (nor did her Birth withſtand)
Of dangling Scepters in her dirty Hand.
But firſt the Baſket her fair Arm did ſuit,
Laden with Pippins and *Heſperian* Fruit.
This firſt Step rais'd, to th'wond'ring Pit ſhe ſold
The lovely Fruit, ſmiling with Streaks of Gold.

---

* Mr. *Hart* the Player, and Lord *Buckhurſt.*

Fate

Fate now for her did its whole Force engage,
And from the Pit, she's mounted on the Stage:
There in full Lustre did her Glories shine,
And, long eclips'd, spread forth their Light divine:
There's HART's and ROWLEY's Soul she did ensnare,
And made a *King* the Rival to a Play'r.
The *King* o'ercomes; and to the Royal Bed
The Dunghill-Offspring is in Triumph led.
Nor let the Envious her first Rags object
To her, that's now in tawd'ry Gayness deck'd;
Her Merit does from this much greater show,
Mounting so high, that took her Rise so low.
Less fam'd that * NELLY was, whose Cuckold's Rage
In ten Years Wars did half the World engage.
She's now the darling Strumpet of the Croud,
Forgets her State, and talks to them aloud;
Lays by her Greatness, and descends to prate
With those 'bove whom she's rais'd by wond'rous Fate;
True to th' Proteftant Interest and Cause,
True to th' establish'd Government and Laws;
The choice Delight of the whole *Mobile*,
Scarce MONMOUTH's Self is more belov'd than She.
Was this the Cause that did their Quarrel move,
That both are Rivals in the People's Love?
No, 'twas her matchless Loyalty alone,
That bids Prince *Perkin* pack up and be gone.

Ill-bred thou art, says Prince. NELL does reply,
Was Mrs. BARLOW *better bred than I?*
Thus sneak'd away the *Nephew*, overcome;
By's *Aunt-in-Law's* severer Wit struck dumb.

---

* *Helen* of *Troy.*

F 5.   HER

HER Virtue, Loyalty, Wit, and noble Mind,
In the foregoing Doggrel you may find.
Now, for her Piety, one Touch, and then
To RYMER I'll refign my Mufe and Pen;
'Twas this that rais'd her Charity fo high,
To vifit thofe that did in Durance lie;
From *Oxford* Prifons many did fhe free,
There dy'd her Father, and there glory'd fhe,
In giving others Life and Liberty;
So pious a Rememb'rance ftill fhe bore
E'en to the Fetters that her Father wore;
Nor was her Mother's Fun'ral lefs her Care,
No Coft, no Velvet, did the Daughter fpare;
Fine gilded 'Scutcheons did the Herfe enrich,
To celebrate this Martyr of the Ditch;

Burnt Brandy did in flaming Brimmers flow,
  Drunk at her Fun'ral; while her well pleas'd Shade
Rejoic'd, e'en in the fober Fields below,
  At all the Drunkennefs her Death had made.

Was ever Child with fuch a Mother blefs'd?
Or ever Mother fuch a Child poffefs'd?
Nor muft her Coufin be forgot, preferr'd
From many Years Command in the Black Guard,
To be an Enfign; ———
Whofe tatter'd Colours well do reprefent
His firft Eftate i'th' Ragged Regiment.

  THUS we, in fhort, have all the Virtues feen
Of the incomparable Madam GWYN;
Nor wonder others are not with her fhown;
She who no Equal has, muft be *alone.*

❀❀❀❀❀❀❀❀❀❀❀❀❀❀❀

The COMMONS Petition *to King* CHARLES II.

IN all Humanity we crave
Our Sovereign may be our Slave;
And humbly beg, that he may be
Betráy'd by us moſt loyally.
And if he pleaſe once to lay down
His Scepter, Dignity and Crown,
We'll make him, for the Time to come,
The greateſt Prince in *Chriſtendom.*

❀❀❀❀❀❀❀❀❀❀❀❀❀❀❀

The King's *Anſwer.*

CHARLES *at this Time having no need,*
Thanks you as much as if he did.

❀❀❀❀❀❀❀❀❀❀❀❀❀❀❀

The Royal ANGLER.

MEthinks I ſee our mighty Monarch ſtand,
His pliant *Angle* trembling in his Hand,
Pleas'd with the Sport, good Man; nor does he know
His eaſy Scepter bends and trembles ſo;
Fine Repreſentative, indeed! of God,
Whoſe Scepter's dwindled to a Fiſhing-Rod.
Such was DOMITIAN in his *Romans* Eyes,
When his great Godſhip ſtoop'd to catching Flies; }
Bleſs us! what pretty Sport have *Deities.*

But

But fee, he now does up from *Datchet* come,
Laden with Spoils of flaughter'd *Gudgeons* Home.
Nor is he warn'd by their unhappy Fate ;
But greedily he fwallows ev'ry Bait,
A Prey to every *King-Fifher* of State :
For how he *Gudgeons* takes you have been taught ;
Then liften now, how he himfelf is caught.
So well, alas ! the fatal Bait is known,
Which R o w l e y does fo greedily take down ;
That, howe'er weak and flender be the String,
Bait it with———and it will hold a *King*.
Almighty Pow'r of Women ! Oh ! how vain
Are *Salique Laws!* for you will ever reign.
Yet L a w s o n, thou, whofe arbitrary Sway
Our King muft more, than we do him, obey ;
Who fhortly fhall of eafy C h a r l e s's Breaft,
And of his Empire, be at once poffefs'd.
Tho' it, indeed, appear a glorious Thing,
Pow'r to command, and to enflave a King ;
Yet, e'er the falfe Appearance has betray'd
A foft, believing, unexperienc'd Maid,
Oh ! yet confider, e'er it be too late,
How near you ftand upon the brink of Fate.
Think who they are, who would for you procure
This great Preferment, to be made a Whore ;
Two rev'rend Aunts, renown'd in *Britifh* Story,
For Luft and Drunkennefs, with *Nell* and *Tory :*
Thefe, thefe are they your Fame would facrifice,
Your Honour fell, and you fhall know the Price.
My Lady *Mary* nothing can defign,
But feed her Luft with what fhe gets for thine.
Old *Richmond*, making thee a glorious Punk,
Shall twice a Day with Brandy now get drunk.

Her

Her Brother BUCKINGHAM shall be restor'd,
NELLY a Countess, LORY be a Lord.
And sure all Honours should on him be thrown,
Both for his Father's Merit, and his own;
For *Dunkirk* first was sold by CLARENDON,
And now *Tangier* is selling by the Son;
A barren Queen the Father brought us o'er,
To make Way for the Son to bring a Whore.

PORTSMOUTH's *Looking-Glass.*

MEthinks I see you newly risen
From your embroider'd Bed, and pissing.
With study'd Mein and much Grimace,
Present yourself before your Glass,
To varnish and smooth o'er those Graces,
You rubb'd off in your Night-Embraces;
To set your Hair, your Eyes, your Teeth,
And all those Charms you conquer with;
Lay Trains of Love, and State-Intrigues,
In Powders, Trimmings, and curl'd Wigs;
And nicely chuse, and neatly spread
Upon your Cheeks the best *French* Red.
Indeed, for *Whites,* none can compare
With those you naturally wear;
And tho' her Highness much delights
To laugh and talk about your *Whites,*
I never could perceive your Grace
Made Use of any for your Face.
Here 'tis you practise all your Art,
To triumph o'er a *Monarch's* Heart.

Tattle.

Tattle, and smile, and wink, and twink on't,
It almost makes me spew to think on't.
These are your Master-Strokes of Beauty,
That keep poor ROWLEY to hard Duty ;
And how can all these be withstood
By frail and am'rous Flesh and Blood ?
These are the Charms that have bewitch'd him,
As if a Conjurer's Rod had switch'd him ;
Made him he knows not what to do,
But loll and fumble here with you.
Amongst your Ladies and his Chits,
At Cards and Council here he sits ;
Yet minds not how they play at either,
Nor cares he when 'tis walking Weather ;
Bus'ness and Power he has resign'd,
And all Things to your mighty Mind.
Is there a *Minister of State*,
Or any *Treasurer* of late,
That's fawning and imperious too,
He owes his Greatness all to you ;
And as you see just Cause to do't,
You keep him in, or turn him out :
Hence 'tis you give us *War* and *Peace*,
Raise Men, disband them, as you please ;
Take away Pensions, retrench Wages,
For Petticoats and lusty Pages ;
Contrive and execute all Laws,
Suiting the Judges to the Cause ?
Learn'd SCROGGS, and honest JEFFERIES,
A faithful Friend to you, whoe'er is ;
He made the Jury come in Booty :
And, for your Service, would hang *Doughty*.
You govern every Council-Meeting,
Make the Fools do as you think fitting :

Your

Your *Royal* Cully has Command,
Only from you, at second Hand;
He does but at the Helm appear,
Sits there and sleeps, while your Slaves steer.
And you are the bright *Northern* Star,
By which they guide this Man of War;
Yet without Doubt, they might conduct
Him better, was you better ———
Many begin to think, of late,
His Crown and C——ds have both one Date;
For as they fall, so falls the State;
And as his Loins prove loose and weak,
The Reins of Government must break.

Spoken Extempore, *upon receiving a Fall
at* Whitehall-Gate, *by attempting to kiss
the Duchess of* Cleveland *as she was step-
ping out of her Chariot.*

BY Heavens! 'twas bravely done,
First to attempt the *Chariot* of the Sun,
And then to fall like PHAETON.

LAIS

✿✿✿✿✿✿✿✿✿✿✿✿✿✿✿✿✿✿

L A I S   J U N I O R:

A Pindarick.

I.

LET Antients boaſt no more
   Their lew'd Imperial Whore,
Whoſe everlaſting Luſt
Surviv'd her Body's lateſt Thruſt;
And when that tranſitory Duſt
Had no more Vigour left in Store,
Was ſtill as freſh and active as before.

II.

Her Glory muſt give Place
To one of modern *Britiſh* Race *,
Whoſe ev'ry daily Act exceeds
The other's moſt tranſcendent Deeds.
She has, at length, made good,
That there is human Fleſh and Blood,
Ev'n able to out-do
All that their looſeſt Wiſhes prompt them to.

III.

When ſhe has jaded quite
Her almoſt boundleſs Appetite,
Cloy'd with the choiceſt Banquets of Delight.
She'll ſtill drudge on in taſtleſs Vice,
As if ſhe ſinn'd for Exerciſe;

---

* The Ducheſs of *Cleveland.*

Diſ-

Difabling ftouteft Stallions ev'ry Hour ;
And when they can perform no more,
She'll rail at them, and kick 'em out of Door.

IV.

Monmouth and *Cav'ndiſh* droop,
As fieſt did *Henningham* and *Scroope* ;
Nay, fcabby *Ned* looks thin and pale,
And ſturdy *Frank* himſelf begins to fail ;
But Woe betide him, if he does,
She'll fet her *Jocky* * on his Toes.
And ſhe ſhall end the Quarrel without Blows.

V.

Now tell me all ye Pow'rs,
Who e'er could equal this *lewd Dame* of ours ?
LAIS herſelf muſt yield,
And vanquiſh'd LUCIA quit the Field :
Nor can that *Princeſs*, one Day fam'd,
  As Wonder of the Earth,
  For *Minotaurus*' glorious Birth,
With Admiration any more be nam'd.
Thofe puny Heroines of Hiſtory,
Eclips'd by her, ſhall all forgotten be,
Whilſt her great Name confronts Eternity.

❁❁❁❁❁❁❁❁❁❁❁❁❁❁❁

Upon NOTHING.

I.

NOthing, thou *elder Brother* ev'n to Shade,
  Thou had'ſt a Being e'er the World was made,
And (well fix'd) art alone of ending not afraid.

---

* *The* Ducheſs's *Lap-Dog.*

II.

II.

, ime and Place were, Time and Place were not,
.ien primitive *Nothing* Something ſtrait begot,
. hen all proceeded from the great united What ?

III.

Something, the nat'ral *Attribute* of All,
Sever'd from Thee, it's ſole *Original*,
Into thy boundleſs Self muſt undiſtinguiſh'd fall.

IV.

Yet Something did thy mighty Pow'r Command,
And from thy fruitful Emptineſs's Hand
Snatch'd *Men, Beaſts, Birds, Fire, Water, Air* and *Land.*

V.

Matter, the wicked'ſt Off-ſpring of thy Race,
By *Form* aſſiſted, flew from thy Embrace,
And *Rebel Light* obſcur'd thy ray'send duſky Face.

VI.

With *Forms* and *Matter ; Time* and *Place* did join ;
Body, thy Foe, did with theſe Leagues combine,
To ſpoil thy peaceful Reign, and ruin all thy Line.

VII.

But Turn-coat *Time* aſſiſts thy Foes in vain,
And, brib'd by Thee, deſtroys their ſhort-liv'd Reign,
And to thy hungry *Womb* drives back thy Slaves again.

VIII.

Theſe *Myſteries* are barr'd from *Laick* Eyes,
And the Divine alone with Warrant pries
Into thy *Boſom,* where the *Truth* in private lies,

IX.

Yet this of Thee the *Wiſe* may truly ſay,
Thou from the *Virtuous* Nothing tak'ſt away ;
And to the Part of Thee, the *Wicked* wiſely pray.

X.

X.

Great *Negative*, how vainly wou'd the Wife
Enquire, define, diftinguifh, teach, devife,
Did'it thou not ftand to point their dull *Philofophies*.

XI.

Is, or *Is not*, the two great Ends of Fate,
And *True* or *Falfe* the Subject of Debate,
That perfect or deftroy the vaft Defigns of Fate.

XII.

When they have rack'd the Politician's Breaft,
Within thy *Bofom* moft fecurely reft ;
And when reduc'd to Thee, are leaft unfafe, and beft.

XIII.

But, *Nothing*, why does *Something* ftill permit
That Sacred *Monarchs* fhou'd at Council fit
With *Perfons* highly thought, at beft, for *Nothing* fit ?

XIV.

Whilft weighty *Something* modeftly abftains
From Princes *Coffers*, and from Statefmen's *Brains*,
And *Nothing* there, like ftately *Nothing* reigns.

XV.

Nothing, who dwell'ft with Fools in grave Difguife,
For whom the Rev'rend *Shapes* and *Forms* devife,
Lawn Sleeves, and Furs, and Gowns, when they, like
          Thee, look wife.

XVI.

French Truth, *Dutch* Prowefs, *Britifh* Policy ;
Hibernian Learning, *Scotch* Civility,
Spaniards Difpatch, *Danes* Wit, are mainly feen in Thee.

XVII.

The Great *Man's* Gratitude to his beft *Friend*,
Kings Promifes, *Whores* Vows, toward Thee they tend,
Flow fwiftly into Thee, and in Thee ever end.

A Ram-

✿✿✿✿✿✿✿✿✿✿✿✿✿✿✿

A Ramble *in* St. James's Park.

MUCH Wine had paſt, with grave Diſcourſe,
.Of who ———n.who, and. who do:s worſe,
Such as you uſually do hear
From them that Diet at the *Bear* ;
When I, who ſtill take-Care to ſee
Drunkenneſs relievʼd by Lechery,
Went out into *St. Jamesʼs Park*,
To cool my Head, and fire my Heart ;
But thoʼ *St. James* has thʼ Honour onʼt,
ʼTis conſecrate to ——— and ———
There, by a moſt inceſtuous Birth,
Strange Woods ſpring from the teeming Earth ;
For they relate how, heretofore,
When antient *Piʆ* began to whore,
Deluded all his Aſſignation,
(Jilting, it ſeems, was then in Faſhion)
Poor penſive Lover in this Place
Wouʼd ——— upon his Motherʼs Face ;
Whence Rows of Mandrakes tall did riſe,
Whoſe lewd Tops ———— the very Skies.
Each imitative Branch does twine
In ſome lovʼd Fold of ARETINE ;
And nightly now beneath their Shade,
Are Buggʼries, Rapes, and Inceſts made.
Unto this All-ſin ſheltring Grove,
Whores of the Bulk, and the Alcove,
Great Ladies, Chamber-Maids, and Drudges,
The Rag-Picker, and Hiereſs trudges ;

Carmen,

Carmen, Divines, great Lords, and Taylors,
Pimps, Poets, 'Prentices, and Jailors,
Footboys, fine Fops, do here arrive,
And here promiscuously they ——— ..
Along these hallow'd Walks it was,
That I beheld CORINNA pass;
Whoever had been by to see
The proud Disdain she cast on me,
Thro' charming Eyes, he wou'd have swore,
She dropp'd from Heav'n that very Hour,
Forsaking the Divine Abode,
In Scorn of some despairing God.
But mark what Creatures Women are,
So infinitely vile and fair!

THREE Knights o' th' Elbow and the S'ur,
With wriggling Tails made up to her.

THE first was of your *Whitehall* Blades,
Near Kin to th' Mother of the Maids;
Grac'd by whose Favour he was able
To bring a Friend to th' Waiters Table,
Where he had heard Sir *Edward Sutton*,
Say how the King lov'd *Bansted Mutton*;
Since when, he'd ne'er be brought to eat,
By's Good-will, any other Meat.
In this, as well as all the rest,
He ventures to do like the best:
But wanting common Sense, th' Ingredient
In chusing well not least expedient,
Converts abortive Imitation
To universal Affectation:
So he not only eats and talks,
But feels and smells, sits down and walks;
Nay, looks and lives, and loves by Rote,
In an old taudry Birth-Day Coat.

I

THE second was a *Grays-Inn Wit* *,
A great Inhabiter of the Pit.
Where, Critick like, he sits and *squints,*
Steals Pocket-Handkerchiefs and *Hints*
From's Neighbour and the Comedy,
To court and pay his Landlady.

THE third a Lady's eldest Son,
Within few Years of Twenty-one,
Who hopes, from his propitious Fate,
Against he comes to his Estate,
By these two *Worthies* to be made
A most accomplish'd tearing *Blade.*
One in a Strain 'twixt *Tune* and *Nonesense,*
Cries, *Madam, I have lov'd you long since;*
Permit me your fair Hand to kiss,
When at her Mouth her —— says *Yes.*

IN short, without much more ado,
Joyful and pleas'd away she flew,
And with these three confounded Asses,
From Park to Hackney-Coach she passes.

So a proud Bitch does lead about
Of humble Curs the am'rous Rout,
Who most obsequiously do heat
The fav'ry Scent of salt swoln ——
Some Pow'r more patient, now relate
The Sense of this surprizing Fate.
Gods! that a Thing admir'd by me,
Should taste so much of Infamy?
Had she pick'd out, to rub her A—— on,
Some lusty Clown, or well-hung Parson;

* Captain Ratcliff.

Each

Each Jobb of whofe fpermatick Juice,
Had fill'd her ———— with wholefome Juice,
I the Procceding fhou'd have prais'd,
In Hope fhe'ad quench'd the Fire I rais'd :
Such nat'ral Freedoms are but juft,
There's fomething gen'rous in mere Luft :
But to turn damn'd abandon'd Jade,
When neither Head nor Tail perfwade ;
To be a Whore in Underftanding,
A paffive Pot for Fools to ———— in ;
The Devil play'd Booty fure with thee,
To bring a Blot of Infamy.
But why was I, of all Mankind,
To fo fevere a Fate defign'd ?
Ungrateful ! Why this Treachery
To humble, fond, believing me ;
Who gave you Priv'leges above
The nice Allowances of Love.
Did ever I refufe to bear
The meaneft Part your Luft cou'd fpare ?
When your lewd ———— come fpewing Home,
Drench'd with the ———— of half the Town,
My Dram of ———— was fupp'd up after,
For the digeftive *Surfeit-Water.*
Full-gorged at another Time,
With a vaft Meal of nafty Slime,
Which your devouring ———— had drawn
From Porter's Backs and Footmen's Brawn,
I was content to ferve you up
My ———— full for your Grace-Cup ;
Nor ever thought it an Abufe,
While you had Pleafure for Excufe.
You that cou'd make my Heart away
For Noife and Colours, and betray.

The Secret of my tender Hours
To such Knight-Errant Paramours;
When leaning on your faithless Breast,
Wrapt in Security and Rest,
Soft Kindness all my Pow'rs did move,
And Reason lay dissolv'd in Love.
May stinking Vapour choak your *Womb*,
Such as the Men you doat upon;
May your depraved Appetite,
That could in whiffling *Fools* delight,
Beget such *Frenzies* in your *Mind*,
You may go mad for the *North Wind:*
And fixing all your Hopes upon't,
To have him bluster in your ———
Turn up your long A—e to the Air,
And perish in a wild Despair.
But *Cowards* shall forget to rant,
School-Boys to ———, old *Whores* to paint;
The *Jesuits Fraternity*
Shall leave the Use of *Buggery*;
Crab-Louse, inspir'd with Grace divine,
From earthly Cod, to Heav'n shall climb;
Physicians shall believe in *Jesus*,
And Disobedience cease to please us,
E'er I desist, with all my Power,
To plague this *Woman* and undo her.
But my Revenge will best be tim'd
When she is marry'd, that is loin'd;
In that most lamentable State,
I'll make her feel my Scorn and Hate,
Pelt her with Scandal, Truth, or Lies,
And her poor *Cur* with Jealousies,
Till I have torn him from her *Breech*,
While she whines like a Dog-drawn *Bitch*,

Loath'd

Loath'd and depriv'd, kick'd out of *Town*,
Into some dirty Hole alone,
To chew the *Cud* of Misery,
And know she owes it all to me.
And may no Woman *better thrive,*
Who dare prophane the —— I ——.

BATH *Intrigues.*

The Argument.

How Tall-Boy, K — P —, S — P — *did contend*
For Bridegroom D —, *Friend did fight with Friend;*
But Man of God, *by* Laymen *called Parson,*
Contriv'd, by Turns, how each might rub her A—e *on.*

SAY, Heav'n-born *Muse,* for only thou can'st tell,
How discord dire, between two Widows fell :
What made the fair One, and her well-shap'd Mother,
Duty forget, and pious Nature smother.
Who was most modest, virtuous or fair,
Was not the Cause of Contest, I dare swear.
Nor Wit, nor Breeding, rais'd this Emulation ;
Those Things with them are Trifles out of Fashion.
Great was the Strife rais'd up by envious Fate,
To ruin P—— happy Reign and State.
　When R—— with evil Eye beheld
The three dear Friends, his Heart with Rancour swell'd,
That in one House they were, of one Accord,
Wanton in Bed, and riotous at Board,
Preferring brawny G—— to spiny Lord ;
He vow'd to break this triple League of Love,
And from their Breasts sweet *Friendship* to remove,

G　　　　　　　　　　In

In a foul Day from bawdy *Bath* he flies,
To put in Act his hasted Enterprize.
I' th' Bow'r of Bliss, where sacred B——— dwells,
There lives a Hag deep read in Charms and Spells,
Philters and Potions, that by Magick Skill
Can give an Eunuch Stones, and ——— its Fill;
Babes, at her Call, fly from the breeding Womb,
With Neighbour T——— in loathsome Jakes to roam;
As oft as Finger ——————— rape
The Virgin *Hymen*, she repairs the Gap.
Fam'd thro' the World for the ——— mending Trade }
To her he goes, t'implore her mighty Aid: }
By Men she's call'd the *Mother of the Maids.*   }
Hail, *worthy Dame,* (said he) *replete with Grace,*
Mother o' th' Maids, Daughter of Noble Race!
Whilst Men of God to Betty Blackbourn *go,*
Whilst ——— *and Pen with White and Black does flow,*
My lasting Verse shall magnify thy Fame,
And melting ——— *adore thy holy Name;*
Therefore dear Mother, lend thine equal Ear
To my Complaint, and favour my just Pray'r.
There is a Place, adown a gloomy Vale,*
Where burden'd Nature lays her nasty Tail;
Ten thousand Pilgrims thither do resort
For Ease, Disease, for Lechery and Sport:
Thither two Beldams, and a jilting Wife,
Came to ——— *off the tedious Hours of Life.*
I, willing to contribute to their Joy,   }
Offer'd my Mite to th' young, insatiate Toy,   }
Who banish'd Luck, 'cause ——— *he could not cloy.* }
Her upright Dam, K— P—, the wise old Jew,   }
Told me, I must twelve Times her Womb bedew,   }
E'er her Child S— P— should her Buttocks shew. }

---

* The *Bath.*

Refolv'd to win (like Hercules*) the Prize,*
Twelve times I fcour'd the Kennel 'twixt her Thighs ;
The cheating Jilt, at th' twelfth, a dry Bob cries.
My —— and I, thus crofs-bit, in high Rage
Appeal'd to th' fkilful Sticklers on the Stage ;
With that fair Tall Boy, *and bold* S— P— *come,*
To fqueeze my ——, and pafs their final Doom ;
Saying, if one Priapus *I could fhew,*
One holy Relick of kind pearly Dew,
I the twelfth Time K— P——*'s* A—*fo did fpew,*
To their deciding Teft I did fubmit ;
Priapus *fqueez'd, a Snow-Ball did emit :*
Yet thefe two partial Dames a dry Bob *cry,*
Perform your Bargain (Peer) *or —— and dye.*
Thus was I rook'd of twelve fubftantial ——
By thefe bafe ftinking over-itching ——
Your Aid, your Aid, dear Mother, me infpire
With apt Revenge, to feed my raging Fire.
The gracious Matron, fmiling on him, faid,
Be it as thou defir'ft, my dear-lov'd Lad ;
For this Abufe, the Rump-fed Runts fhall mourn,
'Till flimy —— to grimy A— *hole turn.*
By her Cave's *Mouth a verdant Myrtle grows,*
Bearing Love's Trophies *on his facred Boughs :*
The Crowns *of* Kings *were offer'd to this Shrine,*
D—— and M—— *of the Royal Line ;*
Fair Ladies Hearts, *with mitred* P——— *transfix'd,*
In myftick Manner make the Crucifix.
To th' Tree fhe leads him, from a Bough pulls down
A mighty Tool, a D—— *of Renown ;*
A D—— *long and large as* Hector's *Lance,*
Infcrib'd Honi foit qui Mal y Penfe.
Knight of the Garter made for's vaft Deferts,
As modern Hero *was for's monftrous Parts.*

THIS, pious Son (said she) nail up in Box,
By Carrier send it these Salt-burning Nocks,
Directed thus : *To the Lady most deserving,*
Who'as made most Slaves, and kept most — from starving.
O'ER-JOY'D with hop'd Success, away he flies
To *Bath*, disguis'd, to bear the welcome Prize ;
But when they saw the Image of bless'd Man,
Who can express how fast, how swift they ran
Each for herself to seiz't ! No *Dog* at *Deer*,
Nor *Hawk* at *Hern*, shew'd such a swift Career ;
At once they souse on the beloved Prey,
And sworn Friends do engage in mortal Fray.
Old *K— P—*, dreadful to her Friends and Foes,
Like *Luxemburgh*, in Back and Breast-Plate shows,
Gigantick *Tall-Boy*, famed in the *West*,
For *Cornish Hug*, to th' Fight herself addrest ;
Whilst the Child *S— P—* hop'd to steal away,
By Stratagem, the Glory of the Day.
But all in vain, *Tall-Boy* with one Hand held
Jove's Prize, with th' other crafty *S— P—* fell'd ;
But Looks, nor Menaces, nor crushing Blow,
Cou'd make stout *K— P—* quit her lov'd D———.
Undaunted, she maintain'd a cruel Fight,
For Conquest scratch'd and tore with all her Might.
So have I seen a crump-back *Crab-Louse* stick
With fervent Love to lick creating ——— ;
The more he pulls, the more the loving Wretch
Does strive to stay, and to each Hair does catch ;
'Till murd'ring Man, enrag'd from ——— tears
The Nock-born Brat, and ends his hopeful Years.
So had it far'd with *K— P—*, had not Fate
Sent *Man of God* to end the dire Debate.
What Rage, what Fury (said he) *does ye stir,*
To shed the Blood of Saints in cruel War ?

How will you make the Mother-Church to mourn,
And to Fanaticks be the publick Scorn?
For Shame, dear Souls, reserve your noble Blood
To spend with Man. Abash'd the Warriors stood,
To see the Holy Father in the Place;
But strait on th' Matter putting a good Face,
Thus *K— P—* spake: *To you, O Rev'rend Sir,*
The Justness of the Cause I will transfer;
A Cause too great for Laymen vile to try;
Fit for Plus Ultra's *deep Divinity;*
A Cause for which bless'd Saints above wou'd die!

THE modest *Tall-Boy* so devout appears,
Tho' stealing ——, you'd think she said her Pray'rs;
And tho' she'ad almost won the bloody Field,
With *S— P—* (Babe of Grace) to this does yield.
The Cause being stated, holy Man does pray
For a Blessing on's Endeavours, then does say:
WHEREAS, sage Matrons you do all agree
Your Case to yield to my Integrity,
Fitter for General Council, than weak Me;
D—— a lawful Tool, deny't who can,
I'll prove 'tis made for a Meet-Help for Man;
As unto Rector, Curate is Assistant,
So D—— to fall'n ——, when —— has piss'd on't.
But here's the Elect ordain'd for Propagation,
Who trusts in this is bless'd in Generation:
This has done more than Tunbridge, Bath, or Epsom;
Though m'er so barren, this is sure to help 'em.

THEN pulling out the Rector of the Females,
Nine Times he bath'd him in their piping hot Tails.
Panting, quoth he, *Now Peace be on you all;*
When I am absent, then on D—— call;
As those in Holy Church to Image pray,
When wonder-working Saint is out o' th' Way.

G 3   THUS

Thus all well-pleas'd, to Church away they go,
To sing *Te Deum* for their dear D———.

On *the* CHARMS *of hidden Treasure.*
A PARADOX.

THOU mighty Princess, lovely Queen of Holes,
   Whose Monarchy the bravest Men controuls;
Shut up in awful and Majestick State,
How dost thou make thy poor Adorers wait!
Reserv'd as *Preston-John*, as seldom seen
As the most shyly kept *Sultana* Queen.
Thou Crown of *Sense*, nay, more Superlative,
Thou very Quintessence of all the Five;
No *Civet Cat* had ever such a Smell,
Thy Essence does all other Sweets excell.
How is our Relish by thy Taste increas'd,
When this one Bit is more than a whole Feast!
Beauty of Beauties, Darling of the Eye,
The Face is but a Mark to hit thee by,
Thou art the Spot of *Cupid's* Archery:
Whether your ornamental Locks you wear,
Or go, like *Eastern* Beauties, smooth and bare;
Whether full-grown the manly Beard appears,
Or Virgin-Lips show fewer Hairs than Years;
Yet all true Beauty shines, as on a Throne,
In her full Splendor, from thy Sight alone.
To please thy Friends, and to confute thy Foes,
Thou hast a Mouth beyond fam'd *Cicero's*;
A Mouth, whose silent Rhetorick affords
More strong Persuasives than all *Tully's* Words.

                       'Twas

'Twas fuch a Mouth did *Paris* more convince,
Than *Juno's* Power, or *Pallas'* Eloquence.
'Twas fuch a Mouth *Achilles* did, perfwade,
And *Hercules,* to live in Mafquerade,
Which all the Force of Arms could ne'er have made.
'Twas fuch a Mouth taught *Antbony* to fcorn
The glorious Name to which that Prince was born.
To fuch Perfuafions mighty *Julius* gave
That Crown th' *Egyptian* Army could not fave,
And of a *Conqueror* became a *Slave.*
Still there remains one Senfe, which we may call
One that is all the reft, is more than all.
Who can defcribe thy more than pleafing Touch?
That is a mighty Tafk, for me too much,
Who fcarce am known to her of whom I write,
And had but once the Honour of her Sight.
None can her charming Virtues duly tell,
But he who comes infpir'd from her own Well,
Whofe Virtues does all *Helicon's* excell.

On the WOMEN about TOWN.

TOO long the wife Commons have been in Debate
About Money and Confcience, thofe Trifles of State;
Whilft dangerous Grievances daily increafe,
The Subject can't riot in Safety and Peace,
Unlefs, as againft *Irifh* Cattle before,
They fhould now make an Act againft *Irifh* Whore.
The *Coots* black and white, *Clanbraxil* and *Fox,*
Invade us with Impudence, Beauty, and Pox;
They carry a Fate which none can oppofe,
The Lofs of his Heart, or the Fall of his Nofe:

Should

Should we dully refift, yet would each take upon her
To befeech us to do't, and engage us in Honour.
O ye Powers above! who of Mortals take care,
Make *Women* lefs cruel, more found, or lefs fair.
Is it juft, cruel Fate with Love fhould confpire,
And our——be burnt, by our Hearts taking Fire?

A DREAM.

'TWas when the fable Mantle of the Night
   Had clos'd the Day, and chas'd away the Light;
'Twas when the *Raven* and the *Owl* begins
To make Mens Confcience tremble for their Sins;
Methought I then went armed to my Dear,
Ready to pay what I had promis'd her.
Methought I found her proftrate on her Bed,
Only her Smock cov'ring her *Maidenhead*;
I heav'd it up, fweet Linnen, by your Favour;
I felt, but how my moiften'd Fingers then did favour!
I look'd, and faw the *blind Boy's* happy Cloifter,
Arch'd on both Sides, lie gaping like an Oyfter;
I had a Tool before me, which I put
Up to the Quick, and ftrait the Oyfter fhut:
It fhut, and clung fo faft at ev'ry Stroke,
As does the loving Ivy to the Oak;
I thruft it hard, and ftill was in fome Hope;
The Liquor came, but yet it would not ope;
And then I fainted; but at fecond Bout
It open'd, and made Way to let me out.
It gap'd, and would have made a dead Man fkip
To fee it mump, and wag its upper Lip:
Thus I awak'd; mock'd by my luftful Brain,
I felt my Belly wet, and flept again.

To his MISTRESS.

I.

WHY doſt thou ſhade thy lovely Face ? O why
    Does that eclipſing Hand of thine deny
The Sun-ſhine of the Sun's enliv'ning Eye ?

II.

Without Thy Light, what Light remains in me ?
Thou art my Life, my Way ; my Light's in Thee ;
I live, I move, and by thy Beams I ſee.

III.

Thou art my Life ; if Thou but turn away,
My Life's a thouſand Deaths: Thou art my Way ;
Without Thee *Love*, I travel not, but ſtray.

IV.

My Light Thou art ; without thy glorious Sight,
My Eyes are darken'd with eternal Night:
My Love, Thou art my Way, my Life, my Light.

V.

Thou art my Way ; I wander if Thou fly :
Thou art my Light ; if hid, how blind am I !
Thou art my Life ; if thou withdraw'ſt, I die.

VI.

My Eyes are dark and blind, I cannot ſee ;
To whom, or whither ſhould my Darkneſs flee,
But to that Light ; and who's that Light but Thee ?

VII.

As Thou art All, ſhine forth, and draw thou nigher ;
Let me be bold, and die for my Deſire ;
A *Phenix* likes to periſh in the Fire.

G 5   VIII.

VIII.

If my puff Life be out, give Leave to join
My fhamelefs Snuff to the bright Lamp of Thine;
Ah! what's thy Light the lefs, for lighting Mine?

IX.

If I have loft my Path, dear Lover, fay,
Shall I ftill wander in a doubtful Way?
Love, fhall a Lamb of *Ifrael's* Sheep-fold ftray?

X.

My Path is loft, my wand'ring Steps do ftray;
I cannot go, nor can I fafely ftay;
Whom fhould I feek, but Thee, my Path, my Way?

XI.

And yet Thou turn'ft thy Face away, and fly'ft me;
And yet I fue for Grace, and Thou deny'ft me;
Speak, art Thou angry, Love, or only try'ft me?

XII.

Difplay thofe heav'nly Lamps, or tell me why
Thou fhad'ft thy lovely Face: Perhaps no Eye
Can view their Flames, and not drop down and die.

XIII.

Thou art the Pilgrim's Path, the blind Man's Eye,
The dead Man's Life; on Thee my Hopes rely;
If I but them remove, I furely die.

XIV.

Diffolve thy Sun-Beams, clofe thy Wings, and ftray;
See, fee how I am blind, and dead, and ftray:
Oh! Thou that art my *Life*, my *Light*, my *Way!*

XV.

Then work thy Will; if Paffion bid me flee,
My Reafon fhall obey, my Wings fhall be
Stretch'd out no farther than from Me to Thee.

To the AUTHOR of a Play called Sodom*.

TELL me, abandon'd Miscreant, prithee tell
What damned Power invok'd and sent from Hell,
(If Hell were bad enough) did Thee inspire
To write, what Fiends, asham'd, wou'd blushing hear?
Hast thou of late embrac'd some *Succubus*,
And us'd the lewd Familiar for a Muse?
Or didst thy Soul by Inch of Candle sell,
To gain the glorious Name of Pimp to Hell?
If so, go, and its vow'd Allegiance swear,
Without 'Press-Money be its Volunteer.
May he who envies Thee, deserve thy Fate,
Deserve both Heaven's and Mankind's Scorn and Hate.
Disgrace to Libels! Foil to very Shame!
Whom 'tis a Scandal to vouchsafe to name.
What foul Description's foul enough for thee,
Sunk quite below the Reach of Infamy?
Thou covet'st to be lewd, but want'st the Might,
And art all over Devil, but in Wit.
Weak feeble Strainer at mere Ribaldry, ⎫
Whose Muse is impotent to that Degree, ⎬
It must, like Age, be whipt to Lechery. ⎭
Vile Sot, who, clapt with Poetry, art sick,
And void'st Corruption like a shanker'd——:
Like Ulcers thy imposthum'd, addled Brains
Drops into Matter, which thy Paper stains;
Whence nauseous Rhimes by filthy Births proceed,
As Maggots in some T——d ingend'ring Breed.

---

* *One* Fishbourn, *a wretched Scribbler.*

Thy

Thy Mufe has got the F——rs, and they afcend,
As in fome Green-fick Girl at upper End.
Sure Nature made, or meant at leaft to 'ave don't,
Thy Tongue a Cl——ris, thy Mouth a ——.
How well a D—— wou'd that Place become,
To gag it up, and make't for ever dumb:
At leaft it fhou'd be fyring'd——,
Or wear fome ftinking Merkin for a Beard,
That all from its bafe Converfe might be fcar'd,
As they a Door fhut up, and mark'd, beware,
That tells Infeftion and the Plague is there,
Thou *Meorfields* Author, fit for Bawds to quote,
(If Bawds themfelves with Honour fafe may do't).
When Suburb 'Prentice comes to hire Delight,
And wants Incentives to dull Appetite:
There Punk, perhaps, may thy brave Works rehearfe,
F—— the fenfelefs Thing with Hand and Verfe,
Which after fhall (preferr'd to Dreffing-Box)
Hold Turpentine, and Med'cines for the Pox.
Or (if I may ordain a Fate more fit
For thy foul nafty Excrements of Wit)
May they condemn'd to th' publick *Jakes* be lent, ⎫
(For me, I'd fear the Piles in Vengeance fent,   ⎬
Shou'd I with them profane my Fundament,)   ⎭
There bugger-wiping Porters when they fhite,
And fo thy Book itfelf turn *Sodomite*.

* * *

His * HIGHNESS's *Converfion by Father* Patrick.

BEtween Father *Patrick*, and's *Highnefs*, of late
There happ'ned a *ftrong* and a *weighty* Debate;

---

* *King* JAMES II. *when Duke of* York.

And

And RELIGION the Theme: 'Tis ſtrange that they Two
Should diſpute about *that* which neither of them knew;
For I dare boldly ſay, had his *Highneſs* but known
The Weakneſs of *Patrick's*, and the Strength of his own,
It had been a Madneſs, and much like a Curſe,
To change from a True one, to one that's much worſe;
For if it be true (as ſome Waggs make us think)
That a Papiſt *of all his Five Senſes* muſt *wink*,
A Man's *no more a* Man *when* He's *waking* than *ſleeping*,
As long as Father *Patrick* has his *Senſes in keeping.*
But ſure its not ſo, We muſt *All* be miſtaken
And have liv'd in a *Dream*, and are juſt now *awaken*;
For the *Father* was *Mighty* in *Word* and in *Reaſon*,
He urg'd not a *Syllable* but came ſo in *Seaſon*,
That ev'ry Argument was Stronger and Stronger;
So the DUKE cry'd at laſt —— *I can hold out no longer*,
The *Reaſons* that mov'd moſt his *Highneſs* to yield,
And ſo willingly quit to the Father the Field,
Were firſt that they cheated, and leave you in the Lurch,
That told you there could be any More *than* ONE *Church.*
And, next He averr'd to the Duke, for a certain,
No Foot-ſteps *of* Ours *could be found before* MARTIN *.
At theſe two great *Reaſons* ſo full and profound,
The Duke had much ado not to fall in a Swound,
And ſtrait he cry'd out—*Father* Patrick, *I find,*
(*By a ſudden Converſion and Change of my Mind,*)
That neither your Wit, *nor* Learning *could afford*
Such Strength to your Cauſe; 'twas the Finger *of the* Lord:
For now I remember, that ſomewhere 'tis ſaid,
From Babes *and from* Sucklings *his* Truth *is convey'd.*
Therefore, I ſubmit, for my *Conſcience's* Eaſe,
To be led by the *Noſe* as your *Fatherſhip* pleaſe.

---

* Martin Luther.

So

So ends the *Dispute* 'twixt the *Priest* and the *Knight*,
In which, to speak *Truth*, and to do *All-sides* Right,
He manag'd this *Cause* as He did the *Sea-fight*.

The King's EPITAPH.

HERE lies our Sov'reign Lord the King,
   Whose Word no Man rely'd on;
Who never *said a foolish Thing*,
Nor ever *did a wise One*.

On ROME'*s Pardons.*

I.

IF *Rome* can *pardon* Sins, as *Romans* hold,
  And if those Pardons can be bought and sold,
It is no Sin t' *adore* and *worship* Gold.

II.

If they can purchase *Pardons* with a Sum,
For Sins they *may commit* in Time to come,
And for Sins *past*, 'tis very well for *Rome*.

III.

At this Rate, they are happiest who have *most*,
They'll purchase Heav'n at their own *proper cost* :
Alas, the *Poor!* all that are *so*, are *Lost*.

IV.

Whence came this Knack ? Or when did it *begin?*
What *Author* have they ? Or *Who* brought *it in ?*
Did CHRIST e'er keep a *Custom-House* for *Sin?*

V.

V.

Some subtle *Devil*, without more ado,
Did certainly this fly Invention brew,
To gull them of their *Souls* and *Money* too.

On a Falſe MISTRESS.

FArewell *falſe* Woman! know I'll ever be
A dumb Man to thy Sex, and dead to *Thee* :
Thy Breath's infectious, and thy Preſence brings
To me a thouſand ſharp and bitter Stings.
Ye Powers Above ! why did you Woman make,
Without an Angel, and Within a Snake ?
They're Hell's chief Engines, by the Devil made,
To heighten and enlarge his growing Trade :
The only Fiend on Earth, the Devil's Friend,
A thouſand Souls to Hell they daily ſend.
Methinks I hear the Gods cry out aloud,
And theſe black Words came reeling thro' a Cloud :
Beware falſe Woman, know ſhe firſt began
To ruin and undo the State of Man.
Yet, for Revenge, I'll now reſolve to be
A damn'd diſſembling Lover, juſt like Thee :
But all my Buſineſs with ſo vile a Creature,
Shall be, as Cloſe-ſtools, to eaſe Nature.
Bleſs'd is the Man, and happy is his State,
That loves a Woman at no other Rate.

✿◉✿◉✿◉✿◉✿◉✿◉✿◉✿◉✿◉✿◉✿◉✿

SONG.

I.

AT the Sight of my *Phillis,* from every Part
A Spring-Tide of Joy does flow up to my Heart,
Which quickens each Pulse, and swells ev'ry Vein,
Yet all my Delights are still mingled with Pain;
So strange a Distemper sure Love cannot bring :
To my Knowledge, Love was a quieter Thing;
So gentle and tame, that he never was known
So much as to wake me when I lay alone.

II.

But the Boy is much grown, and so alter'd of late,
He's become a more furious Passion than *Hate* ;
Since by *Phillis* restor'd to the Empire of Hearts,
He has new-strung his Bow, and sharpen'd his Darts ;
And strictly the Rights of his Crown to maintain,
He wounds ev'ry Heart, and turns ev'ry Brain.

III.

But my Madness, alas! I too plainly discover ;
For he is at least as much Madman as Lover,
Who for one cruel Beauty does easily quit
All the Nymphs of the Stage, and those of the Pit,
The Joys of *Hyde-Park,* and the *Mall*'s dear Delight,
To live sober all Day, and be chaste all the Night.

SONG.

❀❀❀❀❀❀❀❀❀❀❀❀❀❀

SONG.

I.

MY dear Miftrefs had a Heart
   Soft as thofe kind Looks fhe gave me,
When with Love's refiftlefs Art,
   And her Eyes, fhe did enflave me:

II.

But her Conftancy's fo weak,
   She's fo wild, and apt to wander,
That my jealous Heart would break,
   Should we live one Day afunder.

III.

Melting Joys about her move,
   Killing Pleafures, wounding Bliffes;
She can drefs her Eyes in Love,
   And her Lips can arm with Kiffes.

IV.

Angels liften when fhe fpeaks,
   She's my Delight, all Mankind's Wonder;
But my jealous Heart would break,
   Should we live one Day afunder.

❀❀❀❀❀❀❀❀❀❀❀❀❀❀

SONG.

I.

ROOM, Room for a Blade of the Town,
   That takes Delight in Roaring,
Who all Day long rambles up and down,
   And at Night in the Streets lies fnoring.

II.

II.

That for the noble Name of Spark,
  Dares his Companions rally ;
Commits an Outrage in the Dark,
  Then slinks into an Alley.

III.

To ev'ry Female that he meets
  He swears he bears Affection ;
Defies all Laws, Arrests and Cheats
  By the Help of a kind Protection.

IV.

When he, intending farther Wrongs,
  By some resenting Cully
Is decently run thro' the Lungs,
  And there's an End of BULLY.

SONG.

I.

INsulting Beauty, you misspend
  Those Frowns upon your Slave ;
Your Scorn against such Rebels bend,
Who dare with Confidence pretend,
That other Eyes their Hearts defend
  From all the Charms you have.

II.

Your conqu'ring Eyes so partial are,
  Or Mankind is so dull,
That while I languish in Despair,
Many proud senseless Hearts declare,
They find you not so killing Fair,
  To wish you Merciful.

III.

III.

They an inglorious Freedom boaft;
  I triumph in my Chain,
Nor am I unreveng'd, tho' loft;
Nor you anpunifh'd, tho' unjuft;
When I alone, who love you moft,
  Am kill'd with your Difdain.

ET CÆTERA. *A Song.*

I.

IN a dark, filent, fhady Grove,
  Fit for the Delights of Love,
As on CORINNA's Breaft I panting lay,
My Right-hand playing with *Et Cætera.*

II.

A thoufand Words and am'rous Kiffes,
Prepar'd us both for more fubftantial Bliffes;
And thus the hafty Moments flipt away,
Loft in the Tranfport of *Et Cætera.*

III.

She blufh'd to fee her Innocence betray'd,
And the fmall Oppofition fhe had made;
Yet hugg'd me clofe, and, with a Sigh, did fay,
Once more, my Dear, once more, *Et Cætera.*

IV.

But, Oh! the Power to pleafe this Nymph, was paft;
Too violent a Flame can never laft;
So we remitted to another Day,
The Profecution of *Et Cætera.*

✿✿✿✿✿✿✿✿✿✿✿✿✿✿✿✿✿✿

The DISAPPOINTMENT.

NAked she lay, clasp'd in my longing Arms,
I fill'd with Love, and she all over Charms;
Both equally inspir'd with eager Fire,
Melting thro' Kindness, flaming with Desire;
With Arms, Legs, Lips, close clinging to embrace,
She clips me to her *Breast*, and sucks me to her *Face*.
Her nimble Tongue, (Love's lesser Lightning) play'd
Within my Mouth, and to my Thoughts convey'd
Swift Orders, that I shou'd prepare to throw
The All-dissolving Thunderbolt below.
My flutt'ring Soul, sprung with the pointed *Kiss*,
Hangs hov'ring o'er her balmy *Lips* of *Bliss*:
But whilst her busy *Hand* wou'd guide that Part
Which shou'd convey my Soul up to her Heart,
In liquid Raptures I dissolve all o'er,
Melt into S——m, and —— at ev'ry Pore:
A Touch from any Part of her had don't;
Her *Hand*, her *Foot*, her very Look's a ——.
Smiling, she chides in a kind murm'ring Noise,
And from her *Body* wipes the clammy Joys;
When with a thousand Kisses, wand'ring o'er
My panting Breast, *And is there then no more?*
She cries. *All this to Love and Rapture's due;*
Must we not pay a Debt to Pleasure too?
But I, the most forlorn lost Man alive,
To shew my wish'd Obedience, vainly strive:
I sigh, alas! and kiss, but can not——;
Eager Desires confound my first Intent;
Succeeding Shame does more Success prevent,
And *Rage* at last confirms me Impotent.

Even

Even her fair Hand, which might bid Heat return
To frozen *Age*, and make cold Hermits burn,
Apply'd to my dead *Cinder*, warms no more
Than Fire to *Ashes* cou'd past Flames restore :
Trembling, confus'd, despairing, limber, dry,
A wishing, weak, unmoving Lump I lie ;
This *Dart* of Love, whose piercing Point oft dy'd
With *Virgin Blood*, ten *thousand Maids* has try'd.
Which *Nature* still directed with such *Art*,
That it thro' ev'ry ——— reach'd ev'ry *Heart*,
Stiffly resolv'd, 'twould carelesly invade
Woman and *Boy* ; nor aught its Fury staid,
Where e'er it pierc'd, a —— it found or made ;
Now languid lies in this unhappy Hour,
Shrunk up, and sapless, like a wither'd *Flow'r*.
Thou treach'rous base Deserter of my Flame,
False to my Passion, fatal to my *Fame*,
By what mistaken *Magick* do'st thou prove
So true to Lewdness, so untrue to Love ?
What *Oyster*, *Cinder*, *Beggar*, common *Whore*,
Did'st thou e'er fail in all thy Life before ?
When *Vice*, *Disease*, and *Scandal* lead the Way,
With what officious Haste dost thou obey ?
Like a rude roaring *Hector* in the *Streets*,
That scuffles, cuffs, and ruffles all he meets ;
But if his *King* or *Country* claim his Aid,
The *Rascal Villain* shrinks, and hides his Head :
Even so thy *brutal Valour* is display'd,
Breaks ev'ry *Stew*, does each small *Whore invade* ;
But if great *Love* the Onset does command,
Base Recreant, to thy Prince thou dares not stand.
Worst Part of me, and henceforth hated most,
Thro' all the Town the common —— *Post*,
On whom each Whore relieves her tingling ——
As Hogs on Gates do rub themselves, and grunt ;

                                May'st

May'ſt thou to rav'nous Shankers be a Prey,
Or in conſuming Weepings waſte away :
May Strangury and Stone thy Days attend ;
May'ſt thou ne'er piſs, who did'ſt refuſe to —— ⎫
When all my Joys did on falſe Thee depend ; ⎬
And may ten thouſand abler —— agree ⎭
To do the wrong'd *Corinna* Right for Thee.

The INSENSIBLE.

I.

ONE Day the amorous LYSANDER, ⎤
  By an impatient Paſſion ſway'd,
  Surpriz'd fair CHLORIS, that lov'd Maid,
Who could defend herſelf no longer,
All Things did with his Love conſpire ;
  The gilded Planet of the Day,
In his gay Chariot, drawn by Fire,
  Was now deſcending to the Sea,
And loſt no Light to guide the World,
But what from CHLORIS' brighter Eyes was hurl'd.

II.

In a lone *Thicket,* made for Love,
  Silent as yielding Maids conſent,
  She with a charming Languiſhment
Permits his Force, yet gently ſtrove.
Her Hands his Boſom ſoftly meet,
  But not to put him back deſign'd,
  Rather to draw him on inclin'd,
Whilſt he lay trembling at her Feet.
Reſiſtance 'tis too late to ſhow,
She wants the Pow'r to ſay, —— *Ah !* what d'ye do ?

III.

III.

Her Bright Eyes sweet, and yet severe,
   Where Love and Shame confus'dly strive,
   Fresh Vigour to Lysander give :
And whisp'ring softly in his Ear,
She cry'd — *Cease* — *cease* — *your vain Desire,*
   Or I'll call out — *What would you do ?*
   My dearer Honour, ev'n to you,
I cannot — *must not give* — *retire,*
Or take that Life, whose chiefest Part
I gave you with the Conquest of my Heart.

IV.

But he, as much unus'd to fear,
   As he was capable of Love,
   The blessed Minutes to improve,
Kisses her Lips, her Neck, her Hair ;
Each Touch her new Desires alarms ;
   His burning trembling Hand he prest
   Upon her melting snowy Breast ;
While she lay panting in his Arms,
All her unguarded Beauties lie,
The Spoils and Trophies of the Enemy.

V.

And now, without Respect or Fear,
   He seeks the Object of his Vows ;
   His Love no Modesty allows ;
By swift Degrees advancing where
His daring Hand that Altar seiz'd,
   Where Gods of Love do sacrifice ;
   That awful Throne, that Paradise,
Where Rage is tam'd and Anger pleas'd ;
That living Fountain, from whose Trills
The melted Soul in liquid Drops distills.

VI.

VI.

Her balmy Lips encount'ring his,
    Their Bodies as their Souls they join'd,
    Where both in Transports were confin'd,
Extend themselves upon the Mofs.
CHLORIS half dead and breathlefs lay ;
    Her Eyes appear'd like humid Light,
    Such as divides the Day and Night,
Or falling Stars, whofe Fires decay ;
And now no Signs of Life fhe fhows,
But what in fhort-breath'd Sighs returns and goes.

VII.

He faw how at her Length fhe lay ;
    He faw her rifing Bofom bare,
    Her loofe thin Robes, thro' which appear
A Shape defign'd for Love and Play ;
Abandon'd by her Pride and Shame,
    She does her fofteft Sweets difpenfe,
    Off'ring her Virgin-Innocence
A Victim to Love's facred Flame ;
Whilft the o'er-ravifh'd Shepherd lies,
Unable to perform the Sacrifice.

VIII.

Ready to tafte a thoufand Joys,
    The too tranfported haplefs Swain,
    Found the vaft Pleafure turn'd to Pain :
Pleafure, which too much Love deftroys.
The willing Garment by he laid,
    And Heav'n all open to his View ;
    Mad to poffefs, himfelf he threw
On the defencelefs lovely Maid :
But, Oh ! what envious Gods confpire
To fnatch his Pow'r, yet leave him the Defire?

IX.

IX.

Nature's Support, without whofe Aid
  She can no Human Being give,
  Itfelf now wants the Art to live;
Faintnefs its flacken'd Nerves invade:
In vain th' enraged Youth effay'd
  To call his fleeting Vigour back;
  No Motion 'twill from Motion take;
B' Excefs of Love is Love betray'd;
In vain he toils, in vain commands,
Th' *Infenfible* fell weeping in his Hands.

X.

In this fo am'rous cruel Strife,
  Where Love and Fate were too fevere,
  The poor LYSANDER, in Defpair,
Renounc'd his Reafon with his Life.
Now all the brifk and active Fire,
  That fhould the nobler Part inflame,
  Unactive, frigid, dull became,
And left no Spark for new Defire;
Not all her naked Charms could move,
Or calm that Rage which had debauch'd his Love,

XI.

CHLORIS returning from the Trance,
  Which Love and foft Defire had bred,
  Her tim'rous Hand fhe gently laid,
Or guided by Defign or Chance,
Upon that fabulous *Priapus*,
  That potent God (as Poets feign.)
  But never did young Shepherdefs
(Gath'ring of Fern upon the Plain)
More nimbly draw her Fingers back,
Finding, beneath the verdant Leaves, a Snake,

H   XII.

XII.

Than CHLORIS her fair Hand withdrew,
   Finding that God of her Desires
   Disarm'd of all his pow'rful Fires,
And cold as Flow'rs bath'd in the Morning Dew.
Who can the Nymph's Confusion guess?
   The Blood forsook the kinder Place,
   And strew'd with Blushes all her Face,
Which both Disdain and Shame express;
And from LYSANDER's Arms she fled,
Leaving him fainting on th' gloomy Bed.

XIII.

Like Lightning, thro' the Grove she hies,
   Our *Daphne* from the *Delphic* God;
   No Print upon the grassy Road
She leaves, t'instruct pursuing Eyes.
The Wind that wanton'd in her Hair,
   And with her ruffled Garments play'd,
   Discover'd in the flying Maid
All that the God's e'er made so fair.
Thus *Venus*, when her Love was slain,
With Fear and Haste flew o'er the fatal Plain.

XIV.

The Nymph's Resentments none but I
   Can well imagine and condole;
   But none can guess LYSANDER's Soul,
But those who sway'd his Destiny;
His silent Griefs swell up to Storms,
   And not one God his Fury spares;
   He curs'd his Birth, his Fate, his Stars,
But more the Shepherdess's Charms;
Whose soft bewitching Influence
Had damn'd him to the *Hell of Innocence*.

On

On a Juniper-Tree *cut down to make* BUSKS.

WHILST happy I triumphant stood,
    The Pride and Glory of the Wood,
My Aromatic Boughs and Fruit
Did with all other Trees dispute;
Had Right by Nature to excell,
In pleasing both the Taste and Smell;
But to the Touch, I must confess,
Bore an unwilling Sullenness.
My Wealth, like bashful Virgins, I
Yielding with some Reluctancy:
For which my Value shou'd be more,
Not giving easily my Store.
My verdant Branches all the Year
Did an eternal Beauty wear,
Did ever young and gay appear;
Nor needed any Tribute pay
For Bounties from the God of Day.
Nor do I hold Supremacy,
In all the Wood, o'er ev'ry Tree,
But e'en those two of my own Race,
That grew not in this happy Place.
But that in which I glory most,
And do myself with Reason boast,
Beneath my Shade the other Day
Young PHILOCLES and CHLORIS lay.
Upon my Root he plac'd her Head,
And where I grew, he made her Bed;
Their trembling Limbs did gently press
The kind supporting yielding Moss,

Ne'er

Ne'er half fo blefs'd as now, to bear
A Swain fo young, a Nymph fo fair.
My grateful Shade I kindly lent,
And ev'ry aiding Bough I bent
So low, as fometimes had the Blifs
To rob the Shepherd of a Kifs;
Whilft he in Pleafures far above
The Senfe of that Degree of Love,
Permitted ev'ry Stealth I made,
Unjealous of his Rival Shade.
I faw 'em kindle to Defire,
Whilft with foft Sighs they blew the Fire;
Saw the Approaches of their Joy,
He grew more fierce, and fhe lefs coy :
Saw how they mingled melting Rays,
Exchanging Love a thoufand Ways.
Kind was the Force on ev'ry Side ;
Her new Defires fhe could not hide,
Nor would the Shepherd be deny'd.
Impatient, he waits no Confent,
But what fhe gave by Languifhment.
The bleffed Minute he purfu'd,
Whilft Love her Fear and Shame fubdu'd ;
And now transported in his Arms,
Yields to the Conqu'ror all her Charms.
His panting Breaft to her's now join'd,
They feaft on Raptures unconfin'd,
Vaft and luxuriant, fuch as prove
The Immortality of Love.
For, who but a Divinity
Could mingle Souls to that Degree,
And melt 'em into Extafy ?
Where, like the Phenix, both expire,
Whilft from the Afhes of their Fire,
Sprung up a new and foft Defire.

Like

Like Charmers, thrice they did invoke
The God, and thrice new Vigour took ;
And had the Nymph been half fo kind,
As was the Shepherd well inclin'd,
The Myft'ry had not ended there:
But CHLORIS re-affum'd her Fear,
And chid the Swain for having preft
What fhe (alas!) could not refift ;
Whilft he, in whom Love's facred Flame
Before and After was the fame,
Humbly implores fhe would forget
That Fault, which he would yet repeat.
From active Joys with Shame they hafte
To a Reflection on the paft ;
A thoufand Times the Covert blefs,
That did fecure their Happ'nefs ;
Their Gratitude to ev'ry Tree
They pay, but moft to happy me.
The Shepherdefs my Bark carefs'd,
Whilft he my Root (Love's Pillow) kifs'd,
And did with Sighs their Pate deplore,
Since I muft fhelter 'em no more.
And if before my Joys were fuch,
In having feen and heard fo much,
My Griefs muft be as great and high,
When all abandon'd I muft lie,
Doom'd to a filent Deftiny ;
No more the am'rous Strife to hear,
The Shepherd's Vows, the Virgin's Fear ;
No more a joyful Looker on,
Whilft Love's foft Battle's loft and won.

    With Grief I bow'd my murm'ring Head,
And all my chryftal Dew I fhed,

Which

Which did in CHLORIS Pity move;
CHLORIS, whofe Soul is made of Love.
She cut me down, and did tranflate
My Being to a happier State:
No Martyr for Religion dy'd
With half that unconfid'ring Pride:
My Top was on the Altar laid,
Where Love his fofteft Off'rings paid,
And was, as fragrant Incenfe, burn'd;
My Body into BUSKS was turn'd,
Where I ftill guard the facred Store,
And of *Love's Temple* keep the Door.

The Rehearfal. *A* Satire.

A. WHAT, *Timon*, does old Age begin t'approach,
       That thou droop'ft under one Night's De-
       bauch?
Haft Thou left deep to needy Rogues on Tick,
Who ne'er could pay, and muft be paid next Week?
   Tim. Neither, alas! but a dull dining *Sot*
Seiz'd me i' th' *Mall*, who juft my Name had got:
He runs upon me, cries, Dear Rogue, I'm thine,
With me fome Wits of thy Acquaintance dine.
I tell him I'm engag'd; but, as a Whore
With Modefty enflaves her Sparks the more,
The longer I deny'd, the more he preft:
At laft, I e'en confent to be his Gueft.
He takes me in his Coach; and as we go,
Pulls out a Libel of a Sheet or two,
Infipid as *The Praife of pious Queens*,
Or *Settle's* unaffifted former Scenes;

                                          Which

Which he admir'd, and prais'd at ev'ry Line;
At laſt it was ſo ſharp, it muſt be mine.
I vow'd I was no more a Wit than he,
Unpractis'd and unbleſs'd in Poetry:
A Song to *Phillis* I perhaps might make,
But never rhym'd but for my——Sake;
I envy'd no Man's Fortune, nor his Fame,
Nor ever thought of a Revenge ſo tame.
He knew my Style, he ſwore; and 'twas in vain
Thus to deny the Iſſue of my Brain.
Choak'd with this Flatt'ry, I no Anſwer make,
But ſilent, leave him to his dear Miſtake.
Of a well-meaning Fool I'm moſt afraid,
Who ſillily repeats what was well ſaid.
But this was not the worſt; when he came Home,
He aſk'd, Are *Sedley*, *Buckhurſt*, *Saville*, come?
No, but there are above *Half-wit* and *Huff*,
Kickum, and *Dingboy*. O! 'tis well enough,
They're all brave Fellows, cries mine Hoſt, let's dine,
I long to have my Belly full of Wine;
They'll Write and Fight, I dare aſſure you, O!
They're Men *tam Marti quam Mercurio*.
I ſaw my Error; but 'twas now too late,
No Means nor Hopes appear of a Retreat;
Well, we ſalute, and each Man takes his Seat.
Boy, (ſays the Sot,) is my Wife ready yet?
A Wife, (good Gods!) a Fop, and Bullies too!
For one poor Meal what muſt I undergo?
In comes my Lady ſtrait; ſhe had been fair,
Fit to give Love, and to prevent Deſpair;
But Age, Beauty's incurable Diſeaſe,
Had left her more Deſire than Pow'r to pleaſe;
As Cocks will ſtrike, altho' their Spurs be gone,
She with her old blear Eyes to ſmite begun:

Tho'

Tho' nothing elfe, fhe (in Defpite of Time)
Preferv'd the Affectation of her Prime.
However you begun, fhe brought in Love,
And hardly from that Subject wou'd remove.
We chanc'd to fpeak of the *French* King's Succefs:
My Lady wonder'd much how Heav'n could blefs
A Man that lov'd Two Women at One Time;
But more, how he to them excus'd his Crime.
She afk'd *Huff*, if Love's Flame he never felt?
He anfwer'd bluntly, do you think I'm gelt?
She at his Plainnefs fmil'd, then turn'd to me,
Love in your Minds precedes ev'n Poetry;
You to that Paffion can no ftranger be,
But Wits are given to Inconftancy.
She had run on, I think, till now; but Meat
Came up, and fuddenly fhe took her Seat.
I thought the Dinner wou'd make fome Amends,
When my good Hoft cries out, *Ye're all my Friends*;
Our own plain Fare, and the beft Tierce the Bull
Affords, I'll give you, and your Bellies full.
As for French *Kickfhaws,* Cellery, *and* Champaign,
Ragous, *and* Fricaffes, *in Troth we've none.*
Here's a good Dinner towards, thought I, when ftrait,
Up comes a Piece of Beef full Horfe-Man's Weight,
Hard as the Arfe of *Mordaunt*, under which
The Coachman fweats, as ridden by a Witch.
A Difh of *Carrots*, each of them as long
As——that to fair Countefs did belong
Which her fmall Pillow could not fo well hide,
But Vifitors his flaming Head efpy'd.
Pig, Goofe, and *Capon* follow'd in the Rear,
With all that Country-Bumpkins call *Good Cheer,*
Serv'd up with Sauces all of *Eighty-Eight;*
When our rough Youth wreftled, and threw the Weight.

And

And now the Bottle briſkly flies about,
Inſtead of Ice, wrapt up in a wet Clout.
A Brimmer follows the third Bit we eat;
Small Beer becomes our Drink, and Wine our Meat.
The Table was ſo large, that in leſs Space
A Man might ſave ſix old *Italians* Place:
Each Man had as much Room as *Porter Blunt,*
Or *Harris* had in *Cullen*'s Buſhel——
And now the Wine began to work, mine Hoſt
Had been a Col'nel, we muſt hear him boaſt,
Not of Towns won, but an Eſtate he'ad loſt
For the King's Service, which indeed he ſpent
Whoring and Drinking, but with good Intent.
He talk'd much of a Plot, and Money lent
In *Cromwell*'s Time. Alas! my Lady ſhe
Complain'd our Love was coarſe, our Poetry
Unfit for modeſt Ears; ſmall Whores and Play'rs
Were of our hair-brain'd Youth the only Cares,
Who were too wild for any virtuous League,
Too rotten to conſummate the Intrigue.
Falkland ſhe prais'd, and *Suckling*'s eaſy Pen,
And ſeem'd to taſte their former Parts again.
Mine Hoſt drinks to the *Beſt* in *Chriſtendom,*
And decently my Lady quits the Room.
Left to ourſelves, of ſev'ral Things we prate;
Some regulate the *Stage,* and ſome the *State.*
Half-wit cries up my Lord of *Orrery,*
Ah, how well *Muſtapha* and *Zanger* die!
His Senſe ſo little forc'd, that by one Line
You may the other eaſily divine:

> *And, which is worſe, if any worſe can be,*
> *He never ſaid one Word of it to me.*

This is fine Poetry, you'd ſwear 'twere *Proſe,*
So little on the Senſe the Rhimes impoſe.

D—me,

D—me, (fays *Dingbey*) in my Mind, G—d's W—ds,
Etherege writes airy Songs and foft Lampoons,
The beft of any Man. As for your Nouns,
Grammar, and Rules of Art, he knows 'em not;
Yet wrote two taking Plays, without one Plot.
Huff was for *Settle*, and *Morocco* prais'd,
Said rumbling Words, like Drums, his Courage rais'd,
  Whofe broad-built Bulks the boift'rous Billows bear;
  Zaphee and Sally, Mugadore, Oran,
  'The fam'd Arzile, Alcazar, Tetuan.
Was ever braver *Language* wrote by Man?
Kickum for *Crown* declar'd, faid, in *Romance*,
  He had out-done the very Wits of *France*:
Witnefs *Pandion*, and his *Charles the Eight*,
Where a young *Monarch*, carelefs of his Fate,
Thro' *Foreign Troops* and *Rebels* fhock his State;
Complains another Sight afflicts him more,
(*Viz.*) The *Queen's Galleys* rowing from the Shore,
  Fitting their Oars and Tackling to be gone,
  Whilft fporting Waves fmil'd on the Rifing-Sun.
Waves fmiling on the Sun! I'm fure that's new,
And 'twas well thought on, give the Dev'l his Due.
  Mine Hoft, who had faid nothing in an Hour,
Rofe up, and prais'd the *Indian Emperor*;
  As if our old World modeftly withdrew,
  And here in private had brought forth a-new.
Here are two Lines! Who but he durft prefume
To make th' *Old World* a New *Withdrawing-Room,*
Where of another *World* fhe's brought to-bed?
What a brave Midwife is a *Laureat's Head!*
  But, Pox of all thefe Scribblers, what d'ye think,
Will *Souches* this Year any *Champaign* drink?
Will *Turenne* fight him? Without Doubt, fays *Huff,*
If they Two meet, their Meeting will be rough.
                         D—me,

D—me, (fays *Dingboy*,) the *French* Cowards are ;
They pay, but th' *Englifh*, *Scots*, and *Swifs* make *War*.
In gaudy Troops, at a Review, they fhine,
But dare not with the *Germans* Battle join :
What now appears like Courage, is not fo;
'Tis a fhort Pride, which from Succefs does grow :
On their firft Blow, they'll fhrink into thofe Fears
They fhew'd at *Creffy*, *Agincourt*, *Poictiers* :
Their Lofs was infamous, Honour fo ftain'd,
Is by a Nation not to be regain'd.
What they were then, I know not, now they're brave ;
He that denies it, lies, and is a Slave
(Says *Huff*, and frown'd :) Says *Dingboy*, *That do I* :
And, at that Word, at t'others Head let fly
A greafy Plate, when fuddenly they all
Together, by the Ears, in Parties fall ;
Half-wit with *Dingboy* joins, *Kickum* with *Huff*, ⎫
Their Swords were fafe, and fo we let 'em cuff, ⎬
Till they, mine Hoft, and I, had all enough. ⎭
Their Rage once over, they begin to treat,
And fix frefh Bottles muft the Peace compleat ;
I ran down Stairs, with a Vow never more
To drink Beer-Glaffes, and hear Hectors roar.

ANACREONTIC.

T H E Heavens caroufe each Day a Cup,
No wonder *Atlas* holds them up.
The Trees fuck up the Earth and Ground,
And in their brown Bowls drink around.
The Sea too, whom the Salt makes dry,
His greedy Thirft to fatisfy,

'Ten thousand Rivers drink, and then
Grows drunk, and spews 'em up again.
The Sun (and who so right, as he)
S ts up all Night to drink the Sea.
The Moon quaffs up the Sun, her Brother,
And wishes she could tope another.
Ev'ry Thing fuddles ; then that I,
Is't any Reason, should be dry ?
Well, I'll be content to thirst ;
But too much Drink shall make me, first.

A Session of the POETS.

SINCE the Sons of the Muses grew num'rous and loud,
For th' appeasing so factious and clam'rous a Crowd,
Apollo thought fit, in so weighty a Cause,
To establish a Government, Leader and Laws.
The Hopes of the Bays, at this summoning Call,
Had drawn 'em together, the Devil and all :
All thronging and list'ning, they gap'd for the B'essing,
No Presbyter Sermon had more Crouding and Pressing.

In the Head of the Gang *John Dryden* appear'd,
That ancient grave Wit, so long lov'd and fear'd ;
But *Apollo* had heard of a Story in Town,
Of his quitting the Muses, to wear a black Gown,
And so gave him leave, now his Poetry's done,
To let him turn Priest, now *R*——is turn'd Nun.

This rev'rend Author was no sooner set by,
But *Apollo* had got gentle * *George* in his Eye,
And frankly confes'd, that of all Men that writ,
There's none had more Fancy, Sense, Judgment, and Wit ;

------

* *Sir* George Etherege.

But

But i' th' crying Sin, Idlenefs, he was fo harden'd,
That his long fev'n Years Silence was not to be pardon'd.

Brawny *Wycherley* was the next Man fhew'd his Face;
But *Apollo* e'en thought him too good for the Place.
No Gentleman-Writer that Office fhould bear,
'Twas a Trader in Wit the Laurel fhould wear,
As none but a Citizen makes a Lord-Mayor.

Next into the Croud *Tom Shadwell* does wallow,
And fwears by his Guts, his Paunch, and his Tallow,
'Tis he alone beft pleafes the Age;
Himfelf and his Wife have fupported the Stage.
Apollo well pleas'd with fo bonny a Lad,
To oblige him, he told him, he fhou'd be huge glad,
Had he half fo much Wit as he fancy'd he had.
However, to pleafe fo jovial a Wit,
And to keep him in Humour, *Apollo* thought fit
To bid him drink on, and keep his old Trick
Of railing at Poets, and fhewing his ———

Nat Lee ftept in next, in Hopes of a Prize,
Apollo remember'd he had hit Once in Thrice;
By the Rubies in's Face, he could not deny,
But he had as much Wit as Wine could fupply;
Confefs'd that indeed he'ad a mufical Note,
But fometimes ftrain'd fo hard that he rattl'd i' th' Throat;
Yet owning he'ad Senfe, to encourage him for't,
He made him his *Ovid* in *Auguftus*'s Court.

Poet *Settle* his Trial was the next came about,
He brought him an *Ibrahim* with the Preface torn out,
And humbly defir'd he might give no Offence;
G—d D—me, cries *Shadwell*, he cannot write Senfe;
And *Banks*, cry'd up *Newport*, I hate that dull Rogue.
Apollo confid'ring he was not in Vogue,
Would not truft his dear *Bays* with fo modeft a Fool,
And bid the great Boy fhould be fent back to School.

Tom

Tom Otway came next, *Tom Shadwell's* dear *Zany*,
And swears, for Heroicks, he writes best of any :
Don *Carlos* his Pockets so amply had fill'd,
That his Mange was quite cur'd, and his Lice were all kill'd,
But *Apollo* had seen his Face on the Stage,
And prudently did not think fit to engage }
The Scum of a Play-House for the Prop of an Age. }

In the numerous Herd that encompass'd him round,
Little starch *Johnny Crown* at his Elbow he found ;
His Cravat-string iron'd, he gently did stretch
His Lilly-white Hand out, his Laurel to reach :
Alledging, that he had most Right to the Bays,
For writing Romances, and shiting of Plays.
Apollo rose up, and gravely confest,
Of all Men that writ, his Talent was best ;
For since Pain and Dishonour Man's Life only damn, }
The greatest Felicity Mankind can claim, }
Is to want Sense of Smart, and be past Sense of Shame; }
And to perfect his Bliss in poetical Rapture,
He bid him be dull to the End of the Chapter.

The Poetess * *Afra* next shew'd her sweet Face,
And swore by her Poetry, and her black Ace,
That the Laurel by a double Right was her own,
For the Plays she had writ, and the Conquests she'ad won.
Apollo acknowledg'd 'twas hard to deny her ;
But yet, to deal frankly and ingenuously by her,
He told her, were Conquests and Charms her Pretence,
She ought to have pleaded a dozen Years since.
Anabalutha put in for a Share,
And little *Tom Essence's* Author was there :
Nor could *D'Urfey* forbear for the Laurel to stickle, }
Protesting he had had the Honour to tickle }
The Ears of the Town with his dear Madam *Fickle.* }

---

* *Mrs.* Behn.

With other Pretenders, whofe Names I'd rehearfe,
But they are too long to ftand in my Verfe.
Apollo, quite tir'd with their tedious Harangue,
Finds at laft *Tom Betterton*'s Face in the Gang;
And fince Poets with the kind Players may hang,
By his own Day-light he folemnly fwore,
That in Search of a *Laureat* he'd look out no more.
A general Murmur ran quite thro' the Hall,
To think that the Bays to an Actor fhould fall;
But Apollo, to quiet and pacify all,
E'en told them, to put his Deferts to the Teft,
That he had made Plays as well as the beft,
And was the great'ft Wonder the Age ever bore;
For, of all the Play-Scriblers that e'er writ before,
His Wit had moft Worth and moft Modefty in't;
For he had writ Plays, yet ne'er put 'em in Print.

A Lyrick POEM:
In Imitation of *Cornelius Gallius.*

I.

MY Goddefs LYDIA, heav'nly Fair,
As Lillies fweet, as foft as Air;
Let loofe thy Treffes, fpread thy Charms,
And to my Love give frefh Alarms.

II.

O let me gaze on thofe bright Eyes,
Tho' facred Light'ning from them flies:
Show me that foft, that modeft Grace,
Which paints with charming Red thy Face.

III,

III.

Give me *Ambrosia* in a Kiss,
That I may rival JOVE in Bliss;
That I may mix my Soul with thine,
And make the Pleasure all divine.

IV.

O hide thy Bosom's killing White,
(The Milky Way is not so bright,)
Lest you my ravish'd Soul oppress
With Beauty's Pomp, and sweet Excess.

V.

Why draw'st thou from the Purple Flood
Of my kind Heart the vital Blood?
Thou art all over endless Charms;
O take me, dying, to thy Arms.

APOLLO's *GRIEF, for having killed* HYACINTH *by Accident.*
An Imitation of Ovid.

SWEET HYACINTH, my Life, my Joy,
What have I done, my lovely Boy?
With Kisses I would stop thy Soul;
But, O! the Fates my Bliss controul.
For Thee I languish, wish to die,
And weary grow of Immortality.
Yet with my Harp I'll found thy Praise,
And to the Stars thy Beauties raise.
Straight thou shalt rise with Purple Grace,
And with the same inviting Face;
Thy Blood shall turn the Lilly Red,
(Mourning) I'll wear it on my Head.

The

The World fhall celebrate thy Fame,
And Feafts be call'd by thy dear Name ;
With HYACINTH Heav'n fhall refound,
White Echoes catch th'e charming Sound.
The fatal Lofs, thus fad APOLLO mourn'd,
Of the fair Boy, for whom fo much he burn'd.

WOMAN's *Ufurpation.*

WOMAN was made MAN's Sov'reignty to own,
And He, as Monarch, was to rule alone ;
She was his Vaffal made, to fear and dread
The angry Frowns of MAN, her Lord and Head.
Heav'n did to him the Pow'r delegate,
O'er all the Univerfe he made him Great ;
His Power did the largeft Scepter fway,
The whole Creation did his Laws obey.
No Limits e'er were fet to his Commands,
Tygers and Lions lick'd his facred Hands,
And favage Monfters glory'd in his Bands.
The Legiflative Pow'r was fix'd in him,
Juft MAN ! till WOMAN tempted him to Sin.
The Sun no fooner had begun his Courfe,
Spreading his gaudy Beams o'er the' Univerfe ;
Nature herfelf was hardly full awake ;
The Planets did their Motions rarely make ;
The azure Orb, in which is finely fet
The glitt'ring Stars, fcarce knew their Architect :
Air, Water, Earth and *Fire,* did hardly find
Themfelves pure Elements, and were inclin'd
To mix in Compofition of each Kind ;
MAN fcarce had feen the firft refplendent Light,
E'er WOMAN brought forth everlafting Night ;

Damn'd

Damn'd *Pride* invited her at firſt to Sin,
Ambition next the Devil uſher'd in.
Thoſe, for ten thouſand more, have Inlets made;
And now ſhe's Miſtreſs of the Devil's Trade :
She'll tempt, lie, cozen, ſwear, betray, and cheat,
Hell's blackeſt Arts ten Thouſand Times repeat:
She will no longer in Subjection ſtand,
But M A N muſt truckle to her harſh Command;
Toſs'd with tempeſtuous Storms of haughty Pride, ⎫
Diſorder'd Motions all her Paſſions guide,   ⎬
'Till ſhe deſtroys her loving Lord and Bride.   ⎭
How many ſad Examples do we find,   ⎫
Of Huſbands murder'd by the Female Kind ?   ⎬
Such are th' Effects of her aſpiring Mind.   ⎭
No Laws nor Goodneſs could her Thoughts deter,
And *Satan* was foreſtall'd in ſeeing her ;
From all diviner Edicts out ſhe flew,
And ſwell'd with curſed Pride, no Compaſs knew;
Such is the Rage of her infected Mind,
She damns the Race and Stock of poor Mankind ;
And ſtifling-Brimſtone is the ſweeteſt Scent
That burns, whilſt Devils guard her ſable Tent,
Reſolv'd to execute, and ne'er repent,
Whate'er her wicked Malice can invent.
Since Heaven's ſacred Laws cannot reſtrain
Thy Will, and threaten'd Vengeance is in vain ;
Since to live peaceful is thy greateſt Pain ;
Proceed, and then You'll Queen of Devils reign.

An

An Epiſtle from Ephelia *to* Bajazet, *complaining of his Inconſtancy.*

HOW far are they deceiv'd, who hope in vain
A laſting Leaſe of Joys from Love t'obtain?
All the dear Sweets we're promis'd or expect,
After Enjoyment turn to cold Neglect.
Could Love a conſtant Happineſs have known,
That mighty Wonder had in me been ſhown;
Our Paſſions were ſo favoured by Fate,
As if ſhe meant 'em an eternal Date;
So kind he look'd, ſuch tender Words he ſpoke,
'Twas paſt Belief ſuch Vows ſhould e'er be broke:
Fix'd on my Eyes, how often would he ſay,
He could with Pleaſure gaze an Age away.
When Thoughts too great for Words had made him mute,
In Kiſſes he would tell my Hand his Suit:
So ſtrong his Paſſion was, ſo far above
The common Gallantries that paſs for Love:
At worſt, I thought, if he unkind ſhould prove,
His ebbing Paſſion would be kinder far
Than the firſt Tranſports of all others are:
Nor was my Love or Fondneſs leſs than his;
In him I center'd all my Hopes of Bliſs;
For him my Duty to my Friends forgot,
For him I loſt, alas! What loſt I not?
Fame, all the valuable Things of Life,
To meet his Love by a leſs Name than *Wife*:

How

How happy was I then, how dearly bleſt,
When this great Man lay panting on my Breaſt,
Looking ſuch Things as ne'er can be expreſs'd ?
Thouſand freſh Look he gave me ev'ry Hour,
Whilſt greedily I did his Looks devour ;
'Till quite o'ercome with Charms, I trembling lay,
At ev'ry Look he gave, melting away,
I was ſo highly happy in his Love,
Methought I pitty'd them that dwelt Above.
Think then, thou greateſt, lovelieſt, falſeſt Man.
How you have vow'd, how I have lov'd, and then,
My faithleſs Dear, be cruel if you can.
How I have lov'd, I cannot, need not tell ;
No, ev'ry Act has ſhewn I lov'd too well.
Since firſt I ſaw you, I ne'er had a Thought
Was not entirely yours ; to you I brought
My Virgin Innocence, and freely made
My Love an Off'ring to your noble Bed :
Since then youv'e been the Star by which I ſteer'd,
And nothing elſe but you, I lov'd or fear'd ;
Your Smiles I only live by, and I muſt,
Whene'er you frown, be ſhatter'd into Duſt.
O ! ean the Coldneſs that you ſhew me now,
Suit with the gen'rous Heat you once did ſhow ?
I cannot live on Pity or Reſpect,
A Thought ſo mean would my whole Love infect ;
Leſs than your Love I ſcorn, Sir, to expect.
Let me not live in dull Indiff'rency,
But give me Rage enough to make me die ;
For if from you I needs muſt meet my Fate,
Before you pity, I would chuſe your Hate.

A very Heroical Epistle, in Answer to
EPHELIA.

MADAM,

IF you're deceiv'd, it is not by my Cheat,
For all Disguises are below the Great.
What Man or Woman upon Earth can say
I ever us'd 'em well above a Day ?
How is it then that I inconstant am ?
He changes not, who always is the same.
In my dear Self I center every Thing,
My Servants, Friends, my Mistress, and my King, }
Nay, Heav'n and Earth to that one Point I bring. }
Well-manner'd, honest, generous, and stout,
Names by dull Fools to plague Mankind found out,
Should I regard, I must myself constrain,
And 'tis my Maxim to avoid all Pain.
You fondly look for what none e'er could find ;
Deceive yourself, and then call me unkind ;
And, by false Reason, would my Falshood prove,
For 'tis as natural to Change, as Love.
You may as justly at the Sun repine,
Because alike it does not always shine.
No glorious Thing was ever made to stay ;
My Blazing-Star but visits, and away :
As fatal too it shines, as those i'th' Skies ;
'Tis never seen, but some great Lady dies :
The boasted Favour you so precious hold,
To me's no more than changing of my Gold,
Whate'er you gave, I paid you back in Bliss ;
Then where's the Obligation, pray, of this ?

If

If hereto'ore you found Grace in my Eyes,
Be thankful for it, and let that fuffice;
But Women, Beggars like, ftill haunt the Door,
Where they've receiv'd a Charity before.
O! happy *Sultan!* whom we barb'rous call,
How much refin'd art thou above us all?
Who envies not the Joys of thy *Seraigl?*
Thee, like fome God, the trembling Croud adore,
Each Man's thy Slave, and Woman-kind thy Whore.
Methinks I fee thee udderneath the Shade
Of golden Canopy fupinely laid;
Thy crouding Slaves all filent as the Night,
But at thy Nod, all active as the Light:
Secure in folid Sloth, thou there doft reign,
And feel'ft the Joys of Love without the Pain.
Each Female courts thee with a wifhing Eye,
While thou with awful Pride walk'ft carelefs by,
Till thy kind Pledge at laft marks out the Dame
Thou fancieft moft, to quench thy prefent Flame:
Then from thy Bed fubmiffive fhe retires,
And, thankful for the Grace, no more requires.
No loud Reproach, nor fond unwelcome Sound
Of Women's Tongues thy facred Ear does wound;
If any do, a nimble Mute ftrait ties
The True-love Knot, and ftops her foolifh Cries.
Thou fear'ft no injur'd *Kinfman's* threat'ning Blade,
Nor Midnight Ambufhes by Rivals laid;
While here, with aching Hearts our Joys we tafte,
Difturb'd by Swords, like *Democles's* Feaft.

The four following EPISTLES *from* B. *to* E. *are fup-
pofed to be written from the Lord* Buckhurft, *afterwards Earl of* Dorfet, *to Mr.* Etherege, *afterwards
Sir* George Etherege.

An

✽✽✽✽✽✽✽✽✽✽✽✽✽✽✽✽

An Epistle from B. *to* E.

DReaming last on Mrs. *Farley*,
   M ——— was up this Morning early ;
And I was fain, without my Gown,
To rise i'th' Cold to get him down.
Hard Shift, alas ! but yet a sure,
Although it be no pleasing Cure.
Of old, the fair *Ægyptian* Slattern,
For Luxury that had no Pattern,
To fortify her *Roman* Swinger,
Instead of Nutmegs, Mace, and Ginger,
Did spice his Bowls (as Story tells)
With Warts of Rocks, and Spawns of Shells ;
It had been happy for her Grace,
Had I been in the Rascal's Place ;
I, who do scorn that any Stone
Should raise my ———, but my own,
Had laid her down on ev'ry Couch,
And spar'd her Pearl, and Diamond Brouch,
Until her hot-tail'd Majesty,
Being happily reclaim'd by me,
From all her wild expensive Ways,
Had worn her Gems on Holidays :
But since her ——— has long done itching,
Let us discourse of modern Bitching.
   I must intreat you, by this Letter,
T' enquire for *Whores*, the more the better :
Hunger makes any Man a Glutton.
If *Roberts, Thomas,* Mrs. *Dutton,*

Or any other Bawd of Note,
Inform of a fresh Petticoat;
Enquire, I pray, with friendly Care,
Where their respective Logdings are.
Some do compare a Man to a Bark,
A pretty Metaphor, pray mark,
And with a long and tedious Story,
With all the Tackling lay before ye:
The Sails are Hope, the Masts Desire,
'Till they the gentlest Reader tire.
But howsoe'er they keep a Pudder,
I'm sure the —— is the Rudder;
The pow'rful Rudder, which of Force
To Town must shortly steer my Course;
And if you do not there provide
A Port, where I may safely ride:
Landing in haste in some foul Creek,
'Tis ten to one I spring a Leak.

Next, I must make it my Request,
If you have any Interest,
Or can by any Means discover
Some lamentable Rhiming Lover,
Who shall in Numbers harsh and vile,
His Mistress, Nymph or Goddess stile,
Send all his Labours down to me,
By the first Opportunity.

Or any Knights of your Round Table,
To other Scribblers formidable,
Guilty themselves of the same Crime,
Dress Nonsense up in ragged Rhime,
As once a Week they seldom fail,
Inspir'd with Love and Gridiron Ale.

Or any paultry Poetry,
Tho' from the University;

Who

Who, when the King and Queen were there,
Did both their Wit and Learning fpare,
And have (I hope) endeavour'd fince
To make the World fome Recompence,
Such damned Fuftian when you meet,
Be not too rafh or indifcreet,
Tho' they can find no juft Excufes,
To put 'em to their proper Ufes,
The fatal Privy, or the Fire,
Their nobler Foe ; at my Defire,
Reftrain your natural Profufenefs,
And fpare 'em, tho' you have a Loofenefs.

E———'s *Anfwer.*

AS crafty Harlots ufe to fhrink
From Letchers dos'd with Sleep and Drink,
When they intend to make a Pack,
By filching Sheets, or Shirt from Back ;
So were you pleas'd to fteal away
From me, whilft on your Bed I lay :
But long you had not been departed,
When, pinch'd with Cold, from thence I ftarted ;
Where, miffing you, I ftamp'd and ftar'd,
Like *Bacon*, when he wak'd, and heard
His Brazen Head in vain had fpoke,
And faw it lie in Pieces broke :
Sighing, I to my Chamber make,
And ev'ry Limb as ftiff as Stake,
Unlefs poor ———, which did feel
Like flimy Skin of new-ftript Eel ;

I

Or Pudding that Mifchance had got,
And fpent itfelf half in the Pot.
With Care I cleans'd the fneaking Varlet,
That late had been in Pool of Harlot:
But neither Shirt nor Water cou'd
Remove the Stench of letch'rous Mud.
The Queen of Love from Sea did fpring,
Whence the beft ———— do fmell like Ling :
But fure this damn'd notorious Bitch
Was made o'th' Froth of *Jane Shore*'s Ditch ;
Or elfe her ———— could never ftink
Like Pump that's foul, or nafty Sink.

When this was done, to Bed I went,
And the whole Day in Sleep I fpent ;
But the next Morning, frefh and gay,
As Citizen on Holiday,
I wander'd in the fpacious Town,
Amongft the Bawds of beft Renown :
To *Temple* I a Vifit made ;
Temple ! the Beauty of her Trade !
The only Bawd that ever I,
For want of Whore, could occupy.
She made me Friends with Mrs. *Cuffly*,
Whom we indeed had us'd but roughly ;
For by a gentle Way I found,
The Whore would — under ten Pound.
So refty Jades which fcorn to ftir,
Tho' oft provok'd by Whip and Spur,
By milder Ufage may be got
To fall into their wonted Trot.

But what Succefs I farther had,
And what Difcov'ries, good and bad,
I made by roving up and down,
I'll tell you when you come to Town.

Farther,

Farther, I have obey'd your Motion,
Tho' much provok'd by Pill and Potion,
And sent you down some paul.y Rhimes,
The greatest Grievance of our Times;
When such as Nature never made
For Poets, daily will invade
Wit's Empire, both the Stage and Press,
And, which is worse, with good Success.

The second Epistle from B. *to* E.

IF I can guess, the Devil choak me,
What horrid Fury could provoke thee,
To use thy railing scurrilous Wit
'Gainst —— and ——, the Source of it;
For what but —— and —— does raise
Our Thoughts to Songs and Roundelays?
Enables us to *Anagrams*,
And other amorous Flim-flams?
Then we write Plays, and so proceed
To *Bays*, the Poets sacred Weed.
Hast no Respect for God *Priapus?*
That antient Story shall not 'scape us.
Priapus was a *Roman* God,
But in plain *English*, —— and ——;
That pleas'd their Sisters, Wives, and Daughters,
Guarded their Pippins and Pomwaters;
For at the Orchard's utmost Entry
This mighty Deity stood Centry,
Invested in a tatter'd Blanket,
To scare the Magpies from their Banquet:

I 2   But

But this may ferve to fhew we trample
On Rule and Method, by Example
Of modern Authors, who, to fnap at all,
. Will talk of *Cæfar* in the Capitol ;
Of *Cynthia's* Beams, and *Sol's* bright Ray,
Known Foe to Butter-Milk and Whey,
Which foftens Wax, but hardens Clay ;
All this without the leaft Connection,
Which, to fay Truth's enough to vex one ;
But farewell all Poetick Dizzinefs,
And now to come unto the Bufinefs.

 Tell the bright Nymph how fad and penfively,
E'er fince we us'd her fo offenfively,
In difmal Shades, with Arms acrofs,
I fit, lamenting of my Lofs ;
To *Echo*, I her Name commend,
Who has it now at her Tongue's End,
And, Parrot like, repeats the fame ;
For fhould you talk of *Tamerlain* *,
Cuffley, fhe cries, at the fame Time,
Tho' the laft Accents do not rhime,
Far more than *Echo* e'r did yet
For *Phillis* or bright *Amoret.*

 With Pen-knife keen, of mod'ra'e Size,
As bright and piercing as her Eyes,
A glitt'ring Weapon, which would fcorn
To pare a Nail, or cut a Corn,
Upon the Trees of fmootheft Bark
I carve her Name, or elfe her Mark,

---

 * Tamerlane the Great: *Or*, The Scythian Shepherd. *A Tragedy. Written*, 1593, *by* Chriftopher Mar-
loe, *an Author cotemporary with* Shakefpear.

. Which

Which commonly's a bleeding Heart,
A weeping Eye, or flaming Dart.

  Here, on a Beach, like am'rous Sot,
I sometimes carve a True-love's Knot ?
There, a tall Oak her Name does bear,
In a large spreading Character :
I chose the fairest and the best
Of all the Grove ; amongst the rest,
I carv'd it on a lusty Pine,
Which wept a Pint of Turpentine ;
Such was the Terror of her Name,
By the Report of evil Fame ;
Who tired with immod'rate Flight,
Had lodg'd upon his Boughs all Night.
The wary Tree, who fear'd a Clap,
And knew the Virtue of its Sap,
Dropt Balsam into ev'ry Wound,
And in an Hour's Time was found.
But you are unacquainted yet,
With half the Pow'r of *Amoret* ;
For she can drink as well as ——,
Her growing Empire still must thrive.
Our Hearts, weak Forts, we must resign,
When Beauty does its Forces join
With Man's strong Enemy, good Wine.

This I was told by Lord *O-Brian*,
A Man whose Word I much rely on ;
He still kept Touch, and came down hither
When thou wert scar'd with the foul Weather:
But if thou would'st forgiven be,
Say that a Whore detained thee ;
—— whose strong Charms the World bewitches,
The Joy of Kings ! the Beggar's Riches !
The Courtier's Business ! Statesman's Leisure !
The tired Tinker's Ease and Pleasure !

I 3

Of

Of which, alas! I've Leave to prate;
But, O! the Rigour of my Fate!
For want of bouncing *Bona Roba*,
Lascivia est nobis pagina vita proba.
For that Rhime I was fain to fumble:
When *Pegasus* begins to stumble,
Tis Time to rest. *Your very Humble.*

E———'s *Answer.*

SO soft and am'rously you write,
So well describe the pleasing Fight,
That were I still in *Lanthorn* sweating,
Swallowing of *Bolus*, or a spitting;
I should forget each Injury,
The pocky Whores have offer'd me,
And only of my Fate complain,
Because I must from Love abstain;
All-pow'rful Love! whose very Name
Kindles in me an am'rous Flame!
Begins to make my ——— rise,
And long again to fight Love's Prize,
Forgetful of those many Scars
He has received in those Wars.
This shews Love's chiefest Magick lies
In Women's ——— not in their Eyes;
There *Cupid* does his Revels keep,
There Lovers all their Sorrows steep;
For having but once tasted that,
Our Miseries are quite forgot.

This

This may fuffice to let you know,
That I to Love am not a Foe,
Tho' you are pleas'd to think me fo. .
'Tis ftrange his Zeal fhould b'in Sufpicion,
Who dies a Martyr for's Religion.

But now to give you an Account
Of CUFFLEY, that Whore Paramount !
CUFFLEY ! whofe Beauty warms the Age,
And fills our Youth with Love and Rage ;
Who, like fierce Wolves, purfue the Game,
While fecretly the letch'rous Dame
With fome choice Gallant takes her Flight,
And in a Corner lies all Night ;
Then the next Morning we all hunt,
To find whofe Fingers fmell of ———— ;
With Jealoufy and Envy mov'd
Againft the Man that was belov'd :
Whilft you within fome neighb'ring Grove
Indite the Story of your Love,
And with your Pen-Knife keen and bright,
On ftately Trees your Paffion write;
So that each Nymph that paffes through,
Muft envy her and pity you ;
We at the *Fleece,* or at the *Bear,*
With good Cafe-Knife, well whet on Stair,
A gentle Weapon, made to feed
Mankind, and not to make 'em bleed,
A thoufand am'rous Fancies fcrape :
There's not a Pewter-Difh can 'fcape
Without her Name, or Arms, which are
The fame that *Love* himfelf does bear.
Here one, to fhew you *Love's* no Glutton,
I'th' Midft of Supper, leaves his Mutton,

And on a greafy Plate with Care,
Carves the bright Image of the Fair.
    Another, tho' a drunken Sot,
Neglects his Wine, and on the Pot
A Band of naked *Cupids* draws,
With —— no bigger than Wheat-Straws.
Then on a nafty Candleftick
One figures *Love's Hieroglyphick*,
A *Couchant* —— and *Rampant* ——
And that the Sight may more inflame
The Lookers-on, fubfcribes her Name,
CUFFLEY ! her Sex's Pride and Shame :
There's not a Man but does difcover,
By fome fuch Action, he's a Lover ;
But now 'tis Time to give her over.
And let your Lordfhip know you are
The Miftrefs that employs our Care.
Your Abfence makes us melancholy ;
Nor Drink, nor Love, can make us jolly,
Unlefs we've you within our Arms,
In whom there dwells diviner Charms.
Then quit with Speed the penfive Grove *,
And here in Town purfue your Love ;
Where, at your Coming, you fhall find
Your Servant glad, your Miftrefs kind ;
All Things devoted to your Mind.

---

* Knowle, *in* Kent, *the Seat of the Earl of* Dorfet.

ROCHESTER's *Farewell.*

TIR'D with the noifom Follies of the Age,
   And weary of my Part, I quit the Stage ?
For who in Life's dull Farce a Part would bear,
Where Rogues, Whores, Bawds, all the chief Actors are?
Long I with charitable Malice ftrove,
Lafhing the Court, thefe Vermin to remove ;
But thriving Vice under the Rod ftill grew,
As aged Letchers whipt, their Luft renew ;
Yet this my Life has unfuccefsful been,
For who can this *Augean* Stable clean ?
My gen'rous End I will purfue in Death,
And at Mankind rail with my parting Breath.
Firft, then, the *Tangier Bullies* muft appear,
With open Bráv'ry, and diffembled Fear.
Mulgrave, their Head, but Gen'ral have a Care,
Tho' fkill'd in all the Arts that cheat the Fair ;
The undifcerning and impartial *Moor,*
Spares not the Lovers on the Ladies Score.
How many perifh by one fatal Shot !
The Conqueft's all thy Ogling ever got.
Think then (as I prefume you do) how all
The *Englifh* Beauties will lament your Fall ;
Scarce would a greater Grief pierce ev'ry Heart,
Shonld Sir *George Hewet,* or Sir *Carr* * depart,
Had it not better been, than thus to roam,
To ftay and tie the Cravat-ftring at Home ?

---

* *Screp.*

To ſtrut, look big, ſhake Pantaloon, and ſwear
With *Hewet, Dam me,* There's no Action there.
Had'ſt thou no Friend that would tò *Rowley* * write,
To hinder this thy Eagerneſs to fight ?
That without Danger thou a Brave might'ſt be,
As ſure to be deny'd as *Shrewſbury.*
This ſure the Ladie had not fail'd to do;
But who this Courage could ſuſpect in you?
For ſay, what Reaſon could with thee prevail,
To change embroider'd Coat, for Coat of Mail?
Let *Plymouth,* or let *Mordaunt* go, whom Fate
Has made not valiant, but deſperate :
For who would not be weary of his Life,
Who'as loſt his Money, or has got a Wife ?
To the more tolerable Alcaid of *Alcazer,*
One flies from's Creditor, t'other from *Frazier* †.
'Twere Cruelty to make too ſharp Remarks
On all the little, forward, fighting Sparks.
Only poor *Charles,* I can't but pity thee,
When all thy pert young Volunteers I ſee ;
Thoſe Chits in War, who as much Mirth create,
As the Pair-Royal of the Chits of State ;
Their Names ſhall equal, or exceed in Story,
Chit *Sunderland,* Chit *Godolphin,* and Chit *Lory.*
When thou let'ſt *Plymouth* go, 'twas ſuch a Jeſt,
As when thy Brother made the ſame Requeſt ;
Had *Richmond* but got Leave, as well as He,
The Jeſt had been compleat, and worthy Thee.
Well, ſince we muſt, he'll to *Tangier* advance,
It is reſolv'd ; but firſt let's have a Dance.

---

* *The* King.   † *The Duke of* York's *Phyſician,
famous for the Cure of a certain Diſtemper.*

First

Firſt, at her Highneſs' Ball he muſt appear,
And in a parting Country Dance, learn there
With Drum and Fife, to make a Jigg of War.
What is of Soldier ſeen in all the Heap,
Beſides the ·flutt'ring Father in the Cap,
The Scarf, and Yard or two of Scarlet Cloth,
From Gen'ral *Mulgrave*, down to little *Wroth* ?
But now they're all embark'd, and curſe their Fate,
Curſe *Charles* that gave 'em Leave, and much more
    Kate.
Who, than *Tangier* to *England* and the King,
No greater Plague, beſides herſelf, could bring;
And wiſh the *Moors*, ſince now their Hand was in,
As they have got her Portion, had the Queen.
There leave we them, and back to *England* come ;
Where, by the wiſer Sparks that ſtay at Home,
In ſafe Ideas, by their Fancy form'd,
Tangier (like *Maeſtricht*) is at *Windſor* ſtorm'd.
But now we talk of *Maeſtricht*, where is he,
Fam'd for that brutal Piece of Bravery ?
He with his thick impenetrable Skull,
The ſolid-harden'd Armour of a Fool ;
Well might himſelf to all War's Ills expoſe,
Who (come what will) yet had no Brains to loſe.
Yet this is he, the dull unthinking he,
Who muſt (forſooth) our future Monarch be.
This Fool, by Fools *(Armſtrong* and *Vernon)* led,
Dreams that a Crown will drop upon his Head ;
By great Example he this Path doth tread,
Following ſuch ſenſeleſs Aſſes up and down,
(For *Saul* ſought Aſſes when he found a Crown)

But * *Rofs* is rifen, as *Samuel*, at his Call,
To tell that God has left th' ambitious *Saul* :
Never (fays Heaven) fhall the blufhing Sun
See *Proger's* Baftard fill the Regal Throne.
So Heaven fays ; but *Brandon* fays he fhall ;
But whoe'er he protects, is fure to fall.
Who can more certain of Deftruction be,
Than he that trufts to fuch a Rogue as he ?
What Good can come from him, who *York* forfook,
T'efpoufe the Int'reft of this booby Duke ?
But who the beft of Mafters could defert,
Is the moft fit to take a Traytor's Part.
Ungrateful ! This thy Mafter-piece of Sin,
Exceeds e'en that with which thou didft begin ;
Thou great Proficient in the Trade of Hell,
Whofe later Crimes ftill do thy firft excel :
The very Top of Villainy we feize,
By Steps, in Order, and by juft Degrees :
None e'er was perfect Villain in one Day,
The murder'd Boy to Treafon led the Way.
But when Degrees of Villainy we name,
How can we chufe but think of *Buckingham* ?
He who through all of them has boldly ran,
Left ne'er a Law unbroke of God or Man.
His treafur'd Sins of Supererogation,
Swell to a Sum enough to damn a Nation :
But he muft here by Force be let alone,
His Acts require a Volume of their own ;
Where rank'd in dreadful Order, fhall appear
All his Exploits, from *Shrewsbury* to *Le Meer.*
But ftay, methinks I on a fudden find
My Pen to treat on t'other Sex inclin'd :

---

* *The Duke of* Monmouth.

But

But where, in all this Choice, shall I begin?
Where, but with the renowned *Mazarine?*
For all the Bawds the Court's rank Soil doth bear,
(And Bawds and Statesmen grow in Plenty there:)
To thee submit and yield, should we be just
To thy experienc'd and well-travell'd Lust:
Thy well-known Merits claim that thou shoud'st be
First in the glorious Roll of Infamy.
To thee they all give Place, and Homage pay,
Do all thy letcherous Degrees obey;
Thou, Queen of Lust; thy bawdy Subjects, They,
While *Suffex, Braughall, Betty Felton* come,
Thy Whores of Honour, to attend thy Throne:
For what proud Strumpet e'er could merit more,
Than be anointed the Imperial Whore?
For tell me, in all *Europe,* where's the Part
That is not conscious of thy lewd Desert?
The great *Pælean* Youth, * whose Conquests run
O'er all the World, and travell'd with the Sun,
Made not his Valour to more Nations known,
Than thou thy Lust, thy matchless Lust, hast shown,
All Climes, all Countries do with Tribute came
(Thou World of Lewdness) to thy boundless Womb.
Thou Sea of Lust, that never Ebb dost know,
Whither the Rivers of all Nations flow.
Lewd *Miffaline* was but a Type of thee,
Thou highest, last Degree of Letchery:
For in all Ages except Her and You.
Who ever sinn'd so high, and stoop'd so low?
She to th' Imperial Bed each Night did use
To brink the Stink of the exhausted Stews;

---

* Alexander the Great.

Tir'd

Tir'd (but not fatisfy'd) with Man did come,
Drunk with abundant Luft, and reeling Home :
But thou, to our admiring Age doft fhow
More Sin than inn'cent *Rome* did ever know ;
And having all her Lewdneffes out-ran,
Tak'ft up with Devil, having tired Man :
For what elfe is that loathfome ugly Black,
Which you and *Suffex* in your Arms did take ?
Nor does old Age, which now rides on fo faft,
Make thee come fhort of all thy Lewdnefs paft :
Tho' on thy Head grey Hairs, like *Ætna's* Snow,
Are fhed, thou Fire and Brimftone art below.
Thou monft'rous Thing, in whom at once did rage
The Flames of Youth, and Impotence of Age.
My Lady *Harcourt* takes the fecond Place,
Proud with thy Favour, and peculiar Grace ;
Ev'n fhe, with all her Piety and Zeal,
The hotter Flames that burn in thee, does feel.
Thou doft into her kindling Breaft infpire
The luftful Seeds of thy contagious Fire :
So well the Spirit and the Flefh agree,
Luft and Devotion, Zeal and Letchery.
Of what important Ufe Religion's made,
By thofe who wifely drive the cheating Trade.
As Wines prohibited, fecurely pafs,
Changing the Name of their own native Place ;
So Vice grows fafe, drefs'd in Devotion's Name,
Unqueftion'd by the Cuftom-Houfe of Fame.
Wherever too much Sanctity you fee,
Be more fufpicious of hid Villainy.
Whos'ever Zeal is than his Neighbour's more ;
If Man, fufpect him Rogue ; if Woman, Whore :

And

And such a Thing art thou, religious *Hyde*,
So very lewd, and yet so sanctify'd.
Let now the Duchess take no farther Care,
Of num'rous Stallions let her not despair,
Since her indu'gent Stars so kind have been,
To send her *Bromley*, *Hyde*, and *Mazarine*.
This last doth banish'd *Monmouth's* Place supply,
And Wit supplanted is by Letchery.

For *Monmouth*, she had Parts, and Wit, and Sense,
To all which *Mazarine* has no Pretence ;
A Proof, that since such Things as she prevail,
Her Highness' Head is lighter than her Tail.
But stay, I *Portsmouth* almost had forgot,
The common Theme of ev'ry rhiming Sot ;
She'll after railing make us laugh a-while ;
For at her Folly, who can chuse but smile ?
Whilst those who always slight her, great she makes,
And so much Pains to be despis'd she takes ;
Goes saunt'ring with her Highness up to Town,
To an old Play, and in the Dark comes down ;
Still makes her Court to her, as to the Queen,
But still is jostled out by *Mazarine:*
So much more worthy a kind Bawd is thought,
Than even she who her from Exile brought.
O ! *Portsmouth*, foolish *Portsmouth*, not to take
The Offer the great *Sunderland* did make ;
When, cringing at thy Feet, e'en *Monmouth* bow'd,
The Golden Calf that's worshipp'd by the Crowd.
But thou for *York*, who now despises thee,
To leave both him and pow'rful *Shaftsbury*.
If this is all the Policy you know,
This all the Skill in States you boast of so ;

How

How wifely did thy Country's Laws ordain,
Never to let the foolifh Women reign * !
But what muft we expect, who daily fee
Unthinking *Charles* rul'd by unthinking Thee ?

---

* *By the* Salique *Law*, *no Woman is granted Acceffion to the Throne.*

F I N I S.

POEMS

By the EARLS of

ROSCOMON,

AND

DORSET;

The DUKES of

DEVONSHIRE,

BUCKINGHAM, &c.

VOL. II.

LONDON:

Printed in the Year M.DCC.LII.

✿✿✿✿✿✿✿✿✿✿✿✿✿✿

THE

CONTENTS

OF THE

Second VOLUME.

POEMS by the Earl of DORSET, *viz.*

Miscellaneous POEMS by several HANDS, *viz.*

The

The CONTENTS. v

✿❀✿❀✿❀✿❀✿❀✿❀✿❀✿❀✿

POEMS by the Duke of DEVONSHIRE, *viz.*

Horace,

SOME

Some MEMOIRS of the Earl of ROSCOMON:

In a LETTER to a FRIEND.

SIR,

YOU having heard that a great many Particulars concerning the Life of the Earl of ROSCOMON, were once promised to the Public by Dr. *Chetwood* Dean of *Glocester*, but by many Accidents delayed; I have therefore ventured, upon your Request, to give you all such Certainties as may be depended upon, without entering into a Detail of Things that are meerly Traditional.

For a Person so remarkable, I must be plain in telling you, that all former Accounts fall very short of his natural and acquired Accomplishments; the Writers contenting themselves with telling us (as they too frequently do) that he was *Born*, and *Died*; with something very dry and barren between, to support the Honour of their Narrative, as a *true and faithful History*. How despicable these Things are, in the Eyes of Men of Sense and Spirit, you very well know; and I am sure that I should make but a poor Acquittal of my Promise, unless I went a little farther than they have done.

His Name is of very great Antiquity in *Ireland*, as Sir JAMES WARE, and other Historians of that Kingdom, will inform you. His Family, in all Probability,

were dignified with great Honours, soon after the Conquest of that Kingdom, and were originally Natives of *England*. The Earldom which he inherited, came to him by a long Descent, though there does not seem to be much of remarkable Note among them to acquaint the World with, before his Time : Since his Death, indeed, some Branches of his Family, who followed the Fortunes of the late King JAMES, have made considerable Figures abroad, especially in the Army, wherein this Earl took his first Step to Knowledge and Fortune. It appears, that the House he was descended from, were of the *Roman Catholick Religion* ; but his Father * being very early converted from it, his Son WENTWORTH was educated in the *Protestant Persuasion*. I shall pass over the Particulars of his Youth, with only mentioning one Story from Mr. JOHN AUBREY the Antiquary,† which I leave to the Credit of You and the Reader, not without observing, that the Relater was a well-informed tho' credulous Person. " *The Lord* ROSCOMON, *being*
" *a Boy of ten Years of Age, at* Caen *in* Normandy *one*
" *Day was, as it were, madly extravagant in playing,*
" *leaping, getting over the Tea-boards, &c.* *He was*
" *wont to be sober enough* ; *they said,* God *grant this*
" *bodes no ill Luck to him* : *In the Heat of this extrava-*
" *gant Fit, he cries out,* My Father is Dead *A Fort-*
" *night after, News came from* Ireland, *that his Father*
" *was Dead. This Account I had from Mr.* Knolles,
" *who was his Governor and then with him, since Se-*
" *cretary to the Earl of* Stafford : *and I have heard his*
" *Lordship's Relations confirm the same.*"
After the Death of his Father, it seems doubtful what Method was taken in his Education ; tho' by a hint of Mr. DRYDEN's, it looks as if the *Military Ser-*

* JAMES DILLON, Earl of *Roscomon*.　† See Mr. *Aubrey's Miscellanies*, 8vo. Printed for *E. Curll*.

vice was his first Employment, but in what Degree is
uncertain:

> ROSCOMON first *in Fields of Honour known,*
> First *in the peaceful Triumphs of the Gown;*
> He both MINERVAS *justly makes his own.* ‡

That he was at *Oxford*, Mr. WOOD makes plainly to
appear, § and took his *Degrees in Arts*; but whether he
was a Member of that University, or only compliment-
ed them with a short Stay there, is equally uncertain.
He was nominated to be created *Doctor of Laws* in the
Year 1683, when several other Noblemen ‖ *Proceeded*
in the *same*; but what perhaps was a Compliment to
their Birth, was directed to his Lordship's *Merit:* however, he did not take that *Degree.*

The next Notice we have of *Him*, is, as a *Courtier;*
when, by the particular Interest of the KING's Brother,
the Duke of *York*, he was made Captain of the *Band of
Pensioners*, and afterwards, *Master of the Horse* to the
Dutchess of *York*; both which Places he continued in,
as I am assured, to the Time of his Death, contrary to
the Reports of other Writers.

To speak of him as a Gentleman and a Poet, would
be to enumerate all the good Qualities which the best
of either ever enjoyed. In these States, though he never courted, yet he had the Applause of all the knowing
and judicious Men of his Time. Mr. WALLER and
Mr. DRYDEN have spoke of him to such an Advantage,
that if his *Works* were not left to justify their *Opinion*, it
might seem *Flattery.* Besides them, he was acquainted
with, and admired by all the *Wits* of that famous *Æra,*
King CHARLES the *Second's* Reign; and if we may be

B 2   allowed.

---

‡ See his Verses, prefixed to his Lordship's *Essay on
Translated Verse.* Lond. 4to. 1684.

§ See *Athen. Oxon.* Vol. II. Pag. 893.

‖ *Robert Bulkley*, second Son of *Robert* Lord *Bulkley,*
Viscount *Cassels* in *Ireland*; and *Henry Mordaunt*, Earl
of *Peterborow.*

allowed to guefs from his Writings, Mrs. KATHERINE
PHILLIPS, of the *Female Sex,* feems to have been his
Favourite.* But of all the Perfons whom he honoured
with his Friendfhip, none was fo dearly intimate with
him, as the learned and ingenious Dr. CHETWOOD. If
you will be pleafed to read that incomparable Copy of
Verfes of His, before the *Effay on Tranflated Verfe,* you
will be convinced what a near Alliance there was, both
of *Heart* and *Genius,* between thofe eminent Perfons. It
it a great Pity that he does not, for he only can, give us
a full Account of his Lordfhip's Life and Character. His
Genuine Works are well known, † and need no Re-
commendation ; efpecially, not that *borrowed* one of
giving him an Applaufe due to another, as has been
lately done; by an ignorant Editor, in afcribing to his
Lordfhip *Two* Poems, *The Profpect of Death,* by the
Reverend Mr. *Pomfret* ‡ ; and, *The Prayer of Jeremy*
Paraphrafed, by Mr. *Southcot.*‖

---

* He wrote the *Prologue* to the Tragedy of POMPEY,
Tranflated by Her from the *French* of Monfieur *Cor-
neille* ; and another Prologue fpoken to the Duke of *York*
at *Edinburgh,* upon reviving one of her Plays. His
Lordfhip alfo wrote an *Epilogue* to ALEXANDER the
Great, when Acted at *Dublin.* Mrs. PHILLIPS (in a
Letter from *Dublin,* Oct. 19, 1662.) gives him this
Character : " My Lord ROSCOMON is a very ingenious
" Perfon, of excellent natural Parts, and certainly the
" moft hopeful young Nobleman in *Ireland."* See
LETTERS from ORINDA to POLIARCHUS, 12mo. *Lond.*
1729.

† Befides his Poetical Works, (*viz.* 1. His Tranflation of *Horace's* Art of Poetry. 2. An *Effay* on *Tranflated Verfe.* 3. Some fmall Pieces) his Lordfhip, at the
Duke of *Ormond's* Requeft, Tranflated into *French* Dr.
Sherlock's Cafe of Allegiance, *&c.* 1682.

‡ See Mr. *Pomfret's* Poems, Printed for *E. Curll.*

‖ See *Mifcellaneous Poems and Tranflations,* Printed
for *B. Lintot.*

I can tell you no more of him, but that he died in the Clofe of the Year 1684, at St. *James's*, and was buried in *Weftminfter-Abbey*. His Character you may gather from the beft Writings of his Cotemporaries; where you will find him, in fhort, a fine Gentleman, a fincere Friend, an univerfal Mafter of the Sciences; and a Poet whofe Works, all that ever pretended to Poetry have infured us, will laft to the lateft Pofterity: For, as Mr. POPE fays, in his *Effay* on Criticifm,

Such was Rofcomon! *not more Learn'd than Good;*
With Manners generous as his Noble Blood;
To him the Wit of Greece *and* Rome *was known,*
And ev'ry Author's Merit but his own.

  I am, S I R,

      Sincerely, Yours,

London,   GEORGE SEWELL.
Nov. 16, 1717.

❀❀❀❀❀❀❀❀❀❀❀❀❀❀❀❀❀❀❀❀

Mr. *Dryden's* CHARACTER of the Earl of *R O S C O M O N.*

THE Wit of *Greece*, the Gravity of *Rome*,
  Appear exalted in the *Britifh* Loom;
The Mufes' Empire is reftor'd agen,
In *Charles's* Reign and by *Rofcomon's* Pen.
Yet modeftly He does his WORK furvey,
And calls a *finifhed Poem* an ESSAY; §

     B 3   For

§ On *Tranflated Verfe.*

For all the *needful Rules* are fcatter'd here;
Truth fmoothly told, and pleafantly fevere;
(So well is *Art* difguis'd, for *Nature* to appear.)
Nor need thofe *Rules* give *Tranflation* light;
His *own Example* is a Flame fo bright;
That he who but arrives to *Copy* well,
Unguided will *advance*; unknown will *excel.*
Scarce his own *Horace* * could fuch *Rules* ordain,
Or his own *Virgil* ‡ fing a nobler Strain.
To what *Perfection* will our *Tongue* arrive,
How will *Invention* and *Tranflation* thrive;
When Authors *nobly* born will bear that Part!
And not difdain th' inglorious Praife of Art!
When thefe *Tranflate,* and teach *Tranflators* too,
Nor *firftling* Kid, nor any *vulgar* Vow
Should at *Apollo's* grateful Altar ftand;
Rofcomon writes to that aufpicious Hand,
Muse *feed the* BULL *that fpurns the yellow Sand.*
Rofcomon, whom both Courts and Camps commend,
True to his *Prince,* and *Faithful* to his *Friend.*

1684.   **JOHN DRYDEN.**

P. S. Dr. KNIGHTLY CHETWOOD, Dean of *Glocefter,*
Died in the Year 1728. And, it is greatly to be
feared, his MEMOIRS, relating to the Earl of Roscomon, are loft.

---

* His Tranflation of *The Art of Poetry.*
‡ His Tranflation of *The Sixth Eclogue.*

POSTSCRIPT.

SINCE this Edition of the Earl of Roscomon's Works has been in the Prefs, the Publick has been obliged with a fine Edition of Mr. *Waller's* Poems, by Mr. *Fenton*, who has likewise made feveral moft judicious *Obfervations* to illuftrate the Writings of that excellent Poet and his Cotemporaries; among whom, our Author, not being the leaft confiderable, we fhall here give fome Particulars not known to us before, *viz.*

Of my Lord ROSCOMON, fays Mr. *Fenton*, I think I am enabled to give a fuller Account that has hitherto appeared, *viz.*

He was born in *Ireland*, when that was under the Adminiftration of the Earl of *Strafford*, to whom his Lordfhip's *Mother* (defcended from the *Boyntons* of *Bramfton* in *Yorkfhire*) was nearly related: And when He was Baptized, the Lord Lieutenant gave him the Sur-Name of his own Family (*Wentworth*)

His Lordfhip paffed the firft Years of his Infancy in *Ireland*; but Archbifhop *Ufher* having reclaimed his Father from the Church of *Rome*; the Earl of *Strafford*, apprehending that his Family would be expofed to the moft furious Effects of Religious-Revenge, at the Beginning of the *Irifh* Rebellion, fent for his God Son into *England*, and placed him at his own Seat in *Yorkfhire*, under the Tuition of Dr. *Hall*, afterwards Bifhop of *Norwich*, a Perfon of eminent Learning and Piety. By him he was inftructed in *Latin*; and without learning the common Rules of Grammar, which he could never retain in his Memory, he attained to write in the Language with Claffical Elegance and Propriety; and with fo much Eafe, that he chofe to correfpond with thofe Friends who had Learning fufficient to fupport the Commerce.

When

When the Cloud began to gather over *England*, and the Earl of *Strafford* was singled out for a Prey to popular Fury; by the Advice of the Lord Primate *Usher*, he was sent to compleat his Education at *Caen* in *Normandy*, under the Care and Direction of the famous *Bochartus*. After some Years he travell'd to *Rome*, where he grew familiar with the most valuable Remains of Antiquity; applying himself particularly to the Knowledge of Medals, which he gained in Perfection: And spoke *Italian* with so much Grace and Fluency, that he was frequently mistaken there for a Native. Soon after the Restauration he returned to *England*, where he was graciously received by King *Charles* II. and made Captain of the Band of Pensioners. In the Gaieties of that Age he was tempted to indulge a violent Passion for Gaming; by which he frequently hazarded his Life in Duels, and exceeded the Bounds of a moderate Fortune. A Dispute with the Lord *Privy-Seal*, about part of his Estate, obliging him to revisit his Native Country, he resigned his Post in the *English* Court: And soon after his Arrival at *Dublin*, the Duke of *Ormond* appointed him to be Captain of the Guards. His beloved *Horace* observed, that, *The Diseases of the Mind are seldom cured by Change of Air* †; the Truth of which was confirmed by his Lordship's Example: For, he was there as much as ever distempered with the same fatal Affection for Play; which engaged him in one Adventure that well deserves to be related, *viz.*

As he returned to his Lodgings from a Gaming-Table, he was attacked in the Dark by three Ruffians, who were employed to Assassinate him: The Earl defended himself with so much Resolution, that he dispatched one of the Aggressors; whilst a Gentleman, accidentally passing that Way, interposed, and disarmed Another; the Third secured himself by Flight. This
generous

---

† *Cælum non Animum mutant qui transmare currunt.*

generous Affiftant was a disbanded Officer, of a good Family, and fair Reputation; who, by what we call the Partiality of Fortune, to avoid cenfuring the Iniquities of the Times, wanted even a plain Suit of Cloaths to make a decent Appearance at the Caftle. But, his Lordfhip on this Occafion, prefenting him to the Duke of Ormond, with great Importunity prevailed with his Grace, that he might refign his Poft of Captain of the Guards to his Friend; which, for about three Years the Gentleman enjoyed: And upon his Death, the Duke returned the Commiffion to his generous Benefactor.

The Pleafures of the English Court, and the Friendfhips he had there contracted, were powerful Motives for his Return to London. Soon after he came, he was made Mafter of the Horfe to her Royal Highnefs the Dutchefs of York: And married the Lady Frances, eldeft Daughter to RICHARD Earl of Burlington, who before had been the Wife of Colonel Courtney.

About this Time, in Imitation of thofe learned and polite Affemblies, with which he had been acquainted abroad; particularly one at Caen, (in which his Tutor Bochartus died fuddenly, whilft he was delivering an Oration) he began to form a Society for the refining and fixing the Standard of our Language, in which Defign his great Friend Mr. Dryden was a principal Affiftant. A Defign! of which it is much eafier to conceive an agreeable Idea, than any rational Hope ever to fee it brought to Perfection among us. This Project, at leaft, was entirely defeated by the Religious Commotions which enfued on King James's Acceffion to the Throne: At which Time the Earl took a Refolution to pafs the Remainder of his Life at Rome; telling his Friends, it would be beft to fit next to the Chimney when the Chamber fmoaked. Amid thefe Reflections he was feized by the Gout; and being too impatient of Pain, he permitted a bold French Pretender to Phyfick to apply a repelling Medicine, in order to give him prefent

Relief; which drove the Diſtemper into his Bowels; and in a ſhort time put a Period to his Life. The Moment in which he expired, he cried out, with a Voice that expreſſed the moſt intenſe Fervor of Devotion,

  My God, my Father, and my Friend,
  Do not forſake me at my End.§

He was buried with great Funeral Pomp; but his Friends ſeem to have thought his own Writings a more durable Monument, than any they could erect to his Memory. And in them we view the Image of a Mind which was naturally Serious and Solid; richly furniſhed, and adorned, with all the Ornaments of Art, and Sciences; and thoſe Ornaments unaffectedly diſpoſed in the moſt regular, and eligent Order. His Imagination might have probably been more fruitful and ſprightly, if his Judgment had been leſs ſevere: But that Severity (delivered in a Maſculine, Clear, ſuccinct Stile) contributed to make him ſo eminent in the Didactical Manner, that no Man with Juſtice can affirm he was ever equalled by any of our own Nation, without confeſſing at the ſame time that he is inferior to none. In ſome other Kinds of Writing his Genius ſeems to have wanted fire to attain the Point of Perfection: But, who can attain it?

Mr. *Fenton* concludes theſe curious Particulars of the Earl of *Roſcomon's* Life, (which it is ſtrongly to be preſumed were communicated to him by Dean *Chetwood*) with informing us, that, Mr. *Waller* addreſſed the Poem to his Lordſhip, on his Tranſlation of HORACE's *Art of Poetry*. Ann. Ætat. 75.

---

§ See his Tranſlation of the *Dies Iræ, Dies Ille.*

POEMS

P O M E S

BY THE

Earl of *Roscomon.*

The V I S I O N.

TO the *pale* Tyrant,‡ who to horrid Graves
  Condemns fo many thoufand helplefs Slaves,
  Ungrateful. We do gentle *Sleep* compare,
Who, tho' his Victories as num'rous are,
Yet from his Slaves no Tribute does he take,
But woful Cares, that load Men while they wake.
  'When his foft Charms had eas'd my weary Sight
Of all the baneful Troubles of the Light,
Dorinda came, divefted of the Scorn,
Which the un-equall'd Maid fo long had worn.
How oft in vain, had *Love*'s great *God* effay'd
To tame the ftubborn Heart of that bright Maid !
Yet fpite of all the Pride that fwells her Mind,
The humble *God* of *Sleep* § can make her kind
A rifing Blufh increas'd the native Store
Of Charms, which but too fatal were before.
  Once more prefent the VISION to my View,
The *fweet Illufion,* gentle Fate, renew !
How kind, how lovely *fhe,* how ravifh'd *I !*
Shew me, bleft *God of Sleep,* and let me DIE,

The

‡ *Death.* § MORPHEUS.

The SCENE of *Care Selve Beate*, in PASTOR FIDO,* Paraphrased.

DEAR happy Groves, and you the dark Retreat
    Of filent Horror, Reft's eternal Seat!
How well your cool and unfrequented Shade
Suits with the chafte Retirement of a Maid:
O! if kind Heaven had been fo much my Friend,
To make my Fate upon my Choice depend;
All my Ambition I would here confine,
And only this *Elyfium* fhould be mine.
Fond Men, by Paffion wilfully betrayed,
Adore thofe Idols which their Fancy made;
Purchafing Riches with our Time and Care,
We lofe our Freedom in a gilded Snare;
And having all, all to ourfelves refufe,
Oppreft with Bleffings, which we fear to ufe.
Fame is at beft but an unconftant Good,
Vain are the boafted Titles of our Blood:
We fooneft lofe what we moft highly prize,
And, with our Youth, our fhort-liv'd Beauty dies.
In vain our Fields and Flocks increafe our Store,
If our Abundance makes us wifh for more;
How happy is the harmlefs *Country Maid*,
Who, rich by Nature, fcorns fuperfluous Aid!
Whofe modeft Cloaths no wonton Eyes invite,
But, like her Soul, preferves the native White;
Whofe little Store her well taught Mind does pleafe,
Nor pinch'd with Want, nor cloy'd with wanton Eafe,
Who, free from Storms, which on the *Great Ones* fall,
Makes but *few Wifhes*, and enjoys them all;

                    , No

---

* *Paftor Fido*, i. e. *The Faithful Shepherd*, is an *Italian* Paftoral; the whole of which is Tranflated by Sir Richard *Fanfhaw*.

No care but *Love* can difcompofe her Breaft,
Love, of all Cates, the fweeteft and the beft.
While on fweet Grafs her bleating Charge does lie,
Our happy *Lover* feeds upon her *Eye;*
Not *One* on whom, or *Gods,* or *Men* impofe,
But *One* whom *Love* has for this *Lover* chofe:
Under fome fav'rite *Myrtle's* fhady Boughs,
They fpeak their Paffions in repeated Vows;
And Whilft a *Blufh* confeffes how fhe *burns,*
His faithful *Heart* makes as fincere *Returns;*
Thus in the Arms of *Love* and *Peace* they *lie,*
And while they *Live,* their Flames can never *Die.*

✤✤✤✤✤✤✤✤✤✤✤✤✤✤✤✤✤✤✤✤

The GHOST *of the Old Houfe of* Commons, *to the* New *one appointed to meet at* Oxford, 1681.

FROM deepeft Dungeons of eternal Night,
The Seats of Horror, Sorrow, Pains and Spite.
I have been fent to tell You tender Youth
A feafonable and important Truth!
I feel, (O! too late) that no Difeafe
Is like a Surfeit of luxurious Eafe;
And of all other, the moft tempting Things,
Are too much Wealth, and too indulgent Kings,
None ever was fuperlatively ill,
But by Degrees, with Induftry and Skill;
And fome, whofe Meaning has at firft been fair,
Grow Knaves by Ufe, and Rebels, by Defpair.
My Time is paft, and yours will foon begin,
Keep the *firft Blofoms* from the *Blaft of Sin;*
And by the Fate of my tumultuous Ways,
Preferve yourfelf, and bring ferener Days.

The

The bufy fubtile *Serpents* of the *Law*,
Did firft my *Mind* from true *Obedience* draw;
While I did *Limits* to the KING prefcribe,
And took for Oracles the *canting Tribe*,
I chang'd *true* Freedom for the *Name* of Free,
And grew *Seditious* for Variety;
All that oppos'd Me, were to be *accus'd*,
And by the *Laws* I legally *abus'd*;
The Robe was fummon'd, MAYNARD at the Head,
In *legal* Murder, none fo *deeply* read:
I brought him to the Bar, where once He Rood,
Stain'd with the (yet un-expiated) Blood.
Of the brave STRAFFORD, when *Three Kingdoms rung*
With his accumulative *Hackney-Tongue*;
Pris'ners and *Witneffes* were waiting by;
Thefe had been taught to *fwear*, and thofe to *die*,
And to expect their arbitrary Fates,
Some for *ill* Faces, fome for *good* Eftates,
To fright the People and alarm the Town,
BEDLOE and OATES employed the Rev'rend Gown.
But while the *Tripple Mitre* bore the Blame,
The KING's *Three Crowns* were their Rebellious Aim;
I feem'd (and did but feem) to fear the *Guards*,
And took for mine the BETHELS and the WARDS;
Anti-Monarchic Hereticks of State,
Immoral, Atheifts, Rich and Reprobate:
But above all, I got a little Guide, §
Who ev'ry Ford of Villainy had try'd.
None knew fo well the old perricious Way
To ruin *Subjects*, and make *Kings* obey;
And my fmall JEHU, at a furious Rate,
Was driving *Eighty* back to *Forty-Eight*:
This the *King* knew, and was refolv'd to bear;
But I miftook his Patience for his Fear,
All that this happy Ifland could afford,
Was facrific'd to my voluptuous Board.

I*n*

---

§ The Earl of *Shaftfbury*.

In his whole *Paradise*, one only *Tree*
He had excepted by a strict Decree;
A sacred *Tree*, which *Royal Fruit* did bear;
Yet It in Pieces I conspir'd to tear;
Beware, my Child! *Divinity* is there.
This so *out-did* all I *had done* before,
I could attempt, and He endure no more.
My unprepar'd and unrepenting Breath
Was snatch'd away by the swift Hand of Death;
And I, *with all my Sins about me*, hurl'd,
To th' *Utter Darkness* of the *lower World*: ¶
A dreadful Place! which You to soon will see,
If you believe *Seducers* more than me.

¶ *Shakespeare.*

The SPEECH *of* Tom Ross's Ghost, *to his* Pupil *the* Duke *of* Monmouth.

SHame of my Life, Disturber of my Tomb,
Base as thy Mother's prostituted Womb;
Huffing to Cowards, fawning to the Brave,
To Knaves a Fool, to cred'lous Fools a Knave,
The *King's* Betrayer, and the *Peoples* Slave,
Like Samuel, at thy Negromantic Call,
I rise to tell the *God has left thee* Saul.
I strove in vain th' Infected Blood to cure;
Streams will run muddy, when the Spring's impure,
In all your meritorious Life we see
Old Taff's * invincible Sobriety.
Places of *Master of the Horse* and *Spy*,

You

---

* *Shaftsbury.*

You (like *Tom Howard*) did at once fupply :
From SIDNEY's § Blood your *Loyalty* did fpring ;
You fhow us all your *Fathers,* but the *King,*
From whofe too tender, and too bounteous Arms.
(Unhappy he, who fuch a *Viper* warms ;
As dutiful a Subject as a Son)
To your true Parent, the whole Town, you run.
Read, if you can, how th' *old Apoftate* fell,
Out-do his Pride, and merit *more than Hell :*
Both He and You were glorious and bright,
. The *Firft* and *Faireft* of the *Sons of Light ;*
But when, like Him, You offer'd at the Crown,
Like Him, your angry Father kick'd you down.

.. . § *Algernon Sidney,*

STANZAS on a Young LADY who fung finely ; but, was afraid of a Cold.

I

WINTER, thy Cruelty extend,
'Till fatal Tempefts fwell the Sea ;
In vain let finking Pilots pray,
Beneath thy Yoke let Nature bend ;
Let piercing Froft, and lafting Snow,
Thro' Woods and Fields Deftruction fow.

II.

Yet we unmov'd will fit and fmile,
While you thefe leffer Ills create ;
Thefe we can bear ; but, gentle Fate,
And thou bleft Genius of our Ifle,
From Winter's Rage defend her Voice,
At which the lift'ning Gods rejoice.

III.

III.

May that Celeftial Sound each Day
  Whith Extafie tranfport our Souls,
  Whilft al! our Paffions it controuls,
And kindly drives our Cares away ;
Let no ungentle COLD deftroy,
All Tafte we have of Heavenly Joy.

❀❀❀❀❀❀❀❀❀❀❀❀❀❀❀❀❀❀❀❀

On the Death of a Lady's Lap-dog.

THOU, happy Creature, are fecure
  From all the Torments We endure :
Defpair, Ambition, Jealoufy,
Loft Friends, nor Love, difquiet Thee ;
A fullen Prudence drew Thee hence,
From Noife, Fraud and Impertinence ;
Tho' Life, effay'd the fureft Wile,
Gilding itfelf with LAURA's Smile.
How didft Thou fcorn Life's meaner Charms,
Thou, who cou'dft break from LAURA's Arms!
Poor *Cynic* ! Still methinks I hear
Thy awful Murmurs in my Ear ;
As when on LAURA's Lap you lay,
Chiding the worthlefs Croud away.
How fondly Human Paffions turn !
What we then Envy'd, now we Mourn !

An

❀❀:❀❀❀❀❀:❀❀❀❀❀:❀❀❀❀❀

An Imitation *of* Horace, *Book* I. *Ode* 22.
Integer vitæ, &c.

I.

VIRTUE, dear Friend, needs no Defence,
  No Arms but its own Innocence;
Quivers and Bows, and poison'd Darts.
Are only us'd by Guilty Hearts.

II.

An honeft Mind fafely alone,
May travel thro' the Burning *Zone*;
Or thro' the deepeft *Scythian* Snows;
Or where the fam'd *Hydaspes* flows.

III.

While, rul'd by a refiftlefs Fire,
Our great ORINDA* I admire;
The hungry Wolves, that fee me ftray,
Unarm'd and fingle, run away.

IV.

See me in the remoteft Place
That ever *Neptune* did embrace;
When there, her Image fills my Breaft
Helicon is not half fo bleft.

V.

Leave me upon fome *Lybian* Plain,
So fhe my Fancy entertain;
And when the thirfty Monfters meet,
They'll all pay Homage to my Feet,

VI.

The Magic of ORINDA's Name
Not only can their Fiercenefs tame,
But, if that mighty Word I once rehearfe,
They feem fubmiffively to roar in Verfe.

On

---

* Mrs. *Katherine Phillips.*

✿✿✿✿✿✿✿✿✿✿✿✿✿✿✿✿✿✿✿✿✿✿✿✿

On the LAST JUDGMENT.*

I.

THE Day of Wrath, that dreadful Day,
  Shall the whole World in Ashes lay,
As DAVID and the SYBILS say.

II.

What Horror will invade the Mind,
When the strict Judge, who would be kind,
Shall have few Venial Faults to find?

III.

The last loud Trumpet's wondrous Sound,
Shall through the rending Tombs rebound,
And wake the Nations under Ground.

IV.

Nature and Death shall with Surprise,
Behold the pale Offender rise,
And view the Judge with conscious Eyes.

V.

Then shall, with universal Dread,
The sacred Mystic Book be read,
To try the Living and the Dead.

VI.

The Judge ascends his awful Throne;
He makes each secret Sin be known,
And all with Shame confess their own.

VII.

O then! What Int'rest shall I make,
To save my last important Stake,
When the most Just have Cause to quake?

VIII.

---

* This is a Translation of the *Church Hymn*, beginning thus, *Dies Iræ, Dies Illæ,* &c.

VIII.

Thou mighty formidable King,
Thou Mercy's unexhaufted Spring,
Some comfortable Pity bring!

IX.

Forget not what my Ranfom coft,
Nor let my dear-bought Soul be loft,
In Storms of guilty Terror toft.

X.

Thou, who for me didft feel fuch Pain,
Whofe precious Blood the Crofs did ftain,
Let not thofe Agonies be vain.

XI.

Thou, whom avenging Pow'rs obey,
Cancel my Debt (too Great to pay)
Before the fad accounting Day.

XII.

Surrounded with amazing Fears,
Whofe Load my Soul with Anguifh bears,
I figh, I weep; accept my Tears.

XIII.

Thou, who wert mov'd with MARY's Grief,
And, by abfolving of the Thief,
Haft giv'n me Hope, now give Relief.

XIV.

Reject not my unworthy Prayer;
Preferve me from that dang'rous Snare,
Which Death and gaping Hell prepare.

XV.

Give my exalted Soul a Place
Amongft thy chofen Right-Hand Race,
The Sons of God and Heirs of Grace.

XVI.

From that infatiable Abyfs,
Where Flames devour, and Serpents hifs,
Promote me to thy Seat of Blifs.

XVII.

XVII.

Proftrate, my contrite Heart I rend;
My God, my Father, and my Friend,
Do not forfake me in my End.

XVIII.

Well may they curfe their fecond Breath,
Who rife to a reviving Death
Thou great CREATOR of Mankind,
Let Guilty MAN Compaffion find.

Mr.

Mr. *Dryden*'s Character of the Earl of *DORSET*'s Poems.*

THERE is not an *English* Writer this Day living, who is not perfectly convinced, that your Lordship excels all others, in all the several Parts of *Poetry* which you have undertaken to adorn. I will not attempt in this Place, to say any thing particular of your *Lyric* Poems, tho' they are the Delight and Wonder of this Age, and will be the Envy of the next. There is more of *Salt* in your Verses, than I have seen in any of the Moderns, or even in the Ancients; but you have been sparing o the *Gall*, by which Means you have pleased all Readers, and offended none. Your Writings are ever where so full of Candour, that, like HORACE, you may expose the Follies of Men, without arraigning their Vices; and in this excel him, that you add that *Pointedness* of *Thought*, which is visibly wanted in our Great *Roman*. That which is the prime Virtue, and chief Ornament of VIRGIL, which distinguishes him from the rest of Writers, is so conspicuous in your Verses, that it casts a Shadow on all your Cotemporaries; we cannot be seen, or but obscurely, while you are present. I read you with Admiration and Delight. For my own Part, I must avow it freely to the World, that I never attempted any thing in *Satire*, wherein I have not studied your Writings, as the most perfect Model. I have continually laid them before me; and the greatest

A

* See A Discourse *concerning the* Original and Progress of *Satire. Addressed to the Earl of* Dorset.

eft Commendation which my own Partiality can give my Productions, is, that they are *Copies*, and no farther to be allowed, than as they have something more or less of the *Original*. Some few Touches of your Lordship, some *secret Graces* which I have endeavoured to express after *your Manner*, have made *whole* Poems *of mine* to pass with *Approbation*; but, take *Your Verses* all together, and they are *Inimitable*.

Earl of DORSET.

POEMS

P O E M S

BY THE

Earl of DORSET.

On the Countess of Dorchester, Mistress to King James II. Written in the Year 1680.

I.

TELL me, Dorinda, why so gay,
    Why such Embroid'ry, Fringe, and Lace?
    Can any Dresses find a Way,
To stop th' Approaches of Decay,
    And mend a ruin'd Face?

II.

Wilt Thou still sparkle in the Box,
    Still ogle in the Ring?
Canst Thou forget thy Age and Pox?
Can all that shines on Shells and Rocks
    Make Thee a fine young Thing?

III.

So have I seen in Larder dark
    Of Veal a lucid Loin;
Replete with many a brilliant Spark,
(As wise Philosophers remark)
    At once both stink and shine.

On

✛✛✛✛✛✛✛✛✛✛✛✛✛✛✛✛✛✛✛✛✛✛✛✛✛✛✛

On the *SAME.*

I.

PROUD with the Spoils of Royal Cully,
With false Pretence to Wit and Parts ;
She swaggers like a batter'd Bully,
To try the Tempers of Men's Hearts.

II.

Tho' she appear as glitt'ring fine,
As Gems, and Jests, and Paint can make her ;
She ne'er can win a Breast like mine,
The *Devil* and Sir *David* ‖ take her.

On Dolly Chamberlain, *à Sempstress in the* New Exchange.

DOLLY's Beauty and Art,
Have so hemm'd in my Heart,
That I cannot resist the Charm :
In Revenge I will stitch
Up the Hole next her Breech,
With a Needle as long as my Arm.

‖ Sir *David Colyear*, late Earl of *Portmore*.

C   A

A Faithful CATALOGUE of our most Eminent NINNIES.

Written by the Earl of *DORSET*, in the Year 1683.

————— *Quos omnes
Vicini oderunt, noti Pueri atque Puellæ.*
Hor. Sat. I.

CURS'D be thofe dull, unpointed, doggrel Rhimes,
Whofe harmlefs Rage has lafh'd our impious Times.
Rife thou, my Mufe, and with the fharpeft Thorn ;
Inftead of peaceful Bays, my Brows adorn ;
Infpir'd with juft Difdain, and mortal Hate,
Who long have been my Plague, fhall feel thy Weight:
I fcorn a giddy and unfafe Applaufe :
But this (ye Gods) is fighting in your Caufe.
Let *Sodom* fpeak, and let *Gomorrah* tell,
If their curs'd Walls deferv'd the Flames fo well.
Go on, my Mufe, and with bold Voice proclaim
The vicious Lives, and long detefted Fame,
Of fcoundrel Lords, and their lewd Wives Amours,
Pimp Statefmen, Canting Priefts, Court Bawds and Whores:
Exalted Vice its own vile Name does found,
Thro' Climes remote, and diftant Shores renown'd.
Thy Strumpets, *Charles*, have 'fcap'd no Nations Ear,
Cleveland the Van, and *Portfmouth* leads the Rear :
A Brace of Cherubs, of as vile a Breed,
As ever were produc'd of Human Seed.

To

To all but Thee, the Punks were ever kind,
Free as loose Air, and gen'rous as the Wind.
Both steer'd thy P——e, and the Nation's Helm;
And both betray'd thy P——e, and the Realm.
O BARBARA! ‖ thy execrable Name
Is sure embalm'd with everlasting Shame,
Could not the num'rous Host thy Lust suffice,
Which in lascivious Shoals ador'd thy Eyes;
When their bright Beams were through our Orb display'd,
And Kings each Morn their *Persian* Homage paid?
O sacred *James!* may thy dread Noddle be
As free from Danger, as from Wit 'tis free:
But if that good and gracious Monarch's Charms,
Could ne'er confine one Woman to his Arms;
What strange mysterious Spell, what strong Defence,
Can guard that Front, which has not half his Sense?
Poor *Shrewsbury's* Fall, ev'n her own Sex deplore,
Who with so small Temptation turn'd thy Whore.
But *Grafton* bravely does revenge her Fate,
And says, Thou court'st her thirty Years too late;
She scorns such Dwindles; her capacious A——
Is fitter for thy Scepter than thy T——.
Old *Delamer, Shrewsbury,* and *Mordaunt* know,
Why in thy stately Frame she lies so low;
And who but her dull Blockhead would have found
Her Windows small Descent on rising Ground?
Thro' the large Sash they pass (like *Jove* of old).
To her attendant Bawd, in Show'rs of Gold.
Mordaunt (that insolent ill-natur'd Bear)
From the close *Grotto,* when no Danger's near,
Mounts like a rampant Stag, and ruts his Dear.
But when by dire Mischance the harmless Maid
In the dark Closet, with loud Shrieks, betray'd
The naked Letcher, what a woful Grief
It was? Th' Adulteress flew to his Relief,
And sav'd his being murder'd for a Thief.

C 2 Defenceless

‖ The Dutchess of *Cleveland's* Christian Name.

Defenceless Limbs the well-arm'd Host assail'd;
Scarce her own Pray'rs with her own Slaves prevail'd:
Though well prepar'd for Flight, he mourn'd his Weight
And begg'd *Actæon*'s Charge, to 'scape *Actæon*'s Fate:
But wing'd with Fear, tho' untransform'd, he bounds,
And, swift as Hinds, out-strips the yelling Hounds.
Beware Adulterers, betimes beware,
You fall not in the same unhappy Snare;
From *Norfolk*'s Ruin, and his narrow 'Scape,
S——e on contented with a willing Rape,
On a strong Chair, soft Couch, or Side of Bed,
Which never does surprizing Dangers dread.
Let no such Harlots lead your Steps astray,
Her C——s will mount in open Clay;
And from St. *James's* to the Land of *Thule*,
There's not a Whore who S——s so like a Mule:
And yet her blund'ring *Dolt* deserves a worse,
Could Man be plagu'd with a severer Curse.
A fitter Couple sure were never hatch'd;
Some marry'd are indeed, but these are match'd.
But seeing they are lawful Man and Wife,
Why should the Fool and Drazel live in Strife,
While they both lead the same lascivious Life?
Or why should he to *Megg*'s or *Circut*'s come,
When he may find as great a Whore at Home?
Mulgrave ‡ (who all his Summons to big War,
Safely commits to his wife Prince's Care)
Lords it o'er Mankind, and is the first,
By Woman hated, and by Man accurs'd.
Well has his Staff a double Use supply'd,
At once upheld his Body and his Pride.
How haughtily he cries, *Page, fetch a Whore?*
Damn her, she ugly; Rascal, fetch me more;
Bring in that black-ey'd Wench; Woman, come near;
Rot you, you draggled Bitch, What is't your feare?
                                    Trembling.

---

‡ He carried the Lord *Peterborow*'s Challenge to the King.

Trembling fhe comes, and with as little Flame,
As he for the dear Part from whence he came.
Thine, crafty *Seymour*, was a good Defign;
for fure his Iffue ne'er will injure thine :
But thou thy felf muft needs confefs, that fhe
Does juftly curfe thy Politicks and thee.
Her noble Proteftant has got a Flail,
Young, large, and fit to feague her briny Tail;
But now, poor Wench, fhe lies as fhe would burft,
Sometimes with Brandy, and fometimes with Luft.
Tho'*Prince*, as Goats, fhe courts in vain her Drone ;
The *Frigid* he, and the *Torrid Zone.*
Both Friend and Foe he with vaft Ruin mauls,
Who at firft Thruft before, both Sexes falls.
Had I, O! had I his tranfcendant Verfe.
In his own lofty Strains, I would rehearfe
That deep-Intrigue, when he the *Princefs* woe'd,
But lov'd Adult'ry more than Royal Blood.
Young *Offory*, (who lov'd the haughty Peer)
Her Mother's darling Sins could beft declare:
But to her Memory we muft be juft ;
'Tis Sacrilege to rob fuch beauteous Duft.
O *Wharton, Wharton!* what a wretched Tool,
Is a dull Wit, when made, a Woman's Fool ?
Thy rammifh fpendthrift Buttocks 'tis well known, ⎫
Her naufeous Bait has made thee fwallow down, ⎬
Tho' mumbled, and fpit out by half the Town : ⎭
How well my honeft *L——n* fhe knows,
The many Manfions in thy F——— Houfe ?
How often prais'd thy dear curvetting T——,
Which thou rid'ft curb'd, like an unruly Horfe ?
How big with Joy fhe went with thee to Church,
When thou (falfe Varlet) left her in the Lurch ?
Even *E——t,* who refus'd none before,
Scorn'd to pronounce the Banns with fuch a Whore,
To *Pancras Tom,* there fuch as fhe refort ;
(That * Mother-Church too does all Sinners court)A s

---

* St. *Pancras* Church faid to be the Mother of St. *Paul's.*

As she has been thy Strumpet all her Life,
'Tis Time to make her now thy lawful Wife,
That B———y's Spouse may pride it in her Box,
With Face and C——— all martyr'd with the Pox.
In some deep Sawpit, both their Noddles hide;
For 'tis hard guessing which has the best Bride.
Ah *Tom!* thy Brother like a prudent Man,
Has chosen much the better *Haradan*:
She, a good-natur'd candid Devil, shows
Him all the Bawding Jilting Tricks she knows.
Thy *Rook* some trival Cheats her Blockhead learns,
While he the Master *Hocus* ne'er discerns,
To Pox and Plague, O! may she subject be,
As she's from Child-Bed Pain and Peril Free:
Her actual Sins invalidate the first,
With ease she teems, and brings forth unaccurst.
To thee, *Lucina.* she need never call,
Like ripen'd Fruit, her mellow Bastards fall;
And what with needless Labour I disclose,
Her well stretch'd ———; and rivel'd Belly shows.
Whoever, like *Charles D———g,* scorns Disgrace,
Can never want, altho' he lose his Place:
That Toothless Murd'rer, to his just Reproach,
Pimps for his Sister, to maintain a Coach;
And let what will the Church or State befal,
One fulsome crafty Whore maintain'd 'em all.
Scarsdale, tho' loath'd, still the fair Sex adores,
And has a Regiment both of Horse and Whores.
Amidst the common Rout of early Duns,
For *Mustard, Soap, Milk, Small-coal, Swords,* and *Guns:*
Two rev'rend Officers (more highly born)
Wait on his stinking Levee ev'ry Morn,
And in full Pomp his Palace Gates adorn.
But which is most in vogue, is hard to tell,
The public Bawd, or private Centinel;
That blubber'd Oaf, for two dull dribbling Bouts,
Maintains two Bastards made of *Jenney's* Clouts.
E'er it could fetch, 'twas l ke pox'd *Evelyn* spoil'd,
Yet it can't touch a Wench, but she's with Child; But

But who can think that peftilential Breath
Should raife up Life, that always blafts with Death?
'Tis ftrange *Kilgers*, that refin'd *Beau Garcon*
Was never yet at the *Bell-Savage* fhown,
For he's a true and wonderful Baboon.
It therefore wifely was at firft defign'd
He ne'er fhould like to propagate his Kind;
But the dull venom'd Drought in vain employ'd,
Like the falfe Serpent's, was itfelf deftroy'd.
With foul Corruption fure his firft was fed,
And by equiv'cal Generation bred.
An honeft ¶ *Solen* Goofe, compar'd to him,
Is a fine Creature, and of more Efteem.
No learn'd Philofophers need ftrive to know,
Whether his Soul's *ex traduce* or no.
He has none yet, nor never will, I fear;
No Soul of Senfe would ever enter there.
I wonder he dares fpeak, for fear we jerk
His lazy Bones, and make the Monkey work
If aged *Delamer* has left the Trade,
And had enough of coftly Mafquerade,
With Flames renew'd, your old Amours purfue,
Now *Rochefter* has nothing elfe to do.
Well done, old *Hyde*, we all thy Choice adore,
She is the younger, and much better Whore.
But *Hickes* has fure, to his eternal Curfe,
Left his own Strumpet, and efpous'd a worfe.
That blazing Star ftill rifes with the Sun,
And will, I hope, whene'er it fets, go down.
St. *Peter* ne'er deny'd his Lord but thrice,
But good St. *Edward* fcorns to be fo nice:
He, ev'ry Mafs, abjures what he before,
On Tefts and Sacraments fo often fwore.
His Mother-Church will have a fpecial Son
Of him, by whom his Father was undone.
He turn'd, becaufe on Bread alone he'd dine,
And make the Wafer fave his Bread and Wine. *Ma-*

¶ *Thefe Fowls are only bred in fome Part of* Scotland.

Mammon's the God he'll worſhip any Way,
And keeps Conviction ready to a Day.
Forbid it Heav'n, I e'er ſhould live to ſee
Our pious Monarch's gorgeous Chapel be
Fill'd with ſuch Miſcreant Proſelytes as he.
Miſerere Domine! Ave Maria!
Poor Father *Dover* has got a *Gonorrhæa.*
Was e'er (dread *James*) ſo much Affection ſhown?
He'd ſave thy Soul, but cares not for his own.
How *Shrewsbury* prays, that old adult'rous Fap
May find it a *Cormegan* ſwinging Clap!
Unhappy Maid! who Man has never known,
And yet, with perilous Pangs, brought forth a Son!
Our * *Chyre-Medico Dydimus* nothing ſmelt,
'Till he the ſprawling Bantling heard and felt.
And now it ſurely cannot be deny'd
By him, who cur'd the *King* of what he dy'd.
How *Herbert* boaſts, that his wiſe King's-Head Crew
Foretold the diſmal Times we all ſhould rue.
Curs'd be the Screech-Owls! that rebellious Crowd
Preſag'd, indeed, *Rome*'s ſwift Approach, as loud,
As wiſe *Caſſandra*'s boding Voice of old,
The wretched Fate of ancient *Rome* foretold.
But why is he againſt the bringing in
Any Religion that indulges Sin?
He who his other Charges can retrench,
To ſave ten Guineas for a handſome Wench;
Or be content to part with twenty Pound,
If Mrs. *White* inſure her being ſound.
That Ideot thinks the tawdry Harlot's glad
To ſerve him now, for Favours ſhe has had.
But who (dear *Harvey*) ever heard before
Of Gratitude in any common Whore?
She mounts the Price, and goes half Snack herſelf,
And well knows how cully ſuch an Elf.

Poor

---

* Dr. *King*, a Man-Midwife.

Poor *Jenny* I muft needs much more applaud,
A better Whore, and truer Friend and Bawd.
Like the *French* King, he all his Conquefts buys,
And pow'rful Guineas ftill fubdues their Eyes.
How his fmug little black-ey'd Harlot gaz'd
On's hoarded Gold, and fine Apartments prais'd!
But *F——* (not trufting to the Mifer's Truth)
Like *Joseph*'s Sacks, with Money in her Mouth;
Sometimes he'll venture for himfelf to trade,
With aukward Grace, at Balls and Mafquerade.
But what was the proud Coxcomb e'er the near,
Unlefs he got my Lady *Gerhard* there?
Her Qualities to all the World are known,
Fair as his Kin, and honeft as his own.
She makes her Brothel worfe than common Stews,
And loves to S——e in her own Tribe, like *Jews*
Inceft with neareft Blood, Adult'ry, all
Her darling Sins, we may well Deadly call.
Whate'er in Times of Yore fhe may have been,
Her Luft has now parch'd up her rivel'd Skin.
Thou Town of *Edmonton*, I charge, declare
What fhe and *Orkney* did fo often there.
That ‖ fcribbling Fool, who writes to her in Metre,
And only fpeaks his Songs to make 'em fweeter:
Great *Virgil*'s true Reverfe in Senfe and Fate;
For what another writ, procur'd his Hate.
To be but thought a Wit, he loft his Place;
And yet to fhow he is not in that Race,
Will write himfelf, and add to his Difgrace.
His *Valentinian*'s learned Preface fhines,
Like *Memphis*' Siege, or *Bulloign*'s radiant Lines.
Among the Mufes all the Time he fpends,
And his whole Study tow'rds *Parnaffus* bends:
Yet if for his, one handfome Thought be fhown,
Stop the dull Thief; I'll fwear 'tis not his own.

C 5   *Satire*'s

‖ Mr. *Wolfeley.*

Satire's his Joy ; but if he don't improve,
Give me his Hatred, let her take his Love.
That Fop she *Herbert* more than Thee admires ;
He often quenches her lascivious Fires.
In vain poor *Harvey*, with ridic'lous Joy,
Shews her, and ev'ry Fool, his hopeful Boy.
His City Songstress, says, keep such a Pother,
He'll ne'er be able to get her another.
Join, then, propitious Stars, their widow'd Store,
And make them happy, as they were before ;
That is, may the decay'd incestuous Punk
Swill like his Spouse, and he, like her, Die drunk.
Why, *Harding*, has the good old Queen the Grace,
To see thy Bear-like Mien, and Baboon Face ?
Her Court (the God's be prais'd) has long been free
From *Irish* Priggs, and such dull Sots as he.
The wakeful Gen'ral, conscious of thy Charms,
Dreads thine, as much as *Monmouth's* fierce Alarms.
Yet sure there is a greater Ditch between
A greasy whiggish Dolt, and *Charles's* Queen.
There is, and *Harding* soars not yet so high,
His ogling Pigsnies doat on Lady *Di.**
That Gudgeon on soft Baits will only bite,
For easy Conquests are his sole Delight.
And none can say, but that his Judgment's good,
For all our *Kings* are made of Flesh and Blood.
Vernon, the Glory of that lustful Tribe,
Scorns to be meanly purchas'd with a Bribe :
To Fame and Honour hates to be a Slave,
But freely gives what Nature freely gave.
Like Heirs to Crowns, with such Credentials born,
Her hasty Bastards private Entries scorn ;
In midst of Courts, and in the midst of Day,
With little Peril force their easy Way.
But *Woodford* is, methinks, a better Seat,
And for distended Wems a safe Retreat.

'Twas

---

* Lady *Diana Howard.*

'Twas well advis'd old *Kirk* no Dangers fear'd;
No Groans, nor yelling Cries, can there be heard:
In this lewd Town, and thefe cenforious Times,
Where ev'ry Whore rails at each other's Crimes.
Fair *Theodofia!* thy Romantic Name
Had fure been blafted with eternal Shame:
But thy wife Stratagems fo well were laid,
I'd almoft fwear, thou art a very Maid.
Go on, and fcorn our common S——g Rules;
Let *Wincup* make th'inceftuous Uncles Fools:
While *Prudence* pimps, and fuch a Foe combines,
Impregnate more and more by feedy Loins;
Thou ftill art fafe, tho' thy large Womb fhould bear,
Like hers, who teem'd for ev'ry Day o'th' Year,
Proud *Ormond* juftly thinks her *Dutch*-built Shape
A little too unwieldly for a Rape.
Yet being confcious it will tumble down,
At firft Affault, furrenders up the Town.
But no kind Conqueror has yet thought fit
To make it his belov'd imperial Seat.
That batter'd Fort, which they with Eafe deceive,
Pillag'd and fack'd, to the next Foe they leave.
And haughty *Di*, in juft Revenge will try't,
(Altho' fhe ftarve) with any fenfelefs Wight;
Not that to any Principle fhe's firm,
But is debauch'd by damn'd feducing Sp——m.
Shrewsbury well knew the banning Hour, when Seven
The Main throws out, or elfe a Nick, Eleven:
When her decrepit Spend-thrift, trooplefs *Rook*,
Is meek as *Mofes* hid in Fire and Smoak.
Our Sacred Writ does learnedly relate,
For one poor Babe, two Mothers hot Debate:
But our two doughty Heroes, I am told,
Which is the trueft Father, fiercely fcold.
Both Claims feem juft and great; but gen'rous *Hales*,
Who on the right Side, always is, prevails.
He will not only fave its Life, but Soul;
So poor *Paul Kirk* is fobb'd off for a Fool.

But

But 'tis all one; Sir *Courtly Nice* does swear,
He'll go to Mrs. *Grace* of *Exeter*.
But why to *Ireland*, *Bennet?* Is't the Clime,
Dost thou imagine, make an easy Time?
Ungratefully indeed thou did'st requite
The skilful Goddess of the silent Night,
By whose kind Help thou wast so oft before
Deliver'd safely on thy native Shore.
Thy Belly shinn'd, and unusual Load
Make thee believe *Kirk*'s Shoulders were too broad.
And thou'dst be sure we should not hear thee roar :
And if poor *Tussey Mussey* should be tore,
Wisely resolv'd, *Ned* should ne'er see it more :
But since all's well, return, that we may laugh
At *Irish* C——s, which in all Climes are safe.
Justly false *Monmouth* did thy Lord declare,
Thou should'st not in his Crown nor Empire share,
Indeed (dear Pimp) it was a just Design,
Seeing he had so small a Share of thine.
Brave *Framingham,* that thund'ring Son of Arms,
With pow'rful Magic conquer'd both your Charms.
Virtue, thy weak Lieutenant, ran away,
Just like that cursed Miscreant, Coward *Gray*;
And as poor *James* from his new Subjects did,
At last, from thy fair Breast the Gen'ral fled.
His Conversation, Wit, and Parts, and Mien,
Deserv'd, he thought, at least a widow'd Queen.
Nor wert thou sorry, since most Seeds are found
To flourish better, when we change the Ground.
He struck in Years, and spent in Toils and War,
Could please the less than did strong *Delamer* :
Ne'er was a truer Stallion, to his Cost,
He, as he was most able, lov'd thee most.
But politick *Monmouth* thought it too much Grace,
For one t' enjoy too long so great a Place.
Chamberlain next succeeds the lovely Train,
And round his Neck displays a Captive's Chain:

He

He, greater Fool, than any of the reft,
They fay, will marry with the trimming Beaft ;
Which if he does, O ! may his Blood be fhed
On that high Throne where her laft Traytor bled.
Myfterious Pow'rs ! what wond'rous Influence
Governs, that ruling Star, poor Mortal's Senfe ?
What unknown Motives our dread King perfuades,
To make lewd *Ogle* Mother of the Maids.
The gracious Prince had fure much wifer been,
Had he made *Sheppard* Tutrefs to the Queen ;
And then, perhaps, her chaft Inftructions wou'd
Have fav'd a World of unbegotten Blood :
But pious *James,* with Parts profound endu'd.
Will none prefer, but whom he knows are lewd.
A Leafh of Strumpets, all of the Court Breed,
Ladies of wond'rous Honour are indeed.
Ye fcoundrel Nymphs, whom Rags and Scabs adorn,
Than that fmall paultry Whore more highly born ;
If you are wife, apply yourfelves betimes :
None highly merit now, but by their Crimes,
And the King does whate'er he's bid by * *Grimes.* }
Which made the wifer Choice, is now our Strife,
Hall has his Miftrefs, or the Prince his Wife :
Thofe † Traders fure will be belov'd as well,
As all the dainty tender Birds they fell.
The learned Advocate, (that rugged Stump
Of old *Nol's* Honour) always lov'd the Rump ;
And 'tis no Miracle, fince all the *Hoyles*
Were giv'n, they fay, to raife inteftine Broils :
But feeing, to the upright Juror's Praife,
We are return'd to *Ignoramus* Days ;
The Lawyer fwears he greater Hazard runs,
Who F—— one Daughter than a hundred Sons.
Prepoft'rous Fate ! while poor Mifs *Jenny* bawds,
Each foreign Fop her Mother's Charms applauds.

                                        Autumnal .

---

* *By whom fhe got the Reverfion of Mr.* C—*'s Place.*
† *Both Poulterers.*

Autumnal Whore! To ev'ry Nation known!
A Curse to them, and Scandal to her own.
Forgive me, chaster *Harding*, if I name
Her stinking Toes with thine of sweeter Fame.
Thou wond'rous pocky art, and wond'rous poor;
But as she's richer, she's a greater Whore.
What with her Breath, her Armpits, and her Feet,
Ten Civet Cats can hardly make her sweet.
From all the Corners of noisome Town,
The Filth of ev'ry Brute can freely down
To that insatiate Strumpet's Common-Shore,
'Till it broke out, and poison'd her all o'er.
Poor *Buckingham* in unsuccessful Verse,
And Terms too mild, did her lewd Crimes rehearse:
Bold is the Man that ventures such a Flight;
Her *Life's* a *Satire*, which no Pen can write:
And therefore cursed may he ever be,
As when old § *Hyde* was catch'd with *Rem in Re.*

Cætera desunt.

§ *The Earl of* Mulgrave *found her in the Fact with*
Lord Rochester.

To a *Person of* Honour, *on his Incomparable*
Incomprehensible Poems. *

COME on ye Criticks, find one Fault who dare;
    For, read it backward, like a *Witch's* Prayer,
'Twill do as well; throw not away your Jests
On solid Nonsense that abides all Tests.

Wit,

Wit, like Tierce-Claret, when't begins to pall,
Neglected lies, and's of no Use at all,
But, in its full Perfection of Decay,
Turns *Vinegar*, and comes again in Play.
Thou haft a Brain, fuch as thou haft, indeed;
On what elfe fhould thy Worm of Fancy feed?
Yet in a *Filbert* I have often known
Maggots furvive, when all the Kernel's gone.
This Simile fhall ftand in thy Defence,
'Gainft fuch dull Rogues as now and then write Senfe.
Thy Stile's the fame, whatever be thy Theme,
As fome Digeftions turn all Meat to Phlegm.
He lies, dear NED, who fays thy Brain is barren,
Where deep Conceits, like Vermin, breed in Carrion.
Thy ftumbling founder'd Jade can trot as high
As any other *Pegafus* can fly.
So the dull *Eel* moves nimbler in the Mud,
Than all the fwift-finn'd Racers of the Flood.

As fkilful *Divers* to the Bottom fall,
Sooner than thofe that cannot fwim at all,
So in this Way of Writing, without Thinking,
Thou haft a ftrange * *Alacrity in Sinking*.
Thou writ'ft below ev'n thy own nat'ral Parts,
And with acquir'd Dulnefs, and new Arts
Of ftudy'd Nonfenfe, tak'ft kind Readers Hearts.
Therefore, dear NED, at my Advice, forbear,
Such loud Complaints 'gainft Criticks to prefer,
Since thou art turn'd an arrant *Libeller*:
Thou fett'ft thy Name to what thyfelf doft write;
Did ever *Libel* yet fo fharply bite?

---

* *Alluding to an Expreſſion of* Sir John Falftaff's *in* Shakefpear's HENRY IV.

❀❀❀❀❀❀❀❀❀❀❀❀❀❀❀❀❀❀❀

To Sir Thomas St. Serfe, *on his Play called*
Tarugo's Wiles : Or, *The* Coffee-Houſe,
A Comedy.   *Acted at the* Duke of York's
Theatre, 1668.

Taruco gave us Wonder and Delight,
    When he oblig'd the World by Candle-light.
But now he's ventur'd on the Face of Day,
T'oblige and ſerve his Friends a nobler Way ;
Make all our old Men Wits, Stateſmen the Young,
And teach ev'n *Engliſh* Men the *Engliſh* Tongue.
    James, on whoſe Reign *all peaceful Stars* did ſmile, •
Did but attempt th' *Uniting* of our *Iſle*.
What Kings, and Nature, only could deſign,
Shall be accompliſh'd by this Work of thine.
For who is ſuch a *Cockneigh* in his Heart,
Proud of the Plenty of the *Southern* Part,
To ſcorn that Union by which he may
Boaſt 'twas his Country-man that writ this Play ?
    Phoebus himſelf, indulgent to thy Muſe,
Has to thy Country ſent this kind Excuſe,
Fair *Northern* Laſs, it is not thro' Neglect
I court thee at a Diſtance, but Reſpect.
I cannot act, my Paſſion is ſo great,
But I'll make up in Light, what wants in Heat.
On thee I will beſtow my longeſt Days,
And crown thy Sons with everlaſting Bays.
My Beams that reach thee ſhall employ their Pow'rs
To ripen Souls of Men, not Fruits or Flow'rs,
Let warmer Climes my fading Favours boaſt,
Poets and Stars ſhine brighteſt in the Froſt.

                                   Epilogue

────────────────────────────

• *The Motto borne by K.* James I. *was,* Beati Pacifici.

Epilogue *spoken by* TARTUFFE.

MANY have been the vain Attempts of *Wit*,
     Againſt the ſtill-prevailing *Hypocrite*;
Once, and but once, a Poet got the Day,
And vanquiſh'd *Buſie* in a Puppet-play;
And *Buſie* rallying, arm'd with Zeal and Rage,
Poſſeſs'd the Pulpit, and pull'd down the Stage.
To laugh at *Engliſh* Knaves, is dang'rous then,
While *Engliſh* Fools will think 'em honeſt Men:
But ſure no zealous Brother can deny us
Free Leave with this our *Monſieur* ANANIAS.
A Man may ſay, without being call'd an *Atheiſt*,
There are damn'd Rogues among the *French* and *Papiſt*,
That fix Salvation to ſhort Band and Hair,
That belch and ſnuffle to prolong a Pray'r;
That uſe *(enjoy the Creature)* to expreſs
Plain Whoring, Gluttony, and Drunkenneſs;
And, in a decent Way, perform them too
As well, nay better far, perhaps, than you:
Whoſe fleſhly Failings are but Fornication,
We Godly phraſe it *Goſpel-Propagation*,
Juſt as Rebellion was call'd Reformation.
Zeals ſtands but Sentry at the Gate of Sin,
Whilſt all that have the Word paſs freely in.
Silent, and in the Dark, for fear of Spies.
We march, and take Damnation by Surprize.
There's not a roaring Blade in all this Town
Can go ſo far tow'rds Hell for Half-a-Crown,
As I for Sixpence, for I know the Way;
For want of Guides, Men are too apt to ſtray:
Therefore give Ear to what I ſhall adviſe,
Let ev'ry marry'd Man, that's grave and wiſe,

                                                 Take

Take a TARTUFFE of known Ability,
To teach and to increaſe his Family;
Who ſhall ſo ſettle laſting Reformation,
Firſt Get his Son, then Give him Education.

Epilogue *on the Revival of* Ben Johnſon's
Play called, Every Man in his Humour.

INtreaty ſhall not ſerve, nor Violence,
  To make me ſpeak in ſuch a Play's Defence:
A Play, where Wit and Humour do agree
To break all practis'd Laws of Comedy:
The Scene (what more abſurd!) in England lies,
No *Gods* deſcend, nor dancing *Devils* riſe;
No *captive Prince* from unknown Country brought;
No *Battle,* nay, there's ſcarce a *Duel* fought;
And ſomething yet more ſharply might be ſaid;
But I conſider the poor *Author*'s dead.
Let that be his Excuſe.——Now for our own,
  Why,——Faith, in my Opinion, we need none.
The Parts were fitted well; but ſome will ſay,
Pox an 'em, Rogues, what made 'em chuſe this Play?
I do not doubt but you will credit me,
It was not Choice, but meer Neceſſity.
To all our writing Friends, in Town, we ſent,
But not a Wit durſt venture out in Lent.
Have Patience but 'till Eaſter Term, and then
You ſhall have Jigg and Hobby-horſe agen.
Here's Mr. Matthew, our domeſtic Wit,
Does promiſe One o'th' Ten Plays he has writ;

But

---

* Mr. MATTHEW MEDBOURN, *an eminent Actor, belonging to the Duke of* YORK's *Theatre.*

But fince great Bribes weigh nothing with the Juft,.
Know, we have Merits, and to them we truft:.
When any Fafts, or Holidays, defer.
The public Labours of the *Theatre,*
We ride not forth, altho' the Day be fair,
On ambling Tit, to take the Suburb Air;.
But with our *Authors* meet, and fpend that Time
To make up Quarrels between Senfe and Rhime.
Wednefdays and *Fridays* conftantly we fate,
Till after many a long and free Debate,
For divers weighty Reafons 'was thought fit,
Unruly Senfe fhould ftill to Rhime Submit.
This, the moft wholefome *Laws* we ever made,
So ftrictly in this EPILOGUE obey'd,
Sure no Man here will ever dare to *break.*

    [Enter JOHNSON*'s Ghoft.]*

Hold, and give Way, for I myfelf will fpeak;
Can You encourage fo much Infolence,
And add new Faults ftill to the great Offence
Your Anceftors fo rafhly did commit,
Againft the mighty Powers of Art and Wit?
When they condemn'd thofe noble Works of mine,
SEJANUS, and my beft lov'd CATALINE:
Repent, or on your guilty Heads fhall fall
The Curfe of many a Rhiming Paftoral:
The *Three* bold *Beauchamps* * fhall revive again,
And with the *London-*Prentice ‡ conquer Spain,
All the dull Follies of the former Age
Shall find Applaufe on this corrupted Stage.
But if you pay the great Arrears of Praife,
So long fince due to my much-injur'd Plays,
From all paft Crimes I firft will fet you free,
And then infpire fome One to write like Me.

----

* *Alluding to the Three Parts of* Henry VI. *by* Shakefpear.
  ‡ *The* London PRODIGAL. *A Comedy, by* Shakefpear.

                    KNOT.

K N O T T I N G.*

AT Noon, in a Sunshiny Day,
    The brighter LADY of the *May*,
Young CHLORIS innocent and gay,
    Sat KNOTTING in a Shade:

Each slender Finger play'd its Part,
With such Activity and Art,
As would inflame a youthful Heart,
    And warm the most decay'd.

Her fav'rite Swain, by Chance, came by,
He saw no Anger in her Eye;
Yet when the bashful Boy drew nigh,
    She would have seem'd afraid.

She let her ivory Needle fall,
And hurl'd away the twisted Ball;
But strait gave STREPHON such a Call,
    As would have rais'd the Dead.

Dear gentle Youth, is't none but Thee?
With Innocence I dare be free;
By so much Truth and Modesty
    No Nymph was e'er betray'd.

Come lean thy Head upon my Lap;
While thy smooth Cheeks I stroke and clap,
Thou may'st securely take a Nap.
    Which he, poor Fool, obey'd.

She saw him yawn, and heard him snore,
And found him fast asleep all o'er.
She sigh'd, and could endure no more,
    But starting up, she said,

                                    Such

* *This was wrote in* Compliment *to* Queen MARY.

Such Virtue shall rewarded be:
For this thy dull Fidelity,
I'll trust you with my Flocks, not Me,
  Pursue thy grazing Trade;
Go milk thy Goats, and shear thy Sheep,
And watch all Night thy Flocks to keep;
Thou shalt no more be lull'd asleep
  By Me mistaken Maid.

※※※※※※※※※※※※※※※※※※※※※※※

A SONG *to* CHLORIS, *from the Blind* ARCHER.*

I.

AH! CHLORIS, 'tis time to disarm your bright Eyes,
  And lay by those terrible Glances;
We live in an Age that's more civil and wise,
  Than to follow the Rules of Romance.

II.

When once your round Bubbies begin but to pout,
  They'll allow you no long Time of Courting;
And you'll find it a very hard Task to hold out,
  For all Maidens are Mortal at Fourteen.

---

* CUPID.

※※※※※※※※※※※※※※※※※※※※※

A SONG *on* BLACK BESS.

I.

METhinks the poor Town has been troubled too long,
  With PHILLIS and CHLORIS in every Song,
By Fools, who at once can both love and despair,
And will never leave calling 'em cruel and fair.

Which

Which juftly provokes me in Rhime to exprefs
The Truth that I know of bonny BLACK BESS.

II.

This BESS of my Heart, this BESS of my Soul,
Has a Skin white as Milk, and Hair black as a Coal;
She's plump, yet with Eafe you may fpan her round Waift
But her round fwelling Thighs can fcarce be embrac'd
Her Belly is foft, not a Word of the reft;
But I know what think, when I drink to the Beft.

III.

The Plowman and 'Squire, the arranter Clown,
At Home fhe fubdu'd in her Paragon-Gown;
But now fhe adorns both the Boxes and Pit,
And the proudeft Town-Gallants are forc'd to fubmit:
All Hearts fall a leaping wherever fhe comes,
And beat Day and Night, like my Lord *Craven's* Drums.

IV.

I dare not permit her to come to *Whiteball*,
For fhe'd out-fhine the Ladies, Paint, Jewels, and all;
If a Lord fhould but whifper his Love in a Crowd,
She'd fell him a Bargain, and laugh out aloud:
Then the Queen over-hearing what BETTY did fay,
Would fend Mr. *Roper* to take her away.

V.

But to thofe that have had my dear Bafs in their Arms
She's gentle, and knows how to foften her Charms;
And to every Beauty can add a new Grace,
Having learn'd how to lifp and to trip in her Pace;
And with a Head on one Side, and a languifhing Eye,
To kill us by looking as if fhe would die.

SONG

SONG *Written at* SEA, *in the* first Dutch War, 1665, *the Night before an Engagement.*

I.

TO all you Ladies now at Land
    We Men at Sea indite ;
But first wou'd have you underſtand
    How hard it is to write ;
The *Muſes* now, and *Neptune* too,
We muſt implore to write to you.
    With a Fa, la, la, la, la.

II.

For tho' the *Muſes* ſhould prove kind,
    And fill our empty Brain ;
Yet if rough *Neptune* rouſe the Wind,
    To wave the Azure Main,
Our Paper, Pen, and Ink, and we,
Roll up and down our Ships at Sea,
    With a Fa, &c.

III.

Then, if we write not by each Poſt,
    Think not we are unkind ;
Nor yet conclude our Ships are loſt
    By *Dutchmen,* or by *Wind:*
Our Tears we'll ſend a ſpeedier Way,
The Tide ſhall bring 'em twice a Day.
    With a Fa, &c.

IV.

The KING, with wonder and Surpriſe,
    Will ſwear the Seas grow bold ;
Becauſe the Tides will higher riſe,
    Than e'er they us'd of old:

But

But let him know it is our Tears
Brings Floods of Grief to *Whitehall* Stairs.
: *With a Fa,* &c.

V.

Should foggy OPDAM chance to know
  Our sad and dismal Story;
The *Dutch* wou'd scorn so weak a Foe,
  And quite their Fort at *Goeree*:
For what Resistance can they find
From Men who've left their Hearts behind?
  With a Fa, &c.

VI.

Let Wind and Weather do its worst,
  Be You to Us but kind;
Let *Dutchmen* vapour, *Spaniards* curse,
  No Sorrow we shall find:
'Tis then no Matter how Things go,
Or who's our Friend, or who's our Foe.
  With a Fa, &c.

VII.

To pass our tedious Hours away,
  We throw a merry Main;
Or else at serious *Ombre* play;
  But, why should we in vain
Each others ruin thus pursue?
We were undone when we left you.
  With a Fa, &c.

VIII.

But now our Fears tempestuous grow,
  And cast our Hopes away;
Whilst you, regardless of our Woe,
  Sit careless at a Play:
Perhaps permit some happier Man
To kiss your Hand, or flirt your Fan.
  With a Fa, &c.

XI.

IX.

When any mournful Tune you hear,
    That dies in ev'ry Note;
As if it figh'd with each Man's Care,
    For being fo remote:
Think then how often Love we've made
To you, when all thofe Tunes were play'd.
    With a Fa, &c.

X.

In Juftice you cannot refufe,
    To think of our Diftrefs;
When we for Hopes of Honour lofe
    Our certain Happinefs;
All thofe Defigns are but to prove
Ourfelves more worthy of your Love.
    With a Fa, &c.

XI.

And now we've told you all our Loves,
    And likewife all our Fears;
In Hopes this Declaration moves
    Some Pity for our Tears:
Let's hear of no Inconftancy,
We have too much of that at Sea.
    With a Fa, la, la, la, la.

D   *Mifcel-*

Miscellaneous POEMS.

Dryden's Satire to his MUSE.
Written by the Lord Somers.

Quo liceat Libris, non licet ire mibi.   Ovid.
Turpiter huc, illuc ingeniosus erat.   Hor.

HEAR me, dull Proftitute, worfe than my Wife,
Like her, the Shame and Clog of my dull Life;
Whofe firft Effay was in a Tyrant's Praife,*
Bawdy in Prologues, blafphemous in Plays:
So lewd, thou mad'ft me for the *Church* unfit,
And I had ftarv'd, but for a lucky Hit,
When the weak Minifters implor'd my Wit:
Stol'ft me from Bufinefs, where I might have made
A folid Fortune to thy barren Trade.
My Father wifely bid me *be a Clerk*;
Thou whifper'd'ft, Boy, *be thou a tearing Spark.*
I from that fatal Hour new Hopes purfu'd,
Set up for Wit, and aukwardly was lewd ;
Drank 'gainft my Stomach, 'gainft my Confcience fwore,
Againft my Will, I marry'd a rank Whore:
After two Children, and a third Mifcarriage,
By brawny Brothers hector'd into Marriage.
Affected Rapes and Lufts I'ad never known;
As if that all *GOMORRAH* was my own.

Nor.

* *His Panegyrick on* Oliver Cromwell.

Nor Love, nor Wine, could ever see me gay,
To writing bred, I knew not what to say.
With scolding Wife and starving Chits beset,
When I want Money, and no Friend will treat,
Chear'd with one Cup of thy *Castalian* Spring,
I can abuse the Church, my Friend, and King;
Tell him he's jilted, fool'd, led by the Nose,
Then, like ALMANZOR, turn upon his Foes;
Libel his Mistresses, and Stasemen too,
Then o'er his whoring Life old DAVID throw,
By whom URIAH was so basely slain;
But our good *Monarch* spares his CASTLEMAIN,
And OATES his Plots, and Treasons, swears in vain:
Defame the Men that gave me Meat and Cloaths,
And then deny it with a thousand Oaths.
ADRIEL to please, call ROCHESTER a Fool,
SEDLEY a Capuchin, and DORSET dull.
I, like BOROSKY, by the false Count hir'd,
On SCROOP my Blunderbuss of Satire fir'd;
In cool Blood call'd him Fool, Knave, Coward too;
What more to HALL, or CRANBOURN could I do;
Who long enjoy'd e'er I began to Woo?
Thou'lt say, perhaps, What is all this to thee,
If I a Coward, Cuckold, Villain be?
But then thou should'st thy sacred Aid refuse,
When I invoke it to so base a Use;
Blunt, of my murd'ring Pen, the killing Point,
And honestly refuse the odious Hint.
But thou ne'er com'st so gladly to my Call,
As when on Merit unprovok'd I fall.
Is there a Patriot to be defam'd,
Lady abus'd or virtuous Actions blam'd?
Thou, with Officious Haste, rank'st ev'ry Word,
And giv'st thy raging Madman a sharp Sword:
Devils to Witches are not more at Hand,
Than thou, when I an hellish Task Command.
To thee, ungrateful! what has MONMOUTH done,
That, *Parson*-like, thou call'st him ABSALON?

And

And by that Name doft foolifhly infer,
He from old DAVID's Head the Crown would tear,
Was he ambitious, he had kept his Place:
Stood high in DAVID's as People's Grace;
And warlike Chief of the *Prætorian* Bands,
To the whole Nation's Hearts had join'd their Hands;
Of publick Good diffembled his deep Care,
With the falfe JEBUSITE a-while kept fair;
Then in fome great decifive glorious Day,
Make thofe vile Cormorants difgorge their Prey,
Our Church, Religion, Freedom, and our Laws,
Thofe darling Morfels of their longing Jaws.
Wife STANLEY thus, till *Bofworth*'s fatal Day,
Did feeming Faith to cruel RICHARD pay;
But let the Tyrant in the Heat of Fight,
And brought Succefs to HARRY's drooping Right.
MONMOUTH's brave Mind could no Difguife endure,
Still noble Ways preferring to fecure,
While DAVID lavifhes his People's Love,
He buys the Purchafe with Defign t'improve;
And like fome prudent Kinfmen, re-convey
What the wild Heir hath vainly thrown away,
Left the Great Ancient Family decay.
Good honeft DAVID, why would'ft thou have made
Of fuch a Son and Parliament afraid?
Which whilft he fways, what Faction dares difpute,
Or who can fay, He is not abfolute!
Thro' them he may command the People's Purfe,
And fpend their Wealth and Blood without a Curfe.
By Laws they would a Popifh Heir exclude,
Not by rude Force, or a tumultuous Crowd:
Againft *Navarre* the factious Princes leagu'd,
And the right Heir the Papal World intrigu'd:
When a long War had plac'd him on the Throne,
The State-Religion he was forc'd to own;
The harmlefs People took it in good Part,
The zealous Church yet ftabb'd him to the Heart;

Taught

Taught all by Story, there was no Defence,
But they muſt change their Faith, or change their Prince.
Who would not here the like Extreams prevent,
And ſettle Things by Aid of Parliament?
Thou only Court preſiding at the Helm,
Which mak'ſt all others uſeful to the Realm ;
Inferior Judges trembling to decree
What may hereafter be condemn'd by thee :
The Chancellor's and ill Stateſman's only Dread,
For it is thou alone can reach their Head.
By thee fell WOLSEY, and falſe CLARENDON,
Abandon'd by their Kings, but here undone ;
Both over-whelm'd for daring to remove,
Or ſtem the Torrent of their Maſter's Love :
The one fair BULLEN to his Prince deny'd ;
The other made lov'd STUART, RICHMOND's Pride,
And with the Royal Blood for ever, mingled HYDE.
To their own Ruin can all Men agree,
And none the Precipice but Courtiers ſee ?
Courtiers, who importune the Sovereign,
To pardon Robbers, Cut-throats, for their Gain ;
Who live on Ideots, Lunaticks, Forfeits, Fines,
And cannot thrive but when the Nation pines.
Unhappy we, if rul'd by ſuch, whoſe Rent
Conſiſts in Breaches of the Government.
Some few there are with great Eſtates indeed,
Yet labour with imaginary Need :
Strange ſort of Fools, who, for one Penſion more,
Enſlave themſelves, and all they had before.
Others, with Titles and new Earldoms caught,
Would give up all for which the Barons fought :
They're equally unfit for Government,
Who nothing have, or nothing will content.
Who bid thee in ACHITOPHEL's vile Name,
Old DAVID's Errors and his Faults proclaim ?
Or ſay, *Plots True or Falſe are needful Things,*
To ſet up Commonwealths, and pull down Kings?

That .

That DAVID, whom thou doſt with Rev'rence name,
Charm'd into Eaſe, grows careleſs of his Fame,
And brib'd with petty Sums of foreign Gold,
Is grown in BATHSHEBA's Embraces old?
That, like the Prince of Angels, from his Height,
He now comes downward with diminiſh'd Light?
If DAVID once ill Language lay to Heart,
Who ſhall the Poet from the Traytor part?
The People's Voice, of Old the Voice of God,
Thou call'ſt the Voice of an unruly Crowd.
Crowds are the Fools————
That flock to thine and D'URFEY's Loyal Plays,
And give implicit Claps on your third Days:
About the Stage of Mountebank they wait,
And whoop at Cudgels, or a broken Pate,
But have, like thee, no Int'reſt in the State.
Rule as thou wilt the Realm of *Mexico*,
And under Iron-Yokes make *Indians* Bow;
But with old *England* what haſt thou to do?
Who from our Kings an uſeful Pow'r would take;
Nor have they Pow'r; but for the People's Sake
Diſarm themſelves, and *Anarchy* beſpeak.
Kings may do good at their full Stretch of Will,
And need not for a Strain of Law ſtand ſtill.
They ſpare with Mercy, tho' with Judgment kill,
Confin'd, like God, only from doing Ill.
Thus in our Papal Fire, to ſave the Town,
Some Houſes were blown up, and ſome pull'd down:
None blam'd the Order, ſince 'twas underſtood,
A private Miſchief's for the publick Good.
Tho' we all periſh, yet we muſt forbear
The ſacred Title of a Popiſh Heir,
If we thy fooliſh Politicks ſhould hear.
Somewhere there muſt a Sov'reign Power be,
In King, in Lords, in Commons, or all Three,
Deriv'd from God, and only leſs than his,
Which can do all, and nothing do amiſs;

The

The facred Ties of Marriage can diffolve,
And Children in their Parents Crimes involve,
Making thofe Baftards who had elfe been Heirs,
And injur'd Husbands legal Widowers;
Cut off Entails, make new, repeal old Laws,
And of contending Kings decide the Caufe.
Thus from the Helm our learned RICHARD thruft,
Confefs'd their Pow'r, and own'd their Sentence juft.
And on the Throne our brave Fourth EDWARD fate,
Whilft HARRY liv'd a Pris'ner of the State.
ALPHONSO thus depos'd for his weak Life,
PEDRO enjoy'd his Kingdom and his Wife.
There *Jus Divinum* barks not at his Right,
Damns not his Rule by Day, nor Love by Night.
In his Defence, each private Man may kill;
Muft then a Nation perifh and ftand ftill?
If for our Laws, Faith, God, we may not fight,
When can a Chriftian Sword be in the Right?
O! the prodigious Wit, and wond'rous Sting,
To call ACHIT'PHEL's Son, unfeather'd two-legg'd thing!
So by old PLATO Man was once defin'd,
'Till a pull'd Cock that Notion undermin'd.
Thy AMIEL with Bull JONAS felf may vye
For all but Courage, Wit, and Honefty.
As loud he roar'd 'gainft the Prerogative,
As fharply blam'd, as ftingily would give,
'Till his own Wants oblig'd him to receive,
And on his cheated Sire he could no longer live:
Whofe whole Eftate, when he in Truft, had got,
Thy honeft AMIEL grudg'd him Pipe and Pot.
Thy HUSHAI next, a true Friend e'er a Man,
So foon his Dearnefs with his Prince began,
Was but Fourteen when DAVID was Abroad,
Lefs fit for a King's Friendfhip than a Rod;
Which he deferv'd, when he with Tears reply'd,
And in full Houfe the Baby cry'd,
How could one *German* Journey teach his Youth,
And add Experience to his native Truth!

 Abroad

Abroad he learn'd to live upon his Prince,
As ev'ry Fool, Whore, Bully, has done since ;
To other Merit he has no Pretence.
BARZILLAI's Praise I could rehearse again,
And make the second Labour of my Pen ;
Wife, Valiant, Loyal, Rich, of high Descent,
Born t'all that Fortune for her Darlings meant,
Who nobly scorn'd a private Happiness,
When he beheld the Sov'reign in Distress:
To Arms he flew, but, with bold CATO's Fate,
Espous'd the Cause that Fortune seem'd to hate :
Striving to save the Head that wore the Crown,
He pull'd the mighty Ruin on his own.
But why extoll'd *Jerusalem*'s Sagan,
At Drink and Whores indeed a very Dragon ?
Not MAGDALEN, possess'd in all her Prime
With her ten Devils, could have equall'd him.
Why would'st thou call thy ADRIEL a Muse,
And DAVID of his hasty Rise accuse ?
When we all know the same obliging Hand
Gave him his *George*, and CHURCHILL his Command,
Jermin his Countryhouse, and *Bromwick* his Poynt Band.
Or JOTHAM flatter'd with vain fickle Thing,
Famous for Jests upon the Church and King :
One while *Pythagoras*'s harmless Food,
For Thoughts and Politicks must cool his Blood ;
And then again with Whores and lusty Wines,
Revels all Night, and thinks him mad that Dines.
Quibbles, Jokes, Puns, and trifling Wit he has,
And, like the *Swede*, is very rich in Brass ;
Against the Court and DAVID's self he roar'd,
How ill he govern'd, and how worse he whor'd :
Would swear a Parrot had more Wit than *Nelly*,
With her parch'd Face, more wrinkled than P——Belly.
Yet now to Both, like Popish Saints, he prays,
Which shews he will not burn in *James*'s Days :
In his plain Band, and Honesty in Show,
He only aim'd at *Danby*'s Overthrow ;

Which

Which when obtain'd, this Patriot had his Ends,
And farewel all his plain well meaning Friends;
There was no Plot, no Popish Duke to fear,
With DANBY all our Dangers difappear.
DANBY thus fetting, to prevent dark Night;
This paler Moon fhews forth its clearer Light,
Mifguides our Confellors with her glim'ring Ray,
And all our Men of Bus'nefs lofe their Way:
Our Parliament's diffolv'd, new Members meet,
An *Oxford* Journey muft allay their Heat:
But the true *Englifh* Intereft appear'd,
The *Silver Smiths* for their *Diana* fear'd;
Pop'ry would'pafs on us in no Difguife,
No Flow'rs could hide that Serpent from our Eyes,
We're in fuch hafte diffolv'd, that in the Street
New-chofen with diffolving-Members meet;
And then a Paper, in good DAVID's Name,
Muft the Proceedings of the Houfe defame:
Sheriff's and Juries pack'd, Juftices made
Knights of th' Addrefs, and all falfe Colours laid;
To cheat their Party with a vain Conceit,
The People, Parliaments both fear, and hate.
What SAMPSON in a Dungeon, Captive, Blind,
In fpiteful Rage for cruel Foes defign'd,
The Houfe of Commons muft be thought to do
Againft themfelves, and thofe that truft 'em too.
The Head fhall fooner fear its own right Hand,
Parents their fmiling Infants Death Command,
The chearful Birds fit filent in the Spring,
Than Lords or Commons hurt the Realm or King:
They may thy Heroes, that fmall faithful Band,
Precious Counfellors, who dare fingly ftand
'Gainft the collective Wifdom of the Land.
DAVID in Exile had more Friends than thou
Wilt to his beft, his happier Days allow.
Why founds thy Trumpet in the Time of Peace?
Art thou afraid our Diff'rences fhould ceafe,
That thus thou talk'ft of Rebels, Treafons, more
Than any *Irifh* Witnefs ever fwore?   Soldiers

Soldiers of Fortune thus to drive a Trade,
Care not what Ruin, or what Slaughter's made.
  But near me prophesy, and mark we well;
E'er thrice the Rose renews its fragrant Smell,
People and King shall join, like Man and Wife,
And both abhor the Engines of their Strife:
No more shall they endure a Hackney Pen,
And thou, cashier'd, shalt to the Stage again,
Please none but silly Women, or worse Men;
DAVID shall find Duty an empty Word,
(For diff'rent Faiths can never have one Sword;
The Knot of Friendship is but loosely ty'd,
'Twixt those that heavenly Concerns divide.)
He then shall with his Parliament agree,
And Lives and Fortunes shall their Language be:
Monmouth be bless'd for all that he has done,
While thy vile Heroes to their Pardons run.

The INCHANTMENT.

By Mr. OTWAY.

I.

I Did but look and love a while,
  'Twas but for one half Hour;
Then to resist I had no Will,
  And now I have no Power.

II.

To sigh, and wish, is all my Ease;
  Sighs, which do Heat impart,
Enough to melt the coldest Ice,
  Yet cannot warm your Heart.

III;

III.

O! would your pity give my Heart,
  One Corner of your Breast;
'Twould learn of yours the winning Art,
  And quickly steal the rest.

❀❀❀❀❀❀❀❀❀❀❀❀❀❀❀❀❀❀❀❀

The ENJOYMENT.

By the Same.

I.

CLaspt in the Arms of her I love,
  In vain, alas! for Life I strove:
My flutt'ring Spirits, wrapt in Fire,
  By Love's mysterious Art,
Borne on the Wings of fierce Desire,
  Flew from my flaming Heart.

II.

Thus lying in a Trance for dead,
Her swelling Breasts bore up my Head;
When waking from a pleasing Dream,
  I saw her killing Eyes,
Which did in fiery Glances seem
  To say, Now CÆLIA dies.

III.

Fainting, she press'd me in her Arms,
And trembling lay, dissolv'd in Charms;
When, with a shiv'ring Voice, she cry'd,
  Must I alone, then die?
No, no, I languishing reply'd,
  I'll bear thee Company.

IV.

IV.

Melting our Souls thus into one,
Swift Joys our Wishes did out-run:
Then launch'd in rolling Seas of Bliss,
  We bid the World adieu;
Swearing by ev'ry charming Kiss,
  To be for ever true.

The Miller's Tale *from* CHAUCER.
Inscribed to N. Rowe, *Esq*;

By Mr. *SAMUEL COBB,*
Late of *Trinity College* in *Cambridge.* *

The ARGUMENT.

NICHOLAS, *a Scholar of* Oxford, *practiseth with* ALISON, *the Carpenter's Wife of* Osney, *to deceive her Husband; but in the End is rewarded accordingly.*

Whilom in *Oxford* an old *Chuff* did dwell,
    A Carpenter by Trade, as Stories tell;
Who by his Craft had heap'd up many a Hoard,
And furnish'd Strangers both with Bed and Board.
With him a Scholar lodg'd, of slender Means,
But notable for Sciences and Sense,
Yet, tho' he took Degrees in Arts, his Mind
Was mostly to *Astrology* inclin'd:

---

* Mr. Cobb *died in the Year* 1713, *and was interred in the Cloyster of* Christ-Church *Hospital,* London.

A Lad in *Divination* skill'd and shrewd,
Who by Interrogations could conclude,
If Men should ask him, at what certain Hours
The droughty, Earth would gape for cooling Show'rs,
When it should rain, or snow, what should befall
Of fifty Things; I cannot reckon all.

This learned *Clerk* had got a mighty Fame
For Modesty, and *NICHOLAS*, his Name.
Subtile he was, well-taught in CUPID's Trade,
But seem'd as meek and bashful as a Maid.
A Chamber in his Hostelry he kept,
Alone he study'd, and alone he slept,
With sweet and fragrant Herbs the Room was drest,
But he was ten times sweeter than the best,
His Books of various Size, or great or small,
His *Augrim* Stones to cast Accompts withal;
His *Astrolabe* and *Almagist* * apart,
With twenty more hard Names of cunning Art,
On several Shelves were couched nigh his Bed,
And the Press cover'd with a folding Red.
Above, an Instrument of Musick lay,
On which sweet Melody he us'd to play,
So wond'rous sweet, that all the Chamber rung,
And *Angelus ad Virginem* † he sung;
Then would he chaunt in good King DAVID's Note,
Full often blessed was his merry Throat.
And thus the *Clerk* in Books and Musick spent
His Time, and Exhibitions yearly Rent.

This *Carpenter* had a new-married Wife,
Lov'd as his Eyes, and dearer than his Life.
The buxom Lass had twice nine Summers seen,
And her brisk Blood ran high in ev'ry Vein.
The Dotard, jealous of so ripe an Age,
Watch'd her, and lock'd her, like a Bird in Cage:
For she was wild, and in her lovely Prime;
But he, poor Man! walk'd down the *Hill of Time:*

---

* *The Name of a Book of* Astronomy, *written by* Ptolomy. † *The Angel's Salutation to the Virgin* Mary.

He knew his own weak Side, and dreamt in Bed,
She had, or would be planting on his Head.
He knew not CATO, for his Wit was rude,
That Men should wed with their Similitude.
Like should with Like, in Love and Years, engage,
For *Youth* can never be a Rhyme to *Age*.
Hence Jealousies create a nuptial War,
And the warm Seasons with the frigid jar:
But when the Trap's once down, he must endure
His Fate, and *Patience is the only Cure*,
Perhaps his Father, and a hundred more
Of honest Christians, were thus serv'd before.
Fair was his charming Consort, and withal
Sender her Waste, and like a *Weasel's*, small.
She had a Girdle barred all with Silk,
And a clean Apron, white as Morrow Milk.
White as her Smock, embroider'd all before,
Which on her Loins in many Plaits she wore.
Broad was her silken Fillet, set full high,
And oft she twinkled with a liquorish Eye.
Her Brows were arched like a bended *Bow*,
Like *Marble* smooth, and blacker than a *Sloe*,
She softer far than *Wool*, or fleecy *Snow*.
Were you to search the Universe around,
So gay a Wench was never to be found.
With greater Brightness did her Colour shine,
Than a new *Noble* of the freshest Coin.
Shrill was her Song, and loud her piercing Note,
No *Swallow* on a Barn had such a Throat.
To this she skipp'd and caper'd, like a *Lamb*,
Or *Kid*, or *Calf*, when they pursue their Dam.
Sweet as *Metheglin* was her Honey Lip,
Or Hoard of *Apples* which in *Hay* are kept.
Wincing she was, as is a jolly *Colt*,
Long as a Mast, and upright as a Bolt,
Above her Ancles laced was her Shoe;
She was a *Primrose*, and a *Pigsnye too*;
And fit to lig by any Christian's Side,
Or a Lord's Mistress, or a Yeoman's Bride.

Now, *Sir*, what think you how the Cafe befell?
This NICHOLAS (for I the Truth will tell)
Was a meer Wag, and on a certain Day,
When the good Man, the Hufband, was away,
Began to fport and wanton with his Dame,
(For *Clerks* are fly and very full of Game)
And privily he caught her by *That fame.*
My * Lemman Dear, quoth he, I'm all on Fire,
And perifh, if you grant not my Defire.
He clafp'd her round, and held her faft, and cry'd,
O let me, let me——never be deny'd.
At this fhe wreath'd her Head, and fprung aloof,
Like a young frisking *Colt,* whofe tender Hoof
Ne'er felt the Farrier's Hand, and never knew
The Virgin Burden of an Iron Shoe.
Fie NICHOLAS, away your Hand, quoth fhe;
Is this your Breeding and Civility?
Foh! Idle Set! What means th' unmanner'd Clown,
To teaze me thus, and tofs me up and down?
I vow I'll tell, and bawl it o'er the Town.
You're rude, and will you not be anfwer'd, No?
I will not kifs you——prithee, let me go.
   Here NICHOLAS, a young, defigning Knave,
Began to weep, and cant, and Pardon crave.
So fair he fpoke, and importun'd fo faft,
This feeming modeft Spoufe confents at laft;
By good St. THOMAS ¶ fwore, her ufual Oath,
That fhe would meet his Love, tho' mighty loath.
" If you, faid fhe, convenient Leifure wait,
" (You know my Hufband has a jealous Pate)
" I will requite you, for if once the Beaft
" Should chance to find us out, and fmell the Joff,
" I muft be a dead Woman at leaft.
   Let that, quoth NICHOLAS, ne'er vex your Head,
He muft be a meer learned Afs indeed,
And very foolifhly befets his Wife.
Who cannot a dull Carpenter beguile.

---

* *Miftrefs.*   ¶ *St.* Thomas *'a* Becket.

And thus they were accorded, thus they swore
To wait the Time, as I have said before.
And now, when *Nicholas* had wore away
The pleasant Time in harmless am'rous Play,
To his melodious Psaltery he flew,
Play'd Tunes of Love, by which his Passion grew,
Then printed on her Lips a dear *Adieu*.
It happen'd thus, I cannot rightly tell,
If it on *Easter*, or on *Whitson* fell;
That on a Holiday, this modest Dame
To Church with other honest Neighbours came,
In a good Fit, to hear the Parson preach
What the divine Apostles us'd to teach.
Bright was her Forehead, and no Summer's Day,
Shone half so clear, so tempting, and so gay.

 Now to this Parish did a Clerk belong,
Who many a Time had rais'd a holy Song,
His Name was *Absalon*, a silly Man,
Who curl'd his Hair, which strutted like a Fan,
And from his jolly, pert, and empty Head,
In Golden Ringlets on his Shoulders spread.
His Face was red, his Eyes as grey as Goose,
With St. *Paul*'s Windows figur'd on his Shoes.
Full properly he walk'd, in Scarlet Hose;
But light and Silver-colour'd were his Cloaths,
And Surplice white as Blossoms on the Rose.
Thick Poynts and Tassels did the Coxcomb please,
And fetously they dangled on his Knees.
He could let Blood, and shave your Beard and Head,
But a meer Barber-Surgeon by his Trade.
Nay, he could write and read, and that is more
Than Twenty Parish-Clerks could do before.
Nay, he could fill a Bond, and learnt from *France*,
In thirty Motions how to trip and dance;
Could frisk and toss his twirling Legs in Air,
Nice were his Feet, and trod it to a Hair.

Songs

Songs would he play, and not hide his Wit,
Would fqueak a Treble to his fwaling Kit,
His Drefs was finical, his Mufic queer,
And pleas'd a Tapfter's Eyes, or Drawer's Ear,
No Tavern, Brew-houfe, Ale-houfe in the Town,
Was to the gentle *Abfalon* unknown :
But he was very careful of his Wind,
And never let it fally out behind.
To give the Devil his Due, he had an Art,
By civil Speech, to win a Lady's Heart.

   This *Abfalon*, fo jolly, fpruce, and gay,
Went with the *Cenfor* on the Sabbath Day.
He fwung the Incenfe Pot with comely Grace,
But chiefly would he fume a pretty Face.
His wanton Eye, which ev'ry where he caft,
Dwelt on the *Carpenter's* fine Dame at laft.
So fweet and proper was his lovely Wife,
That he could freely gaze away his Life.
Were he a Cat, this pretty Moufe would feel
Too foon his Tallons, a delicious Meal.

   And now had *Cupid* fhot a piercing Dart,
And wet the Feathers in his wounded Heart.
No Off'ring of the handfome Wives he took,
He wonted nothing but a fmiling Look,
The Parifh Fees refus'd, and faid, the Light
Of the fair Moon fhines brighteft in the Night.
Soon as the Cock had bid the Morning rife,
The fmitten Lover to his Fiddle flies ;
A hideous Noife his fqeaking Trilloes make,
And all the drowfy Neighbourhood awake.
At the lov'd Houfe fome am'rous Tunes he play'd,
And thus with gentle Voice he fung, or faid,
Now, dear Lady, if thy Will be,
I pray you that you'll pity me.
And twenty fuch complaining Notes he fung,
Alike the Mufic of his Kit, and Tongue.
At this the ftaring Carpenter awoke,
And thus his Wife (fair *Alifon*) befpoke :

Art

Art thou asleep, or art thou deaf, my Dear?
And cannot *Absalon* at Window hear?
How with his Serenade he charms us all,
Chaunting melodiously beneath our Wall?
Yes, yes, I hear him, *Alison* reply'd,
Too well, God wot; and then she turn'd aside.
Thus went Affairs, 'till *Absalon*, alas!
Was a lost Creature, a meer whining Ass.
All Night he wakes, and sighs, and wears away.
On his broad Locks and Dress the live long Day,
To such a Height his doating Fondness grew,
To kiss the Ground, and wipe her very Shoe.
Where'er she went, he like a Slave pursu'd,
With spiced Ale, and sweet Metheglin woo'd.
All Dainties he could rap and rend he got,
And sent her Tarts and Custards piping hot.
He spar'd no Cost for an expensive Treat,
Of Mead and Cyder, and all Sorts of Meat.
Throbbing he sings with his lamenting Throat,
And rivals PHILOMELA's mournful Note.
With Rigour some, and some with gentle Arts,
Have found a Passage to young Ladies Hearts:
Some Wealth have won, and some have had the Lot
To fall enamour'd of a treating Sot.
   Sometimes he Scaramouched it on high,
And Harlequin'd it with Activity;
Betrays the Lightness of his empty Head,
And how he could cut Capers in a Bed.
But neither this nor that the Damsel move,
For *Nicholas* has swept the Stakes of Love.
The Parish Clerk has nothing met but Scorn,
And may go Fiddle now, or blow his Horn.
Thus gentle *Absalon* is made her Ape,
And all his Passion turn'd into a Jape;
For *Nicholas* is always in her Eye;
True, says the Proverb, that the *Nigh are sly*.
A distant Love may Disappoinment find,
For out of Sight is ever out of Mind.

The Scholar was at Hand, as I have told,
And gave the Parish-Clerk *the Dog to hold.*
Now, *Nicholas,* thy Craft and Cunning try,
That *Abfalon* may *de profundis* cry.

Now when this Carpenter was call'd away,
To work at *Ofney,* on a certain Day;
The fubtile Scholar, and the wanton Spoufe,
Were decently contriving for his Brows:
Agreed, that *Nicholas* fhould fhape a Wile,
Her addle-pated Husband to beguile.
And if fo be the Game fucceeded right,
She then would fleep within his Arms all Night:
For both were in this one Defire concern'd,
Alike they fuffer'd, and alike they burn'd.
Strait a new Thought leap'd crofs the Scholar's Head,
Who at that Inftant to his Chamber fled:
But to relieve his Thirft and Hunger, bore
Of Meat and Liquor a fubftantial Store,
And victuall'd it for a long Day or more.
Alce, fhould your Husband ask for Us, quoth he,
Reply, in Scorn, What's *Nicholas* to Me?
Am I his Keeper? Help your filly Head!
Perhaps the Man is mad, afleep, or dead.
My Maid indeed has thump'd this Hour or more,
And knock'd as if fhe'd thunder down the Door:
But he, a moaping Drone, no Anfwer gave,
Faft as a Church, and filent as the Grave.

Thus did one *Saturday* entire confume,
Since *Nicholas* had lock'd him in his Room.
Nor was he idle, for no *Lent* he kept,
But eat like other Men, and drank, and flept;
Did what he lift, 'till the next Sun was new,
And went to Reft as common Mortals do.

This Carpenter was in a grievous Pain,
Left *Nicholas* fhould over-work his Brain;
By Study lofe his Reafon, or his Life.
Well, by St. *Thomas,* I don't like it, Wife.

The

The World we live in is a ticklifh Place,
And fudden Death has often ftopp'd our Race.
I faw a Corpfe, as to the Church it paft,
And the poor Man at Work but *Monday* laft.
Run *Dick*, quoth he, run fpeedily up Stairs,
Thump at the Door, and fee how ftand Affairs.
Up ftrait he runs, like any Tempeft flies,
And knocks, and bawls, and like a Madman cries,
Ho ! Mafter *Nicholas*, what mean you thus
To fleep all Night and Day, and frighten us ?
He might as well have whiftled to the Wind,
As from good *Nicholas* an Anfwer find.
At laft he fpy'd a Hole full low and deep,
Where ufually the Cat was wont to creep ;
Here was difcover'd to his wond'ring Sight
The Scholar gazing with his Eyes upright,
As if intent upon the Stars and Moon ;
And down runs he to tell his Mafter foon,
In what Array he faw this ftudious Man :
The Carpenter to crofs himfelf began ;
And cry'd St. *Fridefwid*, help us one and all
Little we know what Fate fhall us befal.
This Man with his Aftronomy is got
Into fome Frenzy, and ftark mad, God wot :
This comes of poring on his cunning Books,
Of his Moon-fnuffing, and Star-peeping Looks :
Why fhould a filly Earth-born Mortal pry
On Heav'n, and fearch the Secrets of the Sky ?
Well fare thofe Men, who no more Learning need, }
Than what's contain'd in the Lord's Pray'r and Creed, }
Scholars fufficient, if they can but read ! }
Thus far'd a fage Philofopher § of old,
Who walking out, as 'tis in Story told,
Was fo much with Aftronomy bewitch'd,
That his Star-gazing Clerkfhip was bewitch'd.

III

---

§ *Thales.*

Ill Luck attends the Man who looks too high,
And can a Star, but not a Marlpit fpy.
But, by St. *Thomas,* this fhall never pafs;
Too well I love this gentle *Nicholas.*
I'll ferret him, unlefs the Devil's in it,
From his brown Fit of Study in a Minute.

    Robin, let's try if that Iron Par
And your ftrong Back can make this Scholar ftir;
Now *Robin* was a Lad of Brawn and Bones,
And by the Hafp heav'd up the Door at once;
Which in the Chamber fell with dreadful Sound,
As would a Man like you or me aftound.
But *Nicholas* did nothing do but ftare,
And, like a Statue, gape into the Air.

    This Carpenter was in a piteous Fear,
Becaufe he did not, or he would not, hear;
Thought feem deep Melancholy had impar'd
His Brain, and that of Mercy he defpair'd;
For which the Student in his Arms he took
With Might and Main, and by the Shoulders fhook;
Cry'd, *Nicholas* awake! What, not a Word?
Look down, defpair not——think upon the Lord!
Then the Night-Spell he mumbled to himfelf:
Blefs thee from Friends, and ev'ry wicked Elf!
He croft the Threfhold, where the Dev'l might creep,
And each fmall Hole, through which an Imp might peep.
With folemn *Pater-nofters* blefs the Door,
And *Ave-Mary*'s, after and before.
At this the Clerk fent forth a heavy Sigh,
With Tears, and woful Tone began to cry—— }
And fhall this World be loft fo foon? Ah, why? }
What do I hear? the Carpenter reply'd,
What fay'ft thou, *Nich'las?* Sure thou art befide
Thyfelf: Serve God, as we poor Lab'rers do,
And then no Harm; no Danger will enfue.
Ah! Friend, quoth *Nicholas,* you little think
What I can tell; but firft let's have fome Drink.

                         Then,

Then, my dear Hoſt, thou ſhalt in private learn
Some certain Things, which thee and me concern
It ſhall no Mortal but yourſelf avail;
Then fetch a *Wincheſter* of mighty Ale.
And now when both had drank an equal Share,
Cries *Nicholas*, ſit down and draw your Chair,
But firſt, ſweet Landlord, you muſt take an Oath,
To no Man living to betray the Troth:
For, truſt me, what I'm going to relate
Is Revelation, and as ſure as Fate:
And if you tell, this Vengeance will enſue,
No Hare in *March* will be ſo mad as you.

  Nay, quoth mine Hoſt, I am no Blab, not I,
And hang me, if you catch me in a Lie.
I would not tell, tho' 'twere to ſave my Life,
To Chick, or Child, to Man, or Maid, or Wife.

  Now, *John*, quoth *Nicholas*, I will not hide
What by my Art I have of late deſcry'd;
How, as I por'd upon fair *Cynthia's* Light,
Should fall on *Monday* next, at Quarter-Night,
A Rain ſo ſudden, and ſo long to boot,
That *Noah's* Flood was but a Spoonful to't.
This World, within the Compaſs of an Hour   ⎫
Shall all be drown'd; ſo hideous is the Show'r, ⎬
As will the Cattle and Mankind devour.   ⎭
Cries then this ſilly Man, Alas, my Wife!
My Boſom-Comfort, and my better Life!
And muſt ſhe drown and periſh with the reſt?
My *Aliſon*, the Darling of my Breaſt?
At this well nigh he ſwoon'd, o'erwhelm'd with Grief,
Fetch'd a deep Sigh, And is there no Relief,
No Remedy, he cry'd, no Succour left?
Are we, alas! of ev'ry Hope bereft?
No, by no Means, quoth this deſigning Clerk,
Be of good Heart, and by Inſtruction work:
For if by *Nicholas* you will be led,
And build no Caſtles in your own wild Head,

None

None fo fecure ; for *Solomon* fays true,
Work all by Counfel, and you cannot rue.
If you'll be govern'd, and be rul'd by me,
I'll undertake to fave thy Wife and Thee ;
By my own Art againft the Flood prevail,
And make no Ufe of either Maft or Sail.
Have you not heard how, when the World was naught,
Noah by heav'nly Infpiration taught ;
Ay, ay, quoth *John*, I've in my *Bible* found,
That once upon a Time the World was drown'd:
Haft thou not heard how *Noah* was concern'd
For his dear Wife, and how his Bowels yearn'd,
'Till he had built and furnifh'd out a Bark,
And lodg'd her with her Children in the Ark ?
Now, Expedition is the Soul and Life
Of Bufinefs ; if you love Yourfelf, or Wife,
Run, fly——for in this Cafe it is a Crime
To loiter, or to lofe an Inch of Time.
For *Alifon*, yourfelf, and me, provide
Three Kneading-Troughs, to fail upon the Tide:
But take more fpecial Care that they be large,
In which a Man may fwim as in a Barge.
Let them be victuall'd well, and fee you lay
Sufficient Stores againft a rainy Day ;
Enough to ferve you twenty Hours ; and more,
For then the Flood will 'fwage, and not before.
But one Thing let me whifper in your Ear,
Let not thy fturdy Servant *Robin* hear,
Nor bonny *Gillian* know what I relate ;
I muft not utter the Decrees of Fate.
Afk me not Reafons why I cannot fave
Your trufty Servant Maid, and honeft Knave:
Suffice it thee, unlefs thy Wits be mad,
To have as great a Grace as *Noah* had.
Do you make Hafte, and mind the grand Affair ;
To fave your Wife fhall be my proper Care.
But when thefe Kneading-Tubs are ready made,
Which may fecure us when the Floods invade ;

See

See that you hang them in the Roof full high,
That none our providential Plot defcry;
And when thou haft convey'd fufficient Store
Of Meat, and Drink, as I have faid before,
And put a fharpen'd Ax in ev'ry Boat,
To cut the Cord, and fet all afloat,
Then thro' the Gable of the Houfe, which lies
Above the Stable, and the Garden fpies,
Break out a Hole, fo very large and wide,
Thro' which our Tubs may fail upon the Tide.
    Then wilt thou.fo much Mirth and Pleafure take
In fwimming, as the white Duck and the Drake.
Then will I cry, Ho! *Alifon*, and *John*,
Be merry, for the Flood will pafs anon.
Then wilt thou anfwer, Mafter *Nicholay*,
Good-morrow, for I fee it is broad Day.
Then fhall we reign as Emperors for Life,
O'er all the World, like *Noah* and his Wife.
But one Thing I almoft forgot to tell,
Which now comes into my Head (and mark me well)
That on that very Night we go Abroad,
All muft be hufh'd, and whifper not a Word;
But all the Time employ our holy Mind
In earneft Pray'rs, for thus has Heav'n enjoyn'd.
    You and your Wife muft take a fep'rate Place,
Nor is there any Sin in fuch a Cafe.
To-morrow Night, when Men are faft afleep,
We to our Kneading-Tubs will flyly creep;
There will we fit each in his Ship apart,
And wait the Deluge with a patient Heart.
Go now; I have no longer Time to fpare
In Sermoning, ufe expeditious Care:
Your Apprehenfion needs no more Advice;
One fingle Word's fufficient for the Wife:
And none, dear Landlord, can your Wit inform;
Go, fave our Lives from this impending Storm.
Away hies *John*, with melancholy Look,
And figh'd and groan'd at every Step he took.

To *Alison* he does his Fate deplore,
And tells a Secret which she knew before :
But yet she trembled, like an *Aspen* Leaf,
And seem'd to perish with dissembled Grief ;
Crying, Alas ! what shall I do ?——Be gone——
Helpt us t'escape, or we are all undone :
I am thy true and very wedded Wife,
Go, dear, dear Spouse, and help to save my Life.
   What strong Impressions does Affection give !
By Fancy Men have often ceas'd to live.
Howe'er absurd Things in themselves appear,
Weak Minds are apt to credit what they fear.
   This silly Carpenter is almost *Wood,*
And thinks of nothing else but *Noah's* Flood ;
Believes he sees it, and begins to quake,
And all for *Alison* his Honey's Sake.
He's over-run with Sorrow, and with Fear,
And sends forth many a Groan, and many a Tear,
A Kneading-Trough, a Tub, and * Kemeling,
He gets by Stealth, and sends 'em to his Inn.
He makes three Ladders, whence he climbs aloof,
And privately he hangs them in the Roof.
But first he victuall'd them, both Trough and Tub,
With Bread and Cheese, and Bottles full of mighty Bub ;
Enough o' Conscience to relieve their Fast,
And be sufficient for a Day's Repast.
   But e'er this Preparation had been made,
He sent to *London* both his Man and Maid,
On certain Matters which concern'd his Trade.
   And now came on the fatal *Monday* Night,
Barr'd are the Doors, out goes the Candle-light ;
And when all Things in Readiness were set,
These Three their Ladders take, and up they get.
Now *Pater-noster,* ‡ *Clum,* said *Alison,*
And *Clum,* quoth *Nicholas,* and *Clum,* quoth *John.*
   E   This

---

* *A Brewer's Vessel.*
‡ *A Note of Silence.*

This Carpenter his *Orifons* did fay,
For Men in Fear are very apt to pray.
Silent he waited, when the Skies would pour
This unaccountable and difmal Show'r.

And now, at § *Curfew* Time, dead Sleep began
To fall upon this eafy fimple Man ;
Who, after fo much Care and Bufinefs paft,
And fpent with fad Concern, was quickly faft.
Soft down the Ladder ftole this lovely Pair,
Good *Nicholas*, and *Alifon* the Fair :
Then without fpeaking, to the Bed they creep,
Of *John*, poor Cuckold ! who was faft afleep.
There all the Night they revel, fport, and toy,
And act the merry Scene of am'rons Joy ;
'Till that the Bell of *Lauds* began to ring,
And the fat Fryars in the Chancel fing.

The Parifh Clerk, this am'rous *Abfalon*,
Who over Head and Ears in Love is gone,
At *Ofney* happen'd, with a joval Crew,
To fpend the *Monday* as they us'd to do ;
There pulls a certain Fryar by the Sleeve,
With Pardon begg'd, and, Father, by your Leave.
When faw you *John* the Carpenter, he cries ;
Laft *Saturday* the Cloifterer replies,
Since when I have not feen him with thefe Eyes :
Perhaps abroad he's playing faft and loofe,
Or fetching Timber for the Abbot's Ufe,
And lodges at the *Graunge* a Day or two ;
Or elfe at Home —— I know no more than you.

This made *Nab*'s boiling Blood with Pleafure ftart
The News rejoic'd the Cockles of his Heart.

Now

---

§ Curfew, William the Conqueror, *in the firft Year*
of his Reign, commanded, that in every Town and Village,
a Bell fhould be rung every Night at Eight of the Clock ;
and that all People fhould then put out their Fire and
Candle, and go to Bed. The Ringing of this Bell was
called Curfew, *that is,* Cover Fire.

Now is my Time, thinks he, the Moon is bright,
Nor care I, if I travel all the Night;
For at his Door, since Day began to spring,
I've seen, like him, no Kind of Man or Thing.
   It is resolv'd ———— to *Alison* I'll go,
When the first Morning Cock does crow ;
And to her Window privately repair ;
Then knock, and tell her my tormenting Care :
I'll open all my Breast, and ease my Heart,
For 'tis too much to bear Love's stinging Smart.
Some little Comfort sure I shall not miss,
At least she'll grant the Favour of a Kiss.
My Mouth has itch'd all Day, from whence it seems
That I shall kiss ; besides my pleasant Dreams
Of Feasts and Banquets, whence a Man may guess
That I may haply meet with some Success:
But for an Hour or two before I go,
I'll first refresh me with a Nap or so.
   Now the first Cock had wak'd from his Repose
The jolly *Absalon*, and up he rose.
But first he dresses finical and gay,
And looks like any Beau at Church or Play.
And brisk as Bridegroom on a Wedding Day.
Nicely he combs the Ringlets of his Hair,
And, wash'd with Rosewater, looks fresh and fair ;
Then with his Finger he her Window twang'd,
Whisper'd a gentle Tone, and thus harangu'd.
  Sweet Alison, *my Hony-com', my Dear,*
My Bird, my Cinamon, *your Lover hear.*
Awake and speak one Word before I part ;
But one kind Word, the Balsam to my Heart.
Little you think, alas ! the mighty Woe,
Which for the Love of thee I undergo.
For thee I swelter, and for thee I sweat,
And mourn as Lambkins for the Mother's Teat,
Nor false my Grief, nor does the Turtle Dove
Lament more truly, or more truly love.
I cannot eat nor drink, and all for thee————
Get from my Window, you *Jack Fool*, said she

I love another of a different Hue
From such a silly Dunder-head as you.
If you stand talking at that foolish Rate,
My Chamber-pot shall be about your Pate,
Be gone, you empty Sot, and let me sleep;
At this poor *Absalon* began 'to weep,
And his hard Fate with Sighs and Groans deplore,
Was ever faithful Love thus serv'd before?
Since, then, my Sweet, what I desire's in vain,
Let me but one small Boon, a Kiss obtain.
And will you then be gone, nor loiter here,
Quoth *Alison? Ay certainly my Dear!*
Make ready then—— Now, *Nicholas,* lye still;
'Tis such a Jest that you shall laugh your fill.
    Ravish'd whith Joy, *Nab* fell upon his Knees,
The happiest Man alive in all Degrees;
In silent Raptures he began to cry,
No Lord in Europe *is so blest as I.*
I may expect more Favours for a Kiss
Is an Assurance of a farther Bliss.
The Window now unclasp'd, with slender Voice,
Cries *Alison,* be quick, and make no Noise;
I would not for the World our Neighbours hear,
For they're made up of Jealousy and Fear.
    Then silken Handkerchief from Pocket came,
To wipe his Mouth full clean, to kiss the Dame.
Dark was the Night, as any Coal or Pitch,
When at the Window, she clap'd out her Breech.
The Parish-Clerk ne'er doubted what to do,
But ask'd no Questions, and in haste fell to.
On her blind Side full savourly he prest
A loving Kiss, e'er he smelt out the Jest.
Aback he starts, for he knew well enough,
That Women's Lips are smooth, but these were rough:
What have I done, quoth he? and rav'd and star'd,
Ah me! I've kiss'd a Woman with a Beard.
He curs'd the Hour, and rail'd against the Stars,
That he was born to kiss my Lady's Arse.

Tehre

* *Tebea* she cry'd, and clap'd the Window close,
While *Absalon* with Grief and Anger goes
To meditate Revenge; and to requite
The foul Affront, he would not sleep that Night.
And now with Dust, with Sand, with Straw, with Chips,
He scrubs and rubs the Kisses from his Lips,
Oft would he say, *Alas! O bosess Evil!*
Than meet with this Disgrace so damn'd uncivil,
I rather had went head-long to the Devil.
To kiss a Woman's Breech! Oh, it can't be born!
But by my Soul, I'll be reveng'd by Morn.

　Hot Love, the Proverb says, *grows quickly cool,*
　And *Absalon's* no more an am'rous Fool:

For since his Purpose was so foully crost,
He gains his Quiet, tho' his Love is lost:
And, cur'd of his Distemper, can defy
All whining Coxcombs with a scornful Eye:
But for meer Anger, as he pass'd the Street,
He wept, as does a School-Boy, when he's beat.
In a soft doleful Pace, at last, he came
To an old *Vulcan,* J a r v i s was his Name;
Who late and early at the Forge turmoil'd,
In hammering Iron Bars and Plough-shares toil'd.
Hither repair'd, by one or two a-Clock,
Poor *Absalon,* and gave an easy Knock.
Who's there, that knocks so late Sir J a r v i s cries?
'Tis I, the pensive *Absalon* replies,
Open the Door. *What,* Absalon (queth he)
The Parish Clerk! Ah! Benedicite
Where hast thou been? Some pretty Girl, I wot,
Has led you out so late upon the Trot.
Some merry Meeting on the Wenching Score;
You know my Meaning——but I'll say no more.
This *Absalon* another Distaff drew,
And had more Tow to spin than *Jarvis* knew:

E 3　　　　　　He

---

* *A Note of Laughter.*

He minded not a Bean of all he faid,
For other Things employ'd his careful Head.
At laſt he Silence breaks, *dear Friend*, he cries,
Lend's that hot Pur, which in the Chimney lies:
I have occaſion for't, no Queſtions, aſk,
To bring it back again ſhall be my Taſk.
  With all my Heart, quoth *Jarvis* were it Gold,
Or ſplendid Nobles in a Purſe untold:
With all my Heart, as I'm an honeſt Smith,
I'll lend it thee; but what wil't do therewith?
For that quoth *Abſalon*, nor Care, nor Sorrow,
I'll give a good Account of it To-morrow.
Then up the Cutler in his Hand he caught,
Tripp'd out with ſilent Pace and wicked Thought.
Red-hot it was, as any burning Coal,
With which to *John* the Carpenter's he ſtole.
There firſt he cough'd, and, as his uſual Wont,
Up to the Window came, and tapp'd upon't,
Who's there, quoth *Aliſon?* Some Midnight Rook,
Some Thief, I warrant, with a hanging Look.
Ah! God forbid, quoth this diſſembling Elf,
'Tis *Abſalon*, my Life, my better Self!
A rich Gold Ring I've to my Darling brought,
By a known Graver exquiſitely wrought:
Beſide a Poſie moſt divinely writ
By a fam'd Poet and notorious Wit.
My Mother gave it me ('tis wond'rous fine)
She clapp'd it on my Finger, I on thine,
If thou wilt-deign the Favour of a Kiſs——
Now *Nicholas* by chance roſe up to piſs:
Thinking the better and improve the Jeſt,
He ſhould ſalute his Breech before the reſt.
With eager Haſte and ſecret Joy he went,
And his Poſteriors out at Window ſent.
Here A B S A L O N, the Wag, with ſubtile Tone,
Whiſpers, my Love! my Soul! my A L I S O N!
Speak my ſweet Bird, I know not where thou art ——
At this the Scholar let a rouzing Fart;

So loud the Noife, as frightful was the Stroke
As Thunder, when it fplits the fturdy Oak,
The Clerk was ready, and with hearty Guft,
The red-hot Iron in his Buttocks thruft.
Strait off the Skin, like fhrivel'd Parchment flew,
His Breech as raw as St. BARTHOLOMEW.
The Cutler had fo fing'd his Hinder-part,
He thought he fhould have dy'd for very Smart,
In a mad Fit about the Room he ran,
Help, Water, Water, for a dying Man.
The Carpenter, as one befide his Wits,
Starts at the dreadful found, and up he gets.
The Name of Water rouz'd him from his Sleep;
He rubb'd his Eye-lids, and began to peep.
Alas! thought he, now comes the fatal Hour
And from the Clouds does *Noah*'s Deluge pour.
Up then he fits, and without more ado,
He takes his Ax, and fmites the Cord in two.
Down goes the Bread, and Ale, and Cheefe, and all,
And *John* himfelf had a confounded Fall;
Dropt from the Roof upon the Floor; aftound,
He lies as dead and fwims upon the Ground.
Then *Nicholas*, to play the Counterfeit,
With A L I S O N, cries Murder in the Street,
In came the Neighbours pouring, like the Tide,
To know the Reafon why was Murder cry'd.
There they beheld poor *John*, a gafping Man;
Shut were his Eyes, his Face was pale and wan:
Batter'd his Sides, and broken was his Arm;
But ftand it out he muft, to his own Harm.
For when he aim'd to fpeak in his Defence,
They bore him down, and baffled all his Senfe.
They told the People that the Man was Wood,
And dream'd of nothing elfe but *Noah*'s Flood.
His heated Fancy of this Deluge rung,
That to the Roof three Kneading-Troughs he hung,
With which in Danger he defign'd to fwim,
And we, forfooth, muft carry on the Whim;
He begg'd and pray'd, and fo we humour'd him.

At hearing this, the sneering Neighbours gave
An universal Shout and hideous Laugh.
Now on the Roof, and now on *John* they gape,
And all his Earnest turn into a Jape.
He swore against the Scholar and his Wife,
And never look'd so foolish in his Life.
Whate'er he speaks, the People never mind ;
His Oaths are nothing, and his Words are Wind.
Thus all consent to scoff each serious Word,
And *John* remain'd a Cuckold on Record.

   Thus Doors of Brass, and Bars of Steel are vain,
And watchful Jealousy, and carking Pain,
Is fruitless all, when a good-natur'd Spouse
Designs Preferment for her Husband's Brows.
Thus AL180N, her Cuckold, does defy,
And ABSALON has kiss'd her nether Eye ;
While NICHOLAS is scalded in the Breech,
My Tale is done ; God save us all, and each.

BAUCIS and *PHILEMON*,

Imitated from the 8th Book of Ovid.

By JONATHAN SWIFT, *D. D.*

IN ancient Times, as Story tells,
  The Saints would often leave their Cells,
And strole about, but hide their Quality,
To try good People's Hospitality.
.. It happen'd on a Winter Night,
As Authors of the Legend write ;

Two

Two Brothers Hermits, Saints by Trade,
Taking their Tour in Mafquerade,
Difguis'd in tatter'd Habits went
To a fmall Village down in *Kent*;
Where, in the Strollers canting Strain,
They begg'd from Door to Door in vain.
Try'd ev'ry Tone might Pity win,
But not a Soul would let 'em in.
  Our wand'ring Saints in woful State,
Treated at this ungodly Rate,
Having through all the Village paft,
To a fmall Cottage came at laft,
Where dwelt a good old honeft Yoeman,
Call'd in the Neighbourhood, Philemon.
Who kindly did the Saints invite
In his poor Hut to pafs that Night;
And then the hofpitable Sire
Bid Goody Baucis mend the Fire;
While he from out the Chimney took
A Flitch of Bacon off the Hook,
And freely from the fatteft Side
Cut out large Slices to be fry'd:
Then ftept afide to fetch 'em Drink,
Fill'd a large Jug up to the Brink,
And faw it fairly twice go round;
Yet (what is wonderful) they found
'Twas ftill replenifh'd to the Top,
As if they ne'er had touch'd a Drop.
The good old Couple was amaz'd,
And often on each other gaz'd;
For both were frighted to the Heart,
And juft began to cry——What art!
Then foftly turn'd afide to view
Whether the Lights were burning blue.
The gentle Pilgrims foon aware on't,
Told 'em their Calling and their Errant:
Good Folks, you need not be afraid,
We are but Saints, the Hermits faid:

E 5

No Hurt shall come to You or Yours;
But, for that Pack of churlish Boors,
Not fit to live on Christian Ground,
They and their Houses shall be drown'd;
Whilst you shall see your Cottage rise,
And grow a Church before your Eyes.

They scarce had spoke; when, fair and soft,
The Roof began to mount aloft;
Aloft rose ev'ry Beam and Rafter,
The heavy Wall clim'd slowly after.

The Chimney widen'd, and grew higher,
Became a Steeple with a Spire.
The Kettle to the Top was hoist,
And there stood fasten'd to a Joist;
But with the Upside down, to show
It's Inclination for Below.
In vain, for a superior Force,
Apply'd at Bottom, stops in Course,
Doom'd ever in Suspense to dwell;
'Tis now no Kettle, but a Bell,
A wooden Jack, which had almost
Lost, by Disuse, the Art to roast,
A sudden Alteration feels,
Increas'd by new intestine Wheels;
And, what exalts the Wonder more,
The Number made the Motion slow'r:
The Flyer, though't had leaden Feet,
Turn'd round so quick, you scarce cou'd see't;
But slacken'd by some secret Pow'r,
Now hardly moves an Inch an Hour.
The Jack and Chimney near allay'd,
Had never left each other's Side;
The Chimney to a Steeple grown,
The Jack would not be left alone;
But up against the Steeple rear'd,
Became a Clock, and still adher'd:
And still its Love to Houshold Cares,
By a shrill Voice, at Noon declares,

Warning

Warning the Cook-maid not to burn
That Roaft-meet which it cannot turn.

The groaning Chair began to crawl,
Like a huge Snail, along the Wall;
There ftuck aloft, in publick View,
And, with fmall Change, a Pulpit grew.

The Porringers, that in a Row
Hung high, and made a glitt'ring Show,
To a lefs noble Subftance chang'd,
Were now but leathern Buckets rang'd.

The Ballads pafted on the Wall,
Of *Joan* of *France,* and *Englifh Moll*,
Fair Rofamond, and *Robin Hood*,
The little Children in the Wood;
Now feem'd to look Abundance better,
Improv'd in Picture, Size, and Letter;
And, high in Order plac'd, defcribe
The Heraldry of ev'ry Tribe.

A Bedftead of the antique Mode,
Compact of Timber many a Load,
Such as our Anceftors did ufe,
Was metamorphos'd into Pews;
Which ftill their antient Nature keep,
By lodging Folks difpos'd to Sleep.

The Cottage, by fuch Feats as thefe,
Grown to a Church by juft Degrees.
The Hermits then defir'd their Hoft,
To afk for what he fancy'd moft.
PHILEMON, having paus'd a-while,
Return'd 'em Thanks in homely Stile:
Then faid; my Houfe is grown fo fine,
Methinks I ftill would call it mine:
I'm old, and fain would live at Eafe,
Make me the Parfon, if you pleafe.

He fpoke, and prefently he feels
His Grazier's Coat fall down his Heels;
He fees, yet hardly can believe,
About each Arm a Pudding Sleeve:

His

His Waftcoat to a Caffock grew,
And both affum'd a Sable Hue;
But being old, continu'd juft
As thread-bare, and as full of Duft.
His Talk was now of Tythes and Dues,
Could fmoak his Pipe, and read the News;
Knew how to preach old Sermons next,
Vampt in the Preface and the Text;
At Chrift'nings well could act his Part,
And had the Service all by Heart:
Wifh'd Women might have Children faft,
And thought whofe Sow had farrow'd laft;
Againft Diffenters would repine,
And ftood up firm for *Right Divine*;
From his Head fill'd with many a Syftem,
But Claffic Authors——he ne'er mifs'd 'em.
　　Thus having furnifh'd up a Parfon,
Dame BAUCIS next they play'd their Farce on.
Inftead of home-fpun Coifs, were feen
Good Pinners edg'd with *Colberteen*;
Her Petticoat transform'd apace,
Became black Sattin, flounc'd with Lace.
Plain *Goody* would no longer down,
'Twas *Madam*, in her Grogram Gown.
PHILEMON was in great Surprize,
And hardly could believe his Eyes,
Amaz'd to fee her look fo prim;
And fhe admir'd as much at him.
　　Thus happy, in their Change of Life,
Were feveral Years this Man and Wife;
When on a Day, which prov'd their laft,
Difcourfing on old Stories paft,
They went, by chance, amidft their Talk,
To the Church yard, to take a Walk;
When BAUCIS haftily cry'd out,
My Dear, I fee your Forehead fprout.
Sprout, quoth the Man, What's this you tell us?
I hope you don't believe me Jealous;

　　　　　　　　　　　　　　　　But

But yet, methinks, I feel it true ;
And truly yours is budding too——
Nay, now I cannot ftir my Foot;
It feels as if 'twere taking Root——
   Defcription would but tire my Mufe ;
In fhort, they both were turn'd to *Ews*,
Old Goodman DOBSON of the *Green*,
Remembers he the Trees has feen:
He'll talk of them from Noon 'till Night,
And goes with Folks to fee the Sight.
On *Sundays*, after Ev'ning Pray'r,
He gathers all the Parifh there ;
Points out the Place, of either *Ew*,
Here BAUCIS, there PHILEMON grew :
'Till once a Parfon of our Town,
To mend his Barn, cut BAUCIS down :
At which, 'tis hard to be believ'd,
How much the other Tree was griev'd,
Grew fcrubby, dy'd a-Top, was ftunted ;
So the next Parfon ftubb'd and burnt it.

✝✝✝✝✝✝✝✝✝✝✝✝✝✝✝✝✝✝✝✝✝✝✝✝✝✝✝✝✝✝

On the Death of *Queen* MARY.

By the Duke of Devonshire, 1694.

POEMA est PICTURA loquens,

I.

LONG our divided State
    Hung in the Ballance of a doubtful Fate,
When one bright Nymph the gath'ring Clouds difpell'd,
    And all the Griefs of *Albion* heal'd:
    Her the united Land obey'd
    No more to Jealoufy inclin'd,
Nor fearning Pow'r with fo much Virtue join'd.
She knew her Task, and nicely underftood
    To what Intention Kings are made;
Not for the own, but for the People's Good,
'Twas that prevailing Argument alone
Determin'd her to fill the vacant Throne:
    And yet with Sadnefs fhe beheld
    A Crown divolving on her Head,
By the Exceffes of a Prince mifled,
    When by her Royal Birth compell'd,
To what her God, and what her Country claim'd,
    Tho' by a fervile Faction blam'd,
    How graceful were the Tears fhe fhed!

II.

    When waiting only for a Wind,
Againft our Ifle the Pow'r of *France* was arm'd;
Her ruling Arts in the true Luftre fhin'd,
The Winds themfelves were by her Influence charm'd;
'Twas her Authority and Care fupply'd
The Safety, which our Want of Troops deny'd.   Se.

Secure and undisturb'd the scene
Of *Albion* seem'd; and, like her Eyes, serene.
Vain was th' Invader's force, Revenge, and Pride,
MARIA reign'd, and Heav'n was on our Side.
　The Scepter by herself unsought,
Gave double Proofs of her heroick Mind;
With Skill she sway'd it, and with Ease resign'd.
So the *Dictator*, from Retirement brought,
Repell'd the Danger that did *Rome* alarm,
And then return'd contented to his Farm.

III.

　Fatal to the Fair and Young,
　　Accurs'd Disease! how long
　Have wretched Mothers mourn'd thy Rage,
Robb'd of the Hope and Comfort of their Age!
　From the unhappy Lover's Side,
How often hast thou torn the blooming Bride!
Now, like a Tyrant, rising by Degrees
To worse Extreams, and blacker Villanies,
Practis'd in Ruin for some Ages past,
Thou hast brought forth a general one at last.
　　Common Disasters Sorrow raise;
　　But Heav'n's severer Frowns amaze
　　The Queen! a Word, a Sound,
Of Nations once the Hope and firm Support,
Wealth of the Needy, Guard of the Opprest,
The Joy of all, the Wisest and the Best:
　A Name which Eccho did rebound
With loud Applause from neighb'ring Shores,
Their Admiration, the Delight of ours,
　　Becomes unutterable now.
　　The crouds in that dejected Court,
　　Where languishing MARIA lay,
Want Pow'r to ask the News they want to know:
　Silent their drooping Heads they bow,
Silence itself proclaims th' approaching Woe:
　　Ev'n MARIA's latest Care,

Whom

Whom Winter's Seasons, nor contending Jove,
Nor watchful Fleets could from his glorious Purpose move,
Intrepid in the Storms of war, and in the Midst of fly-
　　　　　　　　(ing Deaths sedate,
Now trembles, now he sinks beneath the mighty Weight.
　　The Hero to the Man gives Way,
Unhappy Isle, for half an Age a Prey
To fierce Dissention, or despotick Sway;
Redeem'd from Anarchy, to be undone
By the mistaken Measures of the Throne.
Thy Monarch's meditating dark Designs,
　　Or boldly throwing off the Mask,
Fond of the Power, unequal to the Task;
　　Thy self without remaining Signs,
　　Of antient Virtue so deprav'd,
　　As ev'n to wish to be enslav'd　　　　(so low,
What more than human Aid could raise Thee from a State
Protect Thee from thyself, thy greatest Foe?
Something Celestial sure, a Heroine
Of matchless Form, and a majestic Mien;
Awful, respected, fear'd, but more belov'd;
More than her Laws her great Example mov'd.
The Bounds that in her godlike Mind
We to her Passions set, severely shin'd,
But that of doing Good was unconfin'd:
　　So just, that absolute Command,
　　Destructive in another Hand,
In hers had chang'd its Nature, had been useful made;
　　Oh had she longer staid,
Less swiftly to her Native Heav'n retir'd!
For her the Harps of *Albion* had been strung,
The tuneful Nine could never have aspir'd
To a more lofty and immortal Song.

The

The Duke of Devonſhire's Alluſion *to the Archbiſhop of* Cambray's Telemachus.

Written in the Year 1707.

CAMBRAY, you ſet, when heav'nly Love you write,
The nobleſt Image in the cleareſt Light!
A Love, by no Self-Intereſt debas'd,
But on th' Almighty's high Perfection plac'd!
A Love, in which true piety conſiſts,
That ſoars to Heav'n without the Help of Prieſts!
Let partial *Rome* the great Attempt oppoſe,
Support the cheat from whence her Income flows:
Her Cenſures may condemn, but not confute,
If beſt your elevated Notions ſuit
With what to Reaſon ſeems th' Almighty's Due.
They have, at leaſt, an Air of being true.
And what can animated Clay produce,
Beyond a Gueſs, in Matters ſo abſtruſe?
But when, deſcending from th' Imperial Height,
You ſtoop of Sublunary Things to write,
MINERVA ſeems the Moral to diſpenſe:
How great the Subject, how ſublime the Senſe!
Not the *Aonian* Bard with ſuch a Flame
E'er ſung of *Ruling Arts*; your lofty Theme
In your TELEMACHUS, his Hero's Son,
We ſee the great Original outdone.
There is in Virtue ſure a hidden Charm,
To force Eſteem, and Envy to diſarm:
Elſe in a flatt'ring Court you ne'er had been deſign'd
T' inſtruct the future Troublers of Mankind.
Happy your native Soil, at leaſt by Nature ſo;
In none her Treaſures more profuſely flow:

The

· The Hills adorn'd with Vines, with Flow'rs the Plain,
Without the Sun's too near Approach, ferene :
But Heav'n in vain does on the Vineyards fmile,
'The Monarch's Glory mocks the Lab'rer's Toil.
What tho'elab'rate Brafs with Nature ftrive,
And proud *Equeftrian* Figures feem alive ;
With various Terrors on their Bafis wrought,
With yielding Citadels, furpriz'd or bought ?
And here the Ruins of a taken Town,
There a bombarded Steeple tumbling down :
Such Prodigies of Art, of coftly Pains,
Serve but to gild th' unthinking Rabble's Chains.
O defpicable State of all that groan
Under a blind Dependency on One !
How far inferior to the Herds that range,
With native Freedom, o'er the Woods and Plains !
With them no Fallacies of Schools prevail,
Nor of a Right Divine, the naufeous Tale,
Can give to one among themfelves the Pow'r,
Without Controul, his Fellows to devour.
To reafoning human Kind alone, belong
The Arts to hurt themfelves by reas'ning wrong.
Howe'er the foolifh Notion firft began,
Of trufting *Abfolute* to lawlefs Man :
Howe'er a Tyrant may by Force fubfift ;
For who would be a Slave that can refift ?
Thofe fet the Cafuift fafeft on the Throne,
Who make the People's Intereft their own ;
And chufing rather to be lov'd than fear'd,
Are Kings of Men, not of a fervile Herd.
O Liberty ! too late defir'd, when loft ;
Like Health, when wanted, thou art valu'd moft !
In Regions where no Property is known,
Thro' which the *Garone* runs, and rapid *Rhone*,
Where Peafants toil for Harveft not their own ;
How gladly would they quit their native Soil,
And change for Liberty their Wine and Oil !

As

As Wretches chain'd and lab'ring at the Oar,
In Sight of *Italy*'s delightful Shore,
Reflect on their unhappy Fate the more :
Thy Laws have still their Force. Above the rest
Of *Gothic* Kingdoms, happy *Albion*, bless!
Long since their antient Freedom they have lost,
And servilely of their Subjection boast.
Thy better Fate the vain Attempts resists
Of faithless Monarchs, and designing Priests ;
Unshaken yet, the Government subsists.
While Streams of Blood the Continent o'erflow,
Redd'ning the *Maese*, the *Danube*, and the *Po* ;
Thy *Thames*, auspicious Isle ! her Thunder sends,
To crush thy Foes, and to relieve her Friends.
Say Muse, since no Surprize, or foreign Stroke,
Can hurt her, guarded by her Walls of Oak,
Since wholesome Laws her Liberty transfer
To future Ages, what can *Albion* fear ?
Can she the dear-bought Treasure throw away?
Have *Universities* so great a Sway ?
The Muse is silent, cautious to reflect
On Manstons where the Muses keep their Seat.
Barren of Thought, and niggardly of Rhyme,
My creeping Number she forbids to climb :
Vent'ring too far, my weary Genius fails,
And o'er my drooping Senses Sleep prevails.
An Antique Pile, near *Thames*'s silver Stream,
Was the first Object of my airy Dream ;
In antient Times a consecrated Fane,
But since apply to Uses more prophane ;
Fill'd with a popular debating Throng,
Oft in the Right, and oftner in the Wrong;
Of Good and Bad the variable Test,
Where the Religion that was voted best
Is still inclin'd to persecute the rest,
On the high Fabrick stood a Monster fell,
Of hideous Form, second to none in Hell.

The

The Fury, to be more abhorr'd and fear'd,
Her Teeth and Jaws with Clods of Gore befmear'd,
Her particolour'd Robe obfcenely ftain'd
With pious Murders, Freemen rack'd and chain'd,
With the implacable and brutifh Rage
Of fierce Dragoons, fparing no Sex nor Age;
With all the horrid Inftruments of Death,
Of tort'ring Innocents t'improve their Faith,
Clouding the Roof with their infeƈtious Breath.
Thus fhe began: " Are then my Labours vain,
" That to the Pow'rs of *France* have added *Spain*?
" Vain my Attempts to make the Empire great;
" And fhall a Woman my Defigns defeat,
" Baffle th'infernal Projeƈts I've begun,
" And break the Meafures of my fav'rite Son?
" Tho' far unlike the Heroes of her Race,
" That made their Humours of their Laws take Place?
" And, flighting Coronation-Oaths, difdain'd
" Their high Prerogative fhould be reftrain'd,
" Tho' her own Ifle is bleft with Liberty,
" Has fhe a Right to fet all *Europe* free?
" Under this Roof, with Management, I may
" The Progrefs of her Arms at leaft delay;
" From a contagious Vapour I will blow,
" Within thefe Walls Breaches fhall wider grow:
" Here let imaginary Fears prevail;
" And give a Colour to affeƈted Zeal:
" From trivial Bills let warm Debate arife;
" Foment Sedition, and retard Supplies.
" If once my treach'rous Arts, and watchful Care,
" Break the Confed'racy, and end the War,
" Ador'd, in Hell I may in Triumph fit,
" And *Europe* to one Potentate fubmit.

Waking at fo deteftable a Sound,
Which would all Order, and all Peace confound,
I cry'd, infernal Hag! be ever dumb;
Thee, with her Arms, let *ANNA* overcome.

Here

Here *ANNA* reigns, a Queen by Heav'n beftow'd,
To right the Injur'd, and fubdue the Proud.
As *Rome* of old gave Liberty to *Greece*,
ANNA th' invaded finking Empire frees.
Th' Allies her Faith, her Pow'r the *French* proclaim,
Her Piety th' Opprefs'd, the World her Fame.
At *ANNA's* Name, dejected, pale, and fcar'd,
The execrable Phantom difappear'd.

THE

FEMALE REIGN;

AN

O D E,

Alluding to the 14th O D E of the
IVth B O O K of HORACE.

Quæ Cura Patrum, quæve Quiritium, &c.

Attempted in the Style of PINDAR.

With a LETTER to a Gentleman in the
UNIVERSITY of *CAMBRIDGE.*

S I R,

THIS comes to congratulate you on the agreeable News of fome late extraordinary Succeffes,
which have blefs'd the Arms of her Majefty and
her

her Allies. I leave you to the printed Papers for a particular Account of thofe Actions which have furpriz'd the World; and, we hope, given the laft Stroke to the languifhing Power of the Common Enemy of *Europe*. They will furnifh noble Topics for the Wit of an Univerfity, like yours, who can embellifh (if that can be done) the Glories of a *Female Reign*, with a jufter Sublimity of Verfe, than what you will find in the following Performance, which was written feveral Months ago, and not run over with a hafty Negligence. The *Ode*, from whence I take my Hint, is accounted by fome Critics not inferior to the 4th of the fame Book, which begins thus:

Qualem Miniftrum Fulminis Alitem, &c,

And was written in Compliment to *Auguftus*, on Occafion of a famous Victory gain'd by *Tiberius*, as this, which I have aim'd to imitate, was written on the Praife of *Claudius Nero*. I need not inform Men of your Reading and Letters what occafion'd both. The Poet, as he does in almoft all his *Odes*, has fhewn a peculiar Artfulnefs and Elegance, and turns all the Panegyric on the Emperor (who was not in the Action) with, *Te Concilium, & tuos præbente Divos*. If you ask wherein I have trod in the Steps of *Horace*, you will find it in the Beginning. I have only kept him in View, and ufed him only where he was ferviceable to my Defign. He took the fame Liberty with *Alcæus*, as appears from fome Fragments of that *Greek* Lyrick, quoted by *Athenæus*. In my Digreffions and Tranfitions I have taken Care to play always in Sight, and make every one of them contribute to my main Defign. This was the Way of *Pindar*; to read whom, according to *Rapin*, will give a truer Idea of the Ode, than all the Rules and Reflections of the beft Critics. I will not pretend to have div'd into him over Head and Ears; but I have endeavour'd to have made myfelf not the greateft Stranger to his Manner of Writing; which generally
consifts

confifts in the Dignity of the Sentiments, and an elegant Variety, which makes the Reader rife up with greater Satisfaction than he fate down : And that which affects the Mind in Compofitions of any Sort, will never be difagreeable to a Gentleman of Ingenuity and Judgment, I have avoided Turns, as thinking that they debafe the Loftinefs of the *Ode*. You will eafily perceive whether I have reach'd that *acer Spiritus & Vis*, recommended by *Horace*, as the Genius of Poetry. Whether you will call the following Lines no *Pindarick Ode*, or irregular Stanzas, gives me no Difturbance ; for however the feeming Wildnefs of this Sort of Verfe ought to be reftrain'd, the *Strophe, Antiftrophe*, &c. will never bear in *Englifh*; and it would fhew a ftrange Depravity in our Tafte, if it fhould, as may be witneffed by the fervile Imitation of the Dactyles and Spondees ufed by Sir PHILIP SIDNEY. But to make an End of this tedious Epiftle : You will fee through the Whole, that her *MAJESTY* is the Chief Heroine of the *Ode*; and the Moral at the End, fhews the folid Glories of a Reign, which is not founded on a pretended Juftice, or criminal Magnanimity.

Yours, &c.

S. COBB.

The FEMALE REIGN; *an* ODE.

I.

WHAT can the *Britifh* Senate give,
     To make the Name of ANNA live ?
By future People to be fung,
The Labour of each grateful Tongue.

Can

Can faithful Regifters, or Rhyme,
In charming Eloquence, or fprightly Wit,
   The Wonders of her Reign tranfmit
To th' unborn Children of fucceeding Time?
Can *Painter's* Oil, or *Statuary's* Art,
   Eternity to her impart?
No! titled Statues are but empty Things,
   Infcrib'd to Royal Vanity,
   The Sacrifice of Flattery
To lawlefs *Nero's*, or *Bourbonian* Kings.
   True Vertue to her kindred Stars afpires,
Does all our Pomp of Stone and Verfe furpafs,
   And mingling with Etherial Fires,
   No ufelefs Ornament requires,
From Speaking Colours, or from Breathing Brafs.

II.

Greateft of Princes! where the wand'ring Sun
Does o'er Earth's habitable Regions roll,
From th' *Eaftern* Barriers to the *Weftern* Goal,
   And fees thy Race of Glory run
   With Swiftnefs equal to his own.
Thee on the Banks of *Flandrian Scaldis* fings
   The jocund Swain, releas'd from *Gallic* Fear:
   The *Englifh* Voice unus'd to hear,
Thee the repeating Banks, Thee ev'ry Valley rings.
   The *Gaul,* untaught to bear the Flames
   Of thofe who drink the *Maefe* or *Thames,*
   From the *Britannick* Valour flies,
   No longer able to withftand
The Thunderbolt launch'd by a Female Hand,
   Or Light'ning darted from her Eyes.

III.

What treble Ruin pious ANNA brings
   On falfe *Electors*, perjur'd *Kings*,
Let the twice fugitive *Bavarian* tell;
Who, from his airy Hope of better State,
By Luft of Sway, irregularly Great,
   Like an Apoftate Angel fell:

Who

Who by Imperial Favour rais'd,
I'th' higheſt Rank of Glory blaz'd;
And had 'till now unrival'd ſhóne
More than a King, contented with his own.
But *Lucifer*'s bold Steps he trod,
Who durſt aſſault the Throne of GOD;
And for contented Realms of bliſsful Light,
Gain'd the ſad Privilege to be
The Firſt in ſolid Miſery,
Monarch of Hell, and Woes, and endleſs Night.
Corruption of the Beſt is Worſt,
And foul Ambition, like an evil Wind,
Blights the fair Bloſſoms of a noble Mind;
And if a Seraph fall, He's doubly curſt.

IV.

Had Guile, and Pride, and Envy grown
In the black Groves of *Styx* alone,
Nor ever had on Earth the baleful Crop been ſown;
The Swain, without Amaze, had till'd
The *Flandrian* Glebe, a guiltleſs Field:
Nor had he wonder'd, when he found
The Bones of Heroes in the Ground.
No Crimſon Streams had lately ſwell'd
The *Dyle*, the *Danube*, and the *Scheld.*
But *Evils* are of neceſſary Growth,
To rouze the Brave, and baniſh Sloth.
And ſome are born to win the Stars,
By Sweat, and Blood, and worthy Scars.
Heroic Virtue is by Action ſeen,
And Vices ſerve to make it keen;
And as Gigantick Tyrants riſe,
NASSAU's and ANNA's leave the Skies,
The Earth-born Monſters to chaſtiſe;
While *Cerberus* and *Hydra* grow
For an ALCIDES, or a MARLBOROUGH.

V.

If, Heav'nly Muſe, you burn with a Deſire
To praiſe the Man whom all admire;

F   Come

Come from thy learn'd *Castalian* Springs,
And stretch aloft thy *Pegasean* Wings :
   Strike the loud *Pindarit* Strings,
   Like the Lark, who soars and sings ;
   And as you sail the liquid Skies,
Cast on § *Menapian* Fields your weeping Eyes :
   For weep they surely must,
   To see the bloody annual Sacrifice ;
   To think how the neglected Dust,
   Which, with Contempt, is basely trod,
Was once the Limbs of Captains, brave and just,
The Mortal Part of some great Demi-God ;
   Who for thrice fifty Years of stubborn War,
   With slaught'ring Arms, the Gun and Sword.
   Have dug the mighty Sepulchre,
   And fell as Martyrs on Record,
Of Tyranny reveng'd, and Liberty restor'd.

VI.

See, where at *Audenard*, with Heaps of Slain,
   Th' Heroic Man, inspir'dly brave,
   Mowing across, bestrews the Plain,
And with new Tenants crowds the wealthy Grave
His Mind unshaken at the frightful Scene,
   His Looks as chearfully serene,
   The routed Battle to pursue,
   At once adorn'd the *Paphian* Queen,
When to her *Thracian* Paramour she flew.
   The gath'ring Troops he kens from far,
And with a Bridegroom's Passion and Delight,
Courting the War, and glowing for the Fight,
The new *Salmoneus* meets the *Celtic* Thunderer.
   Ah, cursed Pride ! Infernal Dream !
   Which drove him to this wild Extream,
   That Dust a Deity should seem ;
Be thought, as thro' the wond'ring Streets he rode,
   Th' immortal Man, or mortal God :

                              With

---

§ Menapii, *were the ancient Inhabitants of* Flanders.

With rattling Brafs, and trampling Horfe,
Should counterfeit th' inimitable Force
 Of Divine Thunder : Horrid Crime !
 But Vengeance is the Child of Time,
 And will too furely be repay'd
 On his prophane devoted Head,
 Who durft affront the Pow'rs above,
 And their eternal Flames difgrace,
Too fatal, brandifh'd by the Rightful Jove,
 Or PALLAS, who fupplies his Place.

VII.

The *Britifh Pallas !* who, as ‡ HOMER's did
  For her lov'd DIOMEDE,
 Her Hero's Mind with Wifdom fills,
And Heav'nly Courage in his Heart inftills.
Hence thro' the thickeft Squadrons does he ride,
 With ANNA's Angels by his Side.
  With what uncommon Speed
 He fpurs his foaming, fiery Steed !
 And pufhes on thro' midmoft Fires,
Where *France's* Fortune with her Sons retires.
Now here, now there, the fweepy Ruin flies ;
 † As when the *Pleiades* arife,
 The *Southern* Wind afflicts the Skies.

F 2   Then

---

‡ HOMER, *in his* Fifth ILIAD, *becaufe his Hero is to
do Wonders beyond the Power of* MAN, *premifes, in the
Beginning, that* PALLAS *had peculiarly fitted him for
that Day's Exploits.*

† *Indomitas prope qualis undas*
 Exercet Aufter, Pleiadum Choro
 Scindente Nubes, impiger Hoftium
  Vexare Turmas, & frementem
  Mittere Equum medios per Ignes.
 Sic tauriformis volvitur Aufidus,
 Qui Regna Dauni præfluit Appuli,
 Cum fævit, horrendam quo cultis
  Diluviem meditatur Agris.

Then, mutt'ring o'er the Deep, buffets th' unruly Brine,
   'Till Clouds and Water feem to join.
Or as a *Dyke* cut by malicious Hands,
   O'erflows the fertile *Netherlands*;
    Thro' the wide Yawn, th' impetuous Sea,
    Lavifh of his new *Liberty*,
Beftrides the Vale, and with tumultuous Noife,
   Bellows along the delug'd Plain,
   Deftructive to the rip'ning Grain,
   Far as th' *Horizon* he deftroys,
                         (Reign
The weeping Shepherd from an Hill bewails the wat'ry

VIII.

   So rapid flows th' unprifon'd Stream!
   So ftrong the Force of MINDELHEIM!
   In vain the Woods of *Audenard*
   Would fhield the *Gaul*, a fencelefs Guard,
   As foon may Whirl-winds be with-held,
     As his Paffage o'er the *Scheld*.
   In vain the Torrent would oppofe,
   In vain arm'd Banks, and num'rous Foes,
   Who with inglorious Hafte retire,
   Fly fafter than the River flows,
    And fwifter than our Fire.
Vendofme from far upbraids their nimble Shame,
   And pleads his Royal Mafter's Fame.
   By CONDE's mighty Ghoft, he cries,
   By TURENNE, LUXEMBURGH, and all
Thofe noble Souls, who fell a Sacrifice
At ¶ *Lens*, at *Fleurus*, and at *Landen* Fight,
Stop, I conjure you, your ignominious Flight:
   But Fear is deaf to Honour's Call.
   Each frowning Threat and foothing Pray'r
   Is loft in the regardlefs Air.

                               As

¶ *Near this Place the Prince of* Conde *gave the Spa-niards a very great Overthrow,* 1684.

As well he may
  The Billows of the Ocean flay,
  While CHURCHILL, like a driving Wind,
  Or high Spring-Tide, purfues behind,
And with redoubled Speed urges their forward Way.
            IX.
Nor lefs, EUGENIUS, thy important Care,
  Thou fecond Thunder-bolt of War!
  Partner in Danger and in Fame;
  With MARLBOROUGH's, the Winds fhall bear
To diftant Colonies, thy conqu'ring Name.
  Nor fhall my Mufe forget to fing
  From Harmony what Bleffings fpring:
To tell how Death did envioufly repine,
  To fee a Friendfhip fo divine;
When in a Ball's deftroying Shape fhe paft,
  And mark'd thy threaten'd Brow at laft:
  But durft not touch that facred Brain,
  Where the Concerns of *Europe* reign;
  For ftrait fhe bow'd her ghaftly Head;
  She faw the Mark of Heav'n, and fled,
As cruel BRENNUS once infulting *Gaul*,
  When he, at *Allia*'s fatal Flood,
  Had fill'd the Plains with *Roman* Blood,
  With confcious Awe forfook the Capitol,
  Where JOVE, Revenger of Profanenefs, ftood.
            X.
But where the Good and Brave command,
What Capitol, what Caftle can withftand?
  Virtue, as well as Gold, can pafs
  Thro' Walls of Stone, and Tow'rs of Brafs.
LISLE, like a Miftrefs, had been courted long,
And always yielded to the Bold and Young;
The faireft Progeny of *Vauban*'s Art,
  'Till SAVOY's warlik Prince withftood
Her frowning Thunders, and thro' Seas of Blood
Tore the bright Darling from th' old Tyrant's Heart.
      F 3   Such

Such * *Buda* faw him, when proud † APTI fell,
 Unhappy, Valiant Infidel !
 Who, vanquifh'd by fuperior Strength,
 Surrender'd up his haughty Breath,
Upon the Breach meafuring his manly Length,
And fhunn'd the *Bow-firing* by a nobler Death.

XI.

Such ‡ HARSCHAM's Field beheld him in his Bloom,
When Victory befpoke him for her own,
 Her Favourite, Immortal Son,
And told of better Years revolving on the Loom :
How he fhould make the *Turkifh Crefcent* wane,
 And choak § *Tibifcus* with the Slain ;
While *Viziers* lay beneath the lofty Pile
Of flaughter'd *Baffaus*, who o'er *Baffaus* roll'd,
 And all his num'rous Acts fhe told,
From *Latian Carpi* down to *Flandrian* LISLE.

         Where

---

 * *He bore a confiderable Share in the Glory of that Day on which* Buda *was taken.*
 † *He was* Baffau *of the City, and loft his Life on the Breach.*

VICEM GERIT ILLA TONANTIS.

 ‡ *This was the fatal Battle to the* Turks *in the Year* 1687. *Prince* EUGENE, *with the Regiments of his Brigade, was the firft that enter'd the Trenches ; and for that Reafon had the Honour to be the firft Meffenger of this happy News to the Emperor.*

 § *This Battle was fought on the* 10th *of* October, 1697. *where Prince* EUGENE *commanded in Chief ; in which there never happen'd fo great and fo terrible a Deftruction to the* Ottoman *Army, which fell upon the principal Commanders more than the common Soldiers ; for no lefs than fifteen* Baffaus (*five of which had been* Viziers *of the Bench*) *were killed, befides the fupreme* Vizier.

Where ev'ry Day new Conquests should produce,
    Labour for Envy and a Muse :
    Where, with her rattling Trumpet's Sound,
      Fame should shake the Hills around ;
Should tell how WEBB, nigh woody *Wynendale,*
Argu'd each Inch of that important Ground.
      So much in Vertue's Scale
    True Valour Numbers can out-do,
And Thousands are but Cyphers to a Few.

XII.

Honour, with open Arms, receives at last
The Heroes who thro' Vertue's Temple past ;
    And show'rs down Laurels from Above,
    On those whom Heav'n and ANNA love.
    And some, not sparingly, she throws
    For the young Eagles, who could try
    The Faith and Judgment of the Sky,
    And dare the Sun with steady Eye,
    For *Hanover's* and *Prussia* Brows,
Eugenes in Bloom, and future *Marlboroughs.*
To *Hanover,* *Brunswiga's* second Grace,
Descendant from a long Imperial Race,
The Muse directs an unaffected Flight,
And prophesies, from so serene a Morn,
    To what clear Glories he is born,
When blazing with a full *Meridian* Light,
He shall the *British* Hemisphere adorn :
When *Mars* shall lay his batter'd Target down,
    And he (since Death will never spare
    The Good, the Pious, and the Fair)
    In his ripe Harvest of Renown,
    Shall after his Great Father sit,
    (If Heav'n so long a Life permit)
    And having swell'd the flowing Tide
    Of Fame, which he in Arms shall get,
    The Purchase of an honest Sweat,
Shall safe in stormy Seas *Britannia's* Vessel guide.

XIII.

Britannia's Veffel, which in A n n a's Reign.,
And prudent Pilotry, enjoys
The Tempeft which the World deftroys,
And rides triumphant o'er the fubject Main ;
O may fhe foon a quiet Harbour gain !
    And fure the promis'd Hour is come,
    When in foft Notes the Peaceful Lyre
    Shall ftill the Trumpet and the Drum,
    ,Shall play what Gods and Men defire,
    And ftrike Bellona's Mufick Dumb.
When War, by Parents curs'd, fhall quit the Field,
Unbuckle his bright Helmet, and to reft
His weary'd Limbs, fits on his idle Shield,
With Scars of Honour plow'd upon his Breaft.
But if the Gallic Pharaoh's ftubborn Heart
Grows frefh for Punifhment, and hardens ftill,
Prepar'd for th' irrecoverable Ill,   (Part :
And force the unwilling Skies to act the laft ungrateful
Thy Forces A n n a, like a Flood, fhall whelm
(If Heav'n does fcepter'd Innocence maintain)
    His famifh'd defolated Realm ;
And all the Sons of Pharamond in vain
    (Who with Difhoneft Envy fee
The fweet forbidden Fruits of diftant Liberty)
Shall curfe their rigid Salic Law, and wifh a Female Reign.

XIV.

    A Female Reign like thine,
    O Anna, Britifh Heroine !
To the afflicted Empires fly for Aid,
Where'er Tyrannic Standards are difplay'd,
From the wrong'd Iber to the threaten'd Rhine.
Thee, where the Golden-fanded Tagus flows
    Beneath fair * Ulyffippo's Wal's,
    The frighted Lufitanian calls :

                                    Thee.

---

* The old Name of Lifbon, faid to be built by Ulyffes.

Thee, they who drink the *Sein*, with thofe
   Who plow *Iberian* Fields, implore,
   To give the lab'ring Wood repofe;
   And univerfal Peace reftore,
Thee, *Gallia*, mournful to furvive the Fate
Of her fall'n Grandeur, and departed State
   By fad Experience taught to own,
That Virtue is a fafer Way to rife,
   A fhorter Paffage to the Skies,
Than *Pelion*, upon *Offa* thrown :
For they, who by deny'd Attempts prefume
   To reach the Starry Thrones, become
Sure Food for Thunder, and condemn'd to howl!
In § *Ætna*, or in † *Arima* to roll,
   By an inevitable Doom,
Gain but an higher Fall, a Mountain for their Tomb.

---

§ † *Two Mountains where* Jupiter *lodged the* Giants.

✿✿✿✿✿✿✿✿✿✿✿✿✿✿✿✿✿✿

An E S S A Y *on* P O E T R Y.

By the the Duke of Buckinghamfhire.

OF Things in which Mankind does moft excel,
   Nature's chief Mafter-piece is Writing well ;
And of all Sorts of Writing, none there are
That can the leaft with *Poetry* compare :
No Kind of Work requires fo nice a Touch ;
And if well finifh'd, nothing fhines fo much.
But Heav'n forbid we fhould be fo prophane,
To grace the *Vulgar* with that facred Name.

'Tis

'Tis not a Flash of Fancy, which fometimes,
Dazling our Minds, fets off the flighteft Rhymes;
Bright as a Blaze, but in a Moment done;
True Wit is everlafting, like the Sun;
Which, tho' fometimes behind a Cloud retir'd,
Breaks out again, and is by all admir'd.
Numbers, and Rhyme, and that harmonious Sound
Which never does the Ear with harfhnefs wound,
Are neceffary, yet but vulgar Arts;
For all in vain thefe fuperficial Parts
Contribute to the Structure of the whole,
Without a Genius too, for that's the Soul:
A Spirit, which infpires the Work throughout,
As that of Nature moves the World about:
A Heat, which glows in every Word that's writ;
'Tis fomething of Divine, and more than Wit;
It felf unfeen, yet all Things by it fhown,
Defcribing all Men, but defcrib'd by none.
Where doft thou dwell? What Caverns of the Brain
Can fuch a vaft and mighty Thing contain?
When I, at idle Hours, in vain thy Abfence mourn,
O where doft thou retire? And why doft thou return
Sometimes with powe'ful Charms to hurry me away
From Pleafures of the Night, and Bus'nefs of the Day?
E'en now, too far tranfported, I am fain
To check thy Courfe, and ufe the needful Rein.
As all is Dullnefs when the Fancy's bad;
So, whithout Judgment, Fancy is but mad;
And Judgment has a boundlefs Influence,
Not only in the Choice of Words or Senfe,
But on the World, on Manners, and on Men:
Fancy is but the Feather of the Pen.
Reafon is that fubftantial ufeful Part,
Which gains the Head, while t'other wins the Heart.
Here I fhould all the various Sorts of Verfe,
And the whole *Art of Poetry* rehearfe:
But who that Tafk can after *Horace* do?
The beft of Mafters and Examples too!

Ecchoes

Ecchoes at beft ; all we can fay is vain,
Dull the Defign, and fruitlefs were the Pain.
'Tis true, the Antients we may rob with Eafe :
But who with that fad Shift himfelf can pleafe ?
Without an Actor's Pride, a Player's Art
Is above his who writes a borrow'd Part.
Yet modern Laws are made for later Faults,
And new Abfurdities infpire new Thoughts.
What Need has *Satyr*, then, to live on Theft,
When fo much frefh Occafion ftill is left ?
Fertile our Soil, and full of rankeft Weeds,
And Monfters worfe than ever *Nilus* breeds.
But hold, the Fools fhall have no Caufe to fear ;
'Tis Wit and Senfe that is the Subject here.
Defects of witty Men deferve a Cure,
And thofe who are fo, will e'en this endure.

First then of S o n g s, which now fo much abo
Without his Song no Fop is to be found ;
A moft offenfive Weapon, which he draws
On all he meets, againft *Apollo*'s Laws.
Tho' nothing feems more eafy, yet no Part
Of *Poety* requires a nicer Art ;
For as in Rows of richeft Pearl there lies
Many a Blemifh that efcapes our Eyes,
The leaft of which Defects is plainly fhown
In fome fmall Ring, and brings the Value down :
So Songs fhall be to juft Perfection wrought ;
Yet where can we fee one without a Fault ?
Exact Propriety of Words and Thought,
Expreffion eafy, and the Fancy high,
Yet that not feem to creep, nor this to fly ;
No Words tranfpos'd, but in fuch Order all,
As, tho' hard wrought, may feem by Chance to fall.
Here, as in all Things elfe, is moft unfit
Bare Ribaldry, that poor Pretence to Wit :
Such naufeous Songs by a late Author made,
Call an unwilling Cenfure on his Shade.
Not that warm Thoughts of the tranfporting Joy,
Can fhock the Chafteft, or the Niceft cloy ;   Bnt

But Words obfcene, too grofs to move Defire,
Like Heaps of Fuel, do but choak the Fire,
On other Themes he well deferves our Praife,
Here palls that Appetite he meant to raife.

Next E L E G Y, of fweet but folemn Voice,
And of a Subject grave, exacts the Choice;
The Praife of Beauty, Valour, Wit, contains ;
And there too oft defpairing Love complains,
In vain, alas ! for who, by Wit, is mov'd ?
The Phœnix She deferves to be belov'd.
But noify Nonfenfe, and fuch Fops as vex
Mankind, take moft with that fantaftic Sex.
This to the Praife of thofe who better knew,
The Many raife the Value of the Few.
But here, as all our Sex too oft have try'd,
Women have drawn my wand'ring Thoughts afide.
Their greateft Fault, who in this Kind have writ,
Is not defect in Words, nor Want of Wit :
But fhould this Mufe harmonious Numbers yield,
And ev'ry Couplet be with Fancy fill'd,
If yet a juft Coherence be not made,
Between each Thought, and the whole Model laid
So right that ev'ry Step may higher rife,
Like Goodly Mountains, 'till they reach the Skies :
Trifles, like fuch perhaps of late have paft,
And may be lik'd awhile, but never laft.
'Tis *Epigram*, 'tis *Point*, 'tis what you will :
But not an *Elegy*, nor writ with Skill ;
No § *Panegyric*, nor a ‖ *Cooper's-Hill*.

A higher Flight, and of a happier Force,
Are O D E S, the Mufes moft unruly Horfe
That bounds fo fierce, the Rider has no Reft,
But foams at Mouth, and moves like one poffeft.
The Poet here muft be indeed infpir'd
With Fury too, as well as Fancy fir'd.

C O W L E Y.

§ *Waller.*   ‖ *Denham.*

COWLEY might boaſt to have perform'd this Part,
Had he with Nature join'd the Rules of Art ;
But ill Expreſſions ſometimes gives Allay
To that rich Fancy which can ne'er decay.
Tho' all appear in Heat and Fury done,
The Language ſtill muſt ſoft and eaſy run,
Theſe Laws may ſeem a little too ſevere ;
But Judgment yields, and Fancy governs there ;
Which, tho' extravagant, this Muſe allows,
And makes the Work much eaſier than it ſhows.
   Of all the Ways that wiſeſt Men could find,
To mend the Age, and mortify Mankind,
SATIRE well writ has moſt ſucceſsful prov'd,
And Cures, becauſe the Remedy is lov'd.
'Tis hard to write on ſuch a Subject more,
Without repeating Things ſaid oft before.
Some vulgar Errors only we remove,
That ſtain a Beauty which ſo much we love.
Of well-choſe Words ſome take not Care enough,
And think they ſhould be, as the Subject, rough.
This Poem muſt be more exactly made,
And ſharpeſt Thoughts in ſmootheſt Words convey'd,
Some thinks if ſharp enough, they cannot fail,
As if their only Buſ'neſs was to rail :
But human Frailty nicely to unfold,
Diſtinguiſhes a *Satyr* from a *Scold.*
Rage you muſt hide, and Prejudice lay down ;
A Satyr's Smile is ſharper than his Frown :
So, while you ſeem to ſlight ſome Rival Youth,
Malice itſelf may ſometimes paſs for Truth.
The * *Laureat* here may juſtly claim our Praiſe,
Crown'd by † *Mac-Fleckno* with immortal Bays ;

Tho'

---

* *Mr.* Dryden.
† *A famous Satyrical Poem of his on Mr.* Shadwell.

Tho' prais'd and punish'd for another's ‡ Rhymes,
His own deserve as great Applause sometimes.
But once his *Pegasus* has born dead Weight, ‖
Rid by some lumpish Minister of State,
Here, rest my Muse, suspend my Cares a while,
A greater Enterprize attends thy Toil.
As some young Eagle that designs to fly
A long unwonted Journey thro' the Sky,
Considers all the dangerous Way before,
Over what Lands and Seas she is to soar;
Doubts her own Strength so far, and justly fears
That lofty Road of airy Travellers:
But yet incited by some fair Design,
That does her Hopes beyond her Fears incline,
Prunes ev'ry Feather, views herself with Care,
At last resolv'd, she cleaves the yielding Air.
Away she flies, so strong, so high, so fast,
She lessens to us, and is lost at last.

So (but too weak for such a weighty Thing)
The Muse inspires a sharper Note to sing:
And why should Truth offend, when only told
To guide the Ignorant, and warm the Bold?
On then, my Muse, advent'rously engage
To give Instructions that concern the Stage.

The Unities of Action, Time, and Place,
which, if observ'd; give PLAYs so great a Grace,
Are, tho' but little practis'd, too well known
To be taught here, were we pretend alone
From nicer Faults to purge the present Age,
Less obvious Errors of the *English* Stage.

First then, *Soliloquies* had need be few,
Extreamly short, and spoke in Passion too;
Our Lovers talking to themselves, for want
Of others, make the Pit their Confident:

Nor

---

‡ *A Copy of Verses, called An Essay on Satire, for which Mr. Dryden was both Applauded and Beaten, tho' not only Innocent, but Ignorant of the whole Matter.*
‖ *The* Hind *and* Panther.

Nor is the Matter mended yet, if thus
They truft a Friend, only to tell it us.
Th' Occafion fhould as naturally fall,
As when ‖ B e l l a r i o confeffes all.
   Figures of Speech, which Poets think fo fine,
Art's needlefs Varnifh, to make Nature fhine,
Are all but Paint upon a beauteous Face,
And in Defcription only claim a Place:
But to mke Rage declaim, and Grief difcourfe,
From Lovers in Defpair fine Things to force,
Muft needs fucceed ; for who can chufe but pity
A dying Hero miferably witty?
But oh! the Dialogues, where Jeft and Mock
Is held up, like a Reft at Shittle-cock!
Or elfe, like Bells, eternally they chime ;
They Sigh in Simile, and die in Rhime,
What Things are thefe, who would be Poets thought,
By Nature not infpir'd, nor Learning taught?
Some Wit they have, and therefore may deferve
A better Courfe than this, by which they ftarve.
But to write Plays! why, 'tis a bold Pretence
To Judgment, Breeding, Wit, and Eloquence :
Nay more, for they muft look within to find
Thofe fecret turns of Nature in the Mind.
Whithout this Part, in vain would be the Whole,
And but a Body all without a Soul.
All this together yet is but a Part,
Of Dialogue, that great and Pow'rful Art,
Now almoft loft, which the old *Græcians* knew, ⎫
From whom the *Romans* fainter Copies drew, ⎬
Scarce comprehended, fince but by a few. ⎭
P l a t o and L u c i a n are the beft Remains
Of all the Wonders which this Art contains :
Yet to ourfelves we Juftice muft allow,
S h a k e s p e a r and F l e t c h e r are the Wonders now.
Confider then, and read them o'er and o'er,
Go fee them play'd, then read them as before ;   For

‖ *In* Philafter, *a Play of* Beaumont *and* Fletcher,

For tho' in many Things they grosly fail,
Over our Passions still they so prevail,
That our own Grief by theirs is rock'd asleep;
The Dull are forc'd to feel, the Wise to weep,
Their Beauties imitate, avoid their Faults.
First on a Plot employ thy careful Thoughts;
Turn it with Time a thousand several Ways:
This oft alone has giv'n Success to Plays.
Reject that vulgar Error, which appears
So fair, of making perfect Characters:
There's no such Thing in Nature, and you'll draw
A faultless Monster, which the World ne'er saw.
Some Faults must be, that his Misfortunes drew,
But such as may deserve Compassion too.
Besides the main Design compos'd with Art,
Each moving Scene must be a Plot apart.
Contrive each little Turn, mark ev'ry Place,
As Painters first chaulk out the future Face:
Yet be not fondly your own Slave for this;
But change hereafter what appears amiss.
Think not so much where shining Thoughts to place,
As what a Man would say in such a Case.
Neither in Comedy will this suffice,
The Player too, must be before your Eyes;
And tho' 'tis Drudgery to stoop so low,
To him you must your utmost Meaning show.
  Expose no single Fop; but lay the Load
More equally, and spread the Folly broad.
The other Way is vulgar; oft we see
The Fool derided by as bad as he.
Hawks fly at noble Game; in this low Way
A very Owl may prove a Bird of Prey.
Ill Poets so, will one poor Fop devour;
But to collect, like Bees, from ev'ry Flow'r,
Ingredients to compose that precious Juice,
Which serves the World for Pleasure and for Use,

In

In spite of Faction, this would Favour get;
But * FALSTAFF seems inimitable yet.
   Another Fault which often does befal,
Is, when the Wit of some great Poet shall,
So overflow, that is, be none at all,
That all his Fools speak Sense, as if possest,
And each, by Inspiration, breaks his Jest.
If once the Justness of each Part be lost,
Well may we laugh, but at the Poet's Cost.
That silly Thing Men call Sheer-Wit, avoid,
With which our Age so nauseously is cloy'd.
Humour is all, Wit should be only brought
To turn agreeably some proper Thought.
But since the Poets we of late have known,
Shine in no Dress so much as in their own;
The better by Example to convince,
Cast but a View on this wrong Side of Sense.
   First a Soliloquy is calmly made,
Where ev'ry Reason is exactly weigh'd;
Which once perform'd, most opportunely comes
A Hero frighted at the Noise of Drums,
For her sweet Sake, whom at first Sight he loves,
And all in *Metaphor* his Passion proves;
But some sad Accident, tho' yet unknown,
Parting this Pair, to leave the Swain alone.
   He streight grows jealous, yet we know not why;
And, to oblige his Rival, needs must die:
But first he makes a Speech, wherein he tells,
The absent Nymph, how much his Flame excels,
And yet bequeaths her generously now
To that dear Rival whom he does not know;
Who streight appears, but who can Fate withstand?
To late, alas! to hold his hasty Hand,
That just has giv'n himself the cruel Stroke,
At which this very Stranger's Heart is broke;

He

---

* *An admirable Character in* Shakespear's HENRY
the IVth.

He more to his new Friend than Miftrefs kind,
Mourns fadly mourns at being left behind;
Of fuch a Death prefers the pleafing Charms
To Love, and living in a Lady's Arms.
How fhameful, and what monft'rous Things are thefe?
And then they rail at thofe they cannot pleafe;
Conclude us only partial to the Dead,
And grudge the Sign of old BEN JOHNSON's Head:
When the intrinfick Value of the Stage,
Can fcarce be judg'd, but by a following Age;
For Dances, Flutes, *Italian* Songs, and Rhime,
May keep up finking Nonfenfe for a Time:
But that may fail, which now fo much o'er rules,
And Senfe no longer will fubmit to Fools.

By painful Steps we are at laft got up
Parnaffus Hill, on whofe bright airy Top
The *Epic Poets* fo divinely fhow,
And with juft Pride behold the reft below.
Heroic Poems have a juft Pretence
To be the utmoft Reach of humane Senfe;
A Work of fuch ineftimable Worth,
There are but two the World has yet brought forth,
HOMER and VIRGIL; with what awful Sound
Do thefe meer Words the Ears of Poets wound!
Juft as a Changeling feems below the reft
Of Men, or rather is a two-legg'd Beaft;
So thefe *Gigantic* Souls, amaz'd, we find
As much above the reft of human Kind,
Nature's whole Strength united; endlefs Fame,
And univerfal Shouts attend their Name.
Read HOMER once, and you can read no more,
For all Things elfe appear fo dull and poor:
Verfe will feem Profe; yet often on him look,
And you will hardly need another Book.
Had * Boffu never writ, the World had ftill,
Like *Indians*, view'd this wond'rous Piece of Skill;

A3

---

* A celebrated *French Author*, who in his *Treatife* upon Epic
Poetry, drew all his Examples from HOMER.

As fomething of Divine the Work admir'd,
Not hop'd to be inftructed, but infpir'd:
But he, difclofing facred Myfteries,
Has fhewn where all the Magick lies.
Defcrib'd the Seeds, and in what Order fown,
That have to fuch a vaft Proportion grown.
Sure from fome Angel he this Secret knew,
Who thro' this Labyrinth has giv'n the Clue.
But what, alas! avails it poor Mankind,
To fee this promis'd Land, yet ftay behind?
The Way is fhewn; but who has Strength to go?
Who can all Sciences exactly know?
Whofe Fancy flies beyond weak Reafon's Sight,
And yet has Judgment to direct it right?
Whofe juft Difcernment, VIRGIL-like, is fuch,
Never to fay too little, or too much?
Let fuch a Man begin without Delay,
But he muft do much more than I can fay;
Muft above COWLEY, nay, and MILTON too, prevail,
Succeed where great TORQUATO, and our greater SPEN-
                                          (CER fail,

To the QUEEN, on the Death of His Royal Highnefs Prince GEORGE of DENMARK, 1708.

By JOSEPH TRAPP, D. D.

WHEN weeping Majefty thro' Clouds appears,
And all *Britannia's* Hope diffolves in Tears,
'Tis univerfal Grief; and all would fhow
Their Zeal to leffen fuch important Woe.
While others various Arts of Comfort ufe;
Accept of mine, Great Princefs, nor refufe
The Confolations of th' officious Mufe,

Who

Who fighs for you, and labours in his Turn,
To heal that Sorrow, while Kingdoms mourn.
　　With Caufe indeed you grieve, with might Caufe
Lament harfh Deftiny's refiftlefs Laws,
When the dear Partner of our Joys and Cares
No more furvives, no more our Counfel fhares;
No longer lives t'adorn your Court, and blefs
Your warlike Reign with all the Sweets of Peace,
To heighten Fortune's Smiles, allay her Frowns,
And eafe the long Fatigues that waits on Crowns,
All was harmonious; no Difpute between
Th' ambiguous Rights of Confort and of QUEEN,
When mutual Tendernefs unqueftion'd fway'd,
And both, or neither, govern'd or obey'd.
How did the pious Royal Pair improve
The brighteft Patterns of Connubial Love!
Which ftill in all fhall Admiration raife;
O! would they imitate, as well as praife.
　　In Life's Decay, to Sicknefs forc'd to yield,
He fought, 'tis true, no Laurels in the Field:
How could he then thofe tedious Toils fuftain,
With lab'ring Lungs that heav'd for Breath with Pain?
How range the thick'ning Squadrons into Form,
Or reach th' uncertain Battle when to ftorm?
As when his Strength, not yet in its Decline,
Stood firm, and gave the Hero Leave to fhine.
When oft renown'd in Northern Wars, he led
His hardy *Danes*, and charged at their Head,
With fwift Deftruction crufh'd the valiant *Swede*;
Refcu'd the finking Brother from the Foe,
And fav'd a King and Kingdom at a Blow.
　　Or when he march'd with WILLIAM's Arms to join,
And fhar'd with him the Glory of the *Boyne*.
Nor, when retir'd, did all his Labours ceafe;
Silent, but not inglorious, was his Eafe.
Your Realms with delegated Rule he aw'd,
Gentle at Home, as rough and brave Abroad.

Thus

Thus always led by Fame's or Virtue's Charms,
An Hero still in Piety, or Arms.
   Tho' all thefe Honours to himfelf are due,
One more confpicuous he derives from you;
Confort to fuch a QUEEN! That deathlefs Name
Shall add the brighteft Luftre to his Fame;
Immortalize his Glory, and out-fhine
All Regal Titles, but the *Right Divine.*
   A Prince fo excellent you needs muft grieve
To lofe, but Heav'n rejoices to receive:
Ceafe then your Sighs; while languifhing you fit,
Britannia's Genius weeping at your Feet,
The Bufinefs of the World fufpended ftands,
Nor circulates without your dread Commands.
   So if that Part which all the Body guides,
Where the Nerves meet, and where the Soul refides,
The leaft Diforder feels, the whole Machine
Is pale without, and all untun'd within:
The vital Springs their active Force forget,
And all the lazy Pulfes faintly beat.
   Enough to Grief you then refign'd your Breaft,
Profufe and lavifh of your Royal Reft;
When negligent of all your Pomp and State,
Clofe by the gafping Prince you penfive fate;
Outwatch'd the Stars with wat'ry fleeplefs Eyes,
With Vows inceffant importun'd the Skies;
And vainly ftruggling with relentlefs Death,
Hung on his trembling Lips and catch'd his flying Breath.
   As much as could from Deftiny be gain'd,
Your unexampled Piety obtain'd:
Long doubtful did his lifted Hand forbear
The threat'ned Stroke, which hov'ring hung in Air,
Your Pray'rs with Heav'n maintain'd a dubious Strife,
His Soul long fluttering on the Verge of Life,
And by a gradual Death at laft fet free,
To foften Fate, and fmooth it's harfh Decree.
   Nor weep, as if your Glory too were dead,
And all your Joys with your lov'd Confort fled,

No

No more he holds your Pow'r in either Hand,
One to controul the Sea, and one the Land:
Yet Sov'reign o'er these Isles you still remain,
And in our willing Hearts triumphant reign:
Yet still your Fleets the liquid Empire keep,
And ride Majestick o'er the boundless Deep.
Abroad your conqu'ring Troops lament your Loss
In dreadful Grief, pernicious to your Foes.
Soon as the News was to the Camp convey'd,
On *Lisle's* retarding Citadel employ'd,
Murm'ring they paus'd, and Tidings to enquire,
With Arms reclin'd, and stopt their Storms of Fire;
But soon discharg'd their Fury on the *Gauls,*
And pour'd fresh Ruin on their shatter'd Walls.
MARLB'ROUGH and EUGENE still your Thunder wield,
In spite of Winter, and maintain the Field;
Always victorious, they the Foe engage,
Like Winter Tempests, with redoubled Rage;
Teaching his scatter'd Troops no more to dare
To stand the sweeping Whirlwind of their War,
Fir'd with new Courage, farther we advance
On hostile Ground, and closely press on *France.*
Britannia's QUEEN, and all *Britannia's* Pow'rs,
Level their Bolts at *Gallia's* haughty Tow'rs,
More terrible in Grief: So Lightnings fly,
Redd'ning the horrid Gloom, when Clouds obscure the Sky.
    Let all your Conquests for his Death attone,
Forget Fate's Triumphs, and improve your own.
Chiefly to you the Godlike Prince is lost;
But think, Oh! think, you grieve at *Europe's* cost,
And least should mourn him, through you lose him most. ⎠
    And you, who near your weeping Sov'reign wait,
And share the melancholy Pomp of State,
Use all your Female Tenderness, and find
The gentlest Arts to recompose her Mind:
Nor with unskilful pious Haste increase
The swelling Passion which you strive to ease;

But

But footh the Pain awhile, and bring Relief,
With all the foftest Elegance of Grief.
In fad complaining Sounds her Sighs return,
And own, your QUEEN has wond'rous Caufe to mourn.
But then intreat her to regard our Fears,
And count the vaft Expence of Royal Tears.
  May Heav'n, and fhe, if Heav'n our Crimes can fpare,
Make that ineftimable Life their Care.
That we implore, with anxious Fears opprefs'd,
Sollicitous for That, and thoughtlefs of the reft.

✿ ✿ ✿ ✿ ✿ ✿ ✿ ✿ ✿ ✿ ✿ ✿ ✿ ✿ ✿ ✿ ✿ ✿ ✿

A POEM on the Death of our Late Moft Gracious Sovereign Queen ANNE; and the Acceffion of His Moft Excellent Majefty King GEORGE, 1714.

Tranflated from the *Latin* of Bifhop Smalridge. By
Mr. S E W E L L.

WHEN her *Britannia* wept ELIZA's Doom,
    And mourn'd with equal Tears *Maria's* Tomb,
As each deferv'd, each equal Mufes drew,
Nor to their Heav'n without a Poet flew;
But now, what bolder Wing her Fame fhall try?
Who follow ANNA thro' the boundlefs Sky?
Who fhall defcribe, in an exalted Strain,
The Wars and Triumphs of a *Female Reign?*
Who Nations in eternal Leagues rehearfe,
And Peace well worthy an eternal Verfe?
  Thou, * *Sacred Dome*, whom Royal Founders claim,
Wonted of old to grace the Royal Name,

                               And

* Chrift-Church.

And with a § hundred tuneful Tongues return
Thy grateful Sorrow to each Prince's Urn.
Do thou with proper Notes the Youth infpire;
Breath VIRGIL's Trumpet, touch the HORACIAN Lyre.
So may thy Walls to ancient Splendor rife,
And thy *Athenian* Turrets mate the Skies!
   And thou, whofe lib'ral Hand my Fortunes rais'd,
O QUEEN! for ever lov'd, for ever prais'd;
Receive the Tribute which my Numbers bring,
While the Mufe ftrikes the *Elegiac* String:
While Life was thine, how much to thee I owe,
How plenteous did thy ftreams of Bleffing flow?
O! how I grieve, for all thy Bounty gave,
To bring this mournful Off'ring to thy Grave,
No Time fhall ever from my Mind deface
Thy Looks, thy Glories, and diviner Grace.
But moft thy ancient Truth, thy pious Soul,
With conftant Glowings in thy Bofom roll:
The dear Rememb'rance ever is impreft,
What Love of true Religion warm'd thy Breaft!
‖ Pleas'd I revolve, as often as I brought
The Suppliant's Prayer, and for the Wretched fought:
How kind you heard, how plenteous pour'd your Store
And tho' I ask'd for much, you granted more.
Thus at your Sight Afflictions grew more mild,
And Fortune loft her Anger as you fmil'd.
   O had but envious Death made fome Delay,
And not fo hafty fnatch'd the Royal Prey:
Then (may her Promifes to me be fhown)
Thy Mufes, *Oxford*, had her Bleffings known.
What Domes, O facred *Mother*, hadft thou feen,
The pious Gift of a religious QUEEN!
How had another *Area* rais'd its Head,
And fcornful o'er its ancient Ruins fpread!
What Walls had rofe! what lofty Turrets crown'd,
Theme for thy Sons in future Days to found.   But

---

§ *The Number of Students.*
‖ *He was Lord Almoner to her Majefty.*

But now, when here the Trav'ller turns his Eyes,
And, ah! the great unfinish'd Labour spies;
A double Pity rises from his View,
He mourns the Publick Loss, and *Oxford too.*
  Who shall *Britannia's* falling State sustain?
Who fix the Empire of the Land and Main?
Who ANNA's Greatness and her Virtues bear,
And sooth with equal Pity all our Care?
  O thou, to whom the Pious Queen resign'd
A Scepter equal to thy mighty Mind,
O come, Auspicious! urge the happy Way,
And bless thy Subjects with a brighter Day.
The Nobles Thee, the Fathers Thee require,
The People Thee, their Guardian God, desire
And haply, if the Care of Publick Weight
Shall call you from the Pomp and Noise of State;
And here incline you in our calm Retreat,
To taste the Pleasures of the Muses Seat.
Then, Mighty Prince, you better here will see
What ANNA left to be perform'd by Thee.
Then better shall this *Royal House* proclaim }
What Reverence she paid to ANNA's Name, }
While to her SUCCESSOR she pays the same, }

‡‡‡‡‡‡‡‡‡‡‡‡‡‡‡‡‡‡‡‡‡‡‡‡‡‡‡‡‡‡

The DREAM.

Occasioned by the Death of Queen ANNE.

By Aaron Hill, *Esq;*

SLow-rising Night had her black Flag unfurl'd,
 And spread her sooty Mantle o'er the World;
The waning Moon shed, Pale, a sickly Light,
And Stars scarce twinkled to th' enquiring Sight:

G   Half

Half the loft Earth, by Darkneſs over-run,
Wept, in cold Dews, the Abſence of the Sun :
The Waves were huſh'd, the Winds forgot to roar,
And Storms, detach'd in Breezes, cours'd the Shore.
The mix'd Creation was involv'd in Sleep,
Fiſhes roll'd, ſlumb'ring, thro' the ſtagnate Deep ;
Beaſts, Birds and Serpents, various Beds poſſeſt,
Some in thick Woods, ſome in dark Caverns, reſt :
Antipathies, in common Sleep, took Part ;
Care curs'd nor thought ; and Woe forgot to ſmart :
Immerg'd in Reſt, my drowſy Senſes lay,
And Death's proud Image practis'd on my Clay ;
But, while, diſdainful of the mean Controll,
No dull Deſires invade my wakeful Soul,
Active, th' Inſpirer, ſkilful to purſue,
Thro' the wild Tracks of mazy Mem'ry flew ;
There, ſcatter'd Images to Union brought,
And form'd this wondrous Viſion to my Thought.

I found myſelf, at Dead of deepeſt Night,
Chear'd by no glimm'ring Spark of Remnant Light,
Lock'd in that ancient, venerable Pile,
Which holds her ſacred Duſt, who lately bleſt our Iſle !
Aſcending Damps the gloomy Concave ſought,
And hung, impriſon'd, to th' impervious Vault.
While my ſhod Feet trac'd ſwift the dusky Round,
Hoarſe Echo's multiply'd the trampling Sound !
The ſweating Stones diſtill'd a noiſome Dew,
And Earthy Scents my Death-fed Noſtrils drew !
Cold Froſts of Fear pierc'd keen thro' ev'ry Part ;
And ſhiv'ring Agues ſhook my Ice-bound Heart ;
A hollow Wind, from whiſtling Murmurs, bore
Its gathering Din more high, and ſtrove to roar !
The tatter'd Trophies fan'd the priſon'd Air :
And chill Amazement ſtiffen'd up my Hair !

While fix'd I ſtood, intent on Rumblings near ;
And diſtant Groans alarm'd my aking Ear !
Sudden, the Temple, § ſhone with ruſhing Light,
And new-born Terrors overwhelm'd my *Sight!*

§ *Weſtminſter-Abbey.*

'Ghosts, from the loos'ning Pavement, raise their Head,
And yawning Graves disclose their shrowded Dead!
Shot up, in Streams, a Mist of Spirits rise,
As morning Exhalations streak the Skies.
Soul-freezing Horror tingled thro' my Blood,
And curdling Fear bound hard the vital Flood!
Unbending Nerves their dying Vigour lost,
And drooping Life scarce held her dangerous Post:
Large Drops of Sweat from every Finger shed,
And all the Frame of Nature shook with Dread.

From the East End, where mouldring Monarchs lie,
And Worms, luxuriant, feast on Royalty;
Where each proud Tomb some Dust of Princes boasts,
There marches out a Troop of Sovereign Ghosts!
Each, in his Shadowy Hand, a Scepter brings,
Th' acknowledg'd Mark of Power in living Kings!
A glitt'ring Diadem each Forehead wore;
Their Robes trail'd loose, and swept the honour'd Floor!
With slow, and stately Stride, the Monarchs tread,
And ev'ry Meaner Spirit bows its Head!
In foremost Ranks, as latest known to Fame,
The grave-brow'd Ghost of awful ANNA came!
Calm, and Serene, the silent Walks they trace,
And halt, regardful, at each solemn Place.
Visit each Tomb, and in mysterious State,
Hail the dry Remnant of the wasted *Great.*

This Pomp of Death, thus, wore half Night away,
And came, at length, where DENMARK's Body lay;
There ANNA staid, and looking careful round,
With shadowy Scepter touch'd the conscious Ground:
'Tis strange, she sigh'd, that he, whom most I blest,
Has never thank'd me, since I came to Rest!

The willing Ghost his marbly Fetters broke,
And rose up, slowly, at the pow'rful Stroke:
An Air of Sorrow bent his serious Head;
His Eyes some seeming Tears, reluctant, shed:
With folded Arms, and discontented Look,
Thrice bow'd he gently, and thus faintly spoke;

G 2　　　　　　　Hail!

Hail! Happy Shade! rest here, unforc'd to reign,
Nor toil, to save a stubborn Land, in vain.
How did just Pity sweeten thy Controll!
How didst thou strain thy Virtue-propping Soul!
How didst thou wish th' unfinish'd Course to run,
And act, in Will, what Power has left undone!
For this, since Death, Detraction wound thy Fame:
And insolent Reproach corrodes thy Name.
Ungrateful People!———Unrepenting State!
Hast thou, O Queen! *deserv'd* th' ungentle Fate?
 He ceas'd;—Each list'ning Monarch shook his Head!
While she, to whom he spoke, thus answering, said,
O Denmark! wonder not at Ills like those,
Angels if crown'd in England, wou'd have Foes.
Desert, like mine, with living Glories paid,
Can fear no Scandal, when become a Shade.
If ought's left wanting to my People's Prayer,
Mourn not th' unfinish'd Progress of my Care.
When Princes some wish'd Good, in vain, pursue;
By them not done, 'tis left for Heav'n to do!
Let us, in Peace, enjoy our silent Bed,
Truth always triumphs, when she serves the Dead.

The WEDDING-DAY.

By the Same.

'TWas one *May* Morning, when the Clouds undrawn,
 Expos'd, in naked Charms, the waking Dawn;
When Night-fal'n Dews, by Days warm Courtship won,
From reeking Roses climb'd to kiss the Sun;
Nature, new-blossom'd, shed her Odours round;
The Dew-bent Primrose kiss'd the breeze swept Ground:
The watchful Cock has thrice proclaim'd the Day,
And glimm'ring Sunbeams, faintly forc'd their Way:

When

When join'd in Hand, and Heart, to Church we went,
Mutual in Vows, and Prisoners by Consent:
AURELIA's Heart beat high, with mix'd Alarms;
But trembling Beauty glow'd with double Charms.
In her soft Breast a modest Struggle rose,
How she shou'd seem to like the Lot she chose:
A Smile, she thought, wou'd dress her Looks too gay,
A Frowm might seem too sad, and blast the Day.
But while nor This, nor That, her Will cou'd bow,
She walk'd, and look'd, and charm'd, and knew not how!

Our Hands, at length, th' unchanging *Fiat* bound,
And our glad Souls sprung out to greet the Sound.
Joys, meeting Joys, unite, and stronger shine;
For Passion, purify'd, grows half Divine:
AURELIA, thou art mine, I cry'd,——and she
Sigh'd soft—Now, *Damon*, Thou art Lord of me.

But wilt thou, whisper'd she, the Knot now ty'd,
Which only Death's keen Weapon can divide,
Wilt thou, still mindful of thy Raptures past,
Permit the Summer of Love's Hope to last?
Shall not cold Wintry Frosts come on too soon?
Ah, say! What means the World by Honey-Moon?
If we so short a Space our Bliss enjoy,
What Toils does Love for one poor Mouth employ!
Women thus us'd, like Bubbles, blown with Air,
Owe to their outward Charms a Sun-gilt Glare:
Like them, we glitter to the distant Eye,
But, grasp'd like them, we do but weep and die!

Let more, said I, thou shou'd'st profane the Bliss,
I'll seal thy dang'rous Lips, with this close Kiss:
Not thus, the Heav'n of Marriage Hopes blaspheme!
But learn, from me, to speak on this lov'd Theme.
There have been Wedlock Joys of swift decay,
Like Lightning, seen at once, and shot away:
But Theirs were Hopes, which, all unfit to pair,
Like Fire and Powder, kiss'd, and flash'd to Air!
Thy Soul and mine, by mutual Courtship won,
Meet like two mingling Flames, and make but one.

G 3   Union

Union of Hearts, not Hands, does Marriage make;
'Tis Sympathy of Mind keeps Love awake:
Our growing Days Increase of Joy shall know,
And thick-sown Comforts leave no Room for Woe.
Thou, the soft swelling Vine, shall fruitful last,
I, the strong Elm, will prop thy Beauties fast;
Thou shalt strow Sweets, to soften Life's rough Way;
And, when hot Passions my proud Wishes sway,
Thou, like some Breeze, shalt in my Bosom play.
Thou, for Protection, shalt on me depend,
And I, on thee, for a soft, faithful Friend.
I, in AURELIA, shall for ever view,
At once, my Care, my Fear, my Comfort, too!
Thou shalt First Partner in my Pleasures be,
But all my Pains shall, Last, be known to thee.

  AURELIA heard, and view'd me with a Smile,
Which seem'd, at once, to cherish and revile!
O God of Love! she cry'd—What Joys were thine,
If all Life's Race were *Wedding-Days* like mine!

The GNAT.

By the Same.

I.

WHile, in the *Mall*, my CÆLIA shone,
    And drew th' adoring World to gaze,
A wanton *Gnat* came buzzing on,
  To gambol in her Blaze.

II.

Enliven'd by her lucid Beams,
  And urging Bliss too nigh;
Th' attractive Beauty's powerful Streams,
  O'erwhelm'd him in her Eye.

The

III.

The glowing Orb, swift catching Fire,
    Now Heat was mix'd with Light;
The Wings, that durst so high aspire,
    She rubb'd to Dust in Spite.

IV.

Mean while, the clouded Sight shone dim,
    Her Sun thro' Mists appears;
Moist Anguish rose above the Brim,
    And flow'd away in Tears.

V.

O Gnat! too Happy! thus too die!
    My CÆLIA weeps thy Fate;
She kills me, every Day, yet I,
    No Pity can create.

VI.

Mysterious Sex! by Custom led,
    Mere Trifles most to prize!
O Truth, to turn a Lover's Head!
    They Murder *Men*, and weep for *Flies*:

❦❦❦❦❦❦❦❦❦❦ ❦❦❦❦❦ ❦❦

SUSANNAH and the TWO ELDERS.

An Imitation of Chaucer.

By Mr. PRIOR.

FAIR *Susan* did her Wifehode well maintayne,
    Algates assaulted sore by Leachers twayne.
Now, an I read aryghte that auncient Song,
The Paramours were Olde, the Dame was Yong.

Had thilke same Tale in other guise been told,
Had they been Yong (pardie) and she been Olde,
Sweet Jesu! that had been much sorer Tryale;
Full marvaillous, I wot, were such Denyale!

       The

✠✠✠✠✠✠✠✠✠✠✠✠✠✠✠✠✠✠✠✠✠✠✠✠✠✠✠✠

The Same *Attempted in a Modern* Stile.

By Mr. C O B B.

WHEN Fair *Susannah*, in a cool Retreat
    Of shady Arbours shunn'd the sultry Heat,
Two wanton Letchers to her Garden came,
And, rushing furious, seiz'd the trembling Dame;
What Female Strength could do, her Arms perform,
And guarded well the Fort they strove to storm.
The Story's antient, and (if rightly told)
Young was the Lady, but the Lovers Old.
    Had the Reverse been true! had Authors sung,
How that the Dame was old, the Lovers Young!
If she had then the blooming Pair deny'd,
With tempting Youth and Vigour on their Side,
Lord! how the Story would have shock'd my *Creed!*
For that had been a Miracle indeed.

❀❀❀❀❀❀❀❀❀❀ ❀❀❀❀❀❀❀❀❀❀❀❀❀❀

EPITAPH *on* Mr. FENTON, 1730.

By Mr. P O P E.

THE modest Stone, what few vain Marbles can,
    May truly say, here lies an *Honest Man* :
A Poet blest beyond a Poet's Fate,
Whom Heav'n kept Sacred from the Proud and Great.
Foe to loud Praise, and Friend to learned Ease,
Content with Science in the Arms of Peace ;

Calmly

Calmly he look'd on either Life, and *Here*
Saw nothing to regret, nor *There* to fear;
From Nature's temp'rate Feaft rofe fatisfy'd;
Thank'd Heav'n that he had Liv'd, and that he Dy'd.

❀ ❀ ❀ ❀ ❀ ❀ ❀ ❀ : ❀ ❀ ❀ : ❀ ❀ ❀ ❀ ❀ ❀ ❀ ❀ ❀

Tranflations of the following Verfes from
LUCAN.

Viĉtrix Caufa Diis placuit, fed Viĉta CATONI.

DRYDEN.

HEaven, manely with the Conqueror did comply,
But *Cato*, rather than fubmit, wou'd die.

ROSCOMON.

The Gods were pleas'd to chufe the conquering Side,
But *Cato* thought he conquer'd when he dy'd.

STEPNEY.

The Gods and *Cato*, did in this divide,
They chofe the Conquering, he the conquer'd Side.

Dr. LOCKHART.

The Gods efpous'd and crown'd the Victor's Side,
But for the Vanquifh'd *Cato* fought and dy'd.

Mr. CAMPBELL.

The Partial Gods, efpous'd the Victor's Side,
But jufter *Cato* for the Vanquifh'd dy'd.

Mr. ROWE.

Juftly to name the better Caufe were hard,
While greateft Names for either Side declar'd,
Victorious CÆSAR, by the Gods was crown'd,
The Vanquifh'd Party was by *Cato* own'd.

G 5

The PROSPECT.

Written in the *Chiosk* at *Pera*, overlooking *Constantinople*, *Dec.* 26, 1717.

By Lady Mary Wortle Montague.

GIVE me, great God, said I, a little Farm,
  In Summer shady, and in Winter warm :
Where a clear Spring gives Birth unto a Brook ;
By Nature gliding down a mossy Rock ;
Not artfully in Leaden Pipes convey'd,
Or great falling in a forc'd Cascade,
Pure, and unsully'd, winding thro' the Shade.

  All bounteous Heav'n has added to my Pray'r,
A softer Climate, and a purer Air,.
Our frozen Isle ‖ now chilling Winter binds ;
Deform'd by Rains, and rough with blustering Winds ;
The wither'd Woods grown white with hoary Frost,
By driving Storms their verdant beauty lost.
The trembling Birds their leafless Covers shun ;
And seek in distant Climes a warmer Sun :
The Water-Nymphs their silenc'd Urns deplore ;
Ev'n *Thames* benumm'd, a River now no more :
The barren Meadows give no more Delight ;
By gliss'ning Snow made painful to the Sight.

  Here Summer reigns with one eternal Smile ;
Succeeding Harvest bless the happy Soil :
Fair fertile Fields, to which indulgent Heav'n
Has ev'ry Charm of ev'ry Season given :
No killing Cold deforms the beauteous Year ;
The springing Flowers no coming Winter fear :
But, as the Parent-Rose decays and dies,
The Infant-Buds with brighter Colours rise ;
Each with fresh Sweets the Mother-Scent supplies ;
Near them the Violet glows, with Odours blest,
And blooms, in more than *Tyrian*-Purple drest :
The rich Jonquils the Golden Gleam display,
And shine in Glories emulating Day :   Their

‖ *England.*

Their cheareful Groves, their living Leaves retain ;
The Streams still murmur, undefil'd by Rain,
And growing Greens adorn the fruitful Plain :
The warbling Birds uninterrupted sing;
Warm with Enjoyment of perpetual Spring :
Here from my Window, I at once survey
The crowded City, and resounding Sea :
In distant Views see *Asian* Mountains rise,
And lose their snowy Summits in the Skies :
Above these Mountains high *Olympus* tow'rs,
The Parliamental Seat of Heav'nly Powers.

New to the Sight, my ravish'd Eyes admire
Each gilded Crescent, and each antique Spire ;
The Marble Mosques, beneath whose ample Domes
Fierce warlike Sultans sleep in peaceful Tombs :
Those lofty Structures, once the Christian Boast,
Their Names, their Beauties, and their Honours lost :
Those Altars bright, with Gold, with Sculpture grac'd,
By barb'rous Zeal of Savage Foes defac'd :
Sophia alone her ancient Sound retain,
Tho' unbelieving Vows her Shrine profane ;
Where holy Saints have dy'd in sacred Cells,
Where Monarchs pray'd, the frantick *Dervise* dwells.

How art thou fall'n, imperial City, low ?
Where are thy Hopes of *Roman* Glory now ?
Where are thy Palaces by Prelates rais'd ?
Where Priestly Pomp in Purple Lustre blaz'd ?
Where *Græcian* Artists all the Skill display'd ?
Before the happy Sciences decay'd :
So vast, that youthful Knight might there reside ;
So splendid, might content a Patiarch's Pride :
Convents, were Emperors profess'd of old,
The labour'd Pillars that their Triumphs told :
Vain Monuments of Men, that once were Great,
Sunk undistinguish'd in one common Fate :
One little Spot the small Recess contains,
Of *Greek* Nobility, the Poor remains ;
Whose Modern *Helens* shew such pow'rful Charms,
As once engag'd, the warring World in Arms :   Those

Those Names, which Royal Anceſtry can boaſt,.
In mean mechanick Arts obſcurely loſt.
Theſe Eyes a ſecond *Homer* might inſpire;
Fix'd at the Loom, deſtroy their uſeleſs Fire.
Griev'd at a View which ſtrikes upon my Mind;
The ſhort-liv'd Vanity of Human Kind.
In gaudy Objects I indulge my Sight.
And turn, where *Eaſtern* Pomp give, Day Delight.
See the vaſt Train in various Habits dreſt ;
By the bright Scymitar, and ſable Veſt,.
The Vizier proud, diſtinguiſh'd from the Reſt.
Six Slaves, in gay Attire, his Bridle hold ;
His Bridle rich with Gems, his Stirups Gold :
His ſnowy Steed adorn'd with laviſh Pride,
Whole Troops of Soldiers mounted by his Side :
Theſe toſs the plumy Creſt, *Arabian* Courſers guide :
With awful Duty, all decline their Eyes ;
No bellowing Shouts of noiſy Clouds ariſe ;
Silence in ſolemn State, the March attends,
'Till at the dread *Divan*, the ſlow Proceſſion ends.
   Yet not theſe Proſpects all profuſely Gay ;.
The gilded Navy that adorns the Sea ; ;
The riſing City, in Confuſion fair,
Magnificently form'd Irregular,.
(Where Woods and Palaces at once ſurprize ;
Gardens on Gardens, Domes on Domes ariſe,.
And endleſs Beauties tire the wand'ring Eyes :)
So ſooth my Wiſhes, or ſo charm my Mind,
At this Retreat; ſecure from Human Kind :
No Knave's ſucceſsful Craft does Spleen excite,
No Coxcomb's taudry ſplendor ſhocks my Sight :
No Mob-Alarms awake my Female Fear :
No Praiſe my Mind, no Envy hurts my Ear :
Ev'n Fame itſelf can hardly reach me here.
Impertinence, with all her tattling Train,.
Fair ſounding *Flattery*'s delicious Bane :
Cenſorious Folly, noiſy Party-rage,
The Thouſands Tongues with which ſhe muſt engage,
Who dares have Vertue in a Vicious Age! [*Horace*.]

Horace. Book III, Ode III. *Imitated.*

By William Walsh, *Esq;*

Justum & tenacem propositi virum. &c.

THE Man that's resolute and just,
　Firm to his Principles and Trust,
　　Nor Hopes, nor Fears can blind ;
No Passions his Designs controul,
Not Love, the Tyrant of the Soul,
　　Can shake his steady Mind,
Not Parties for Revenge engag'd,
Not Threat'nings of a Court enrag'd,
　　Nor Storms where Fleets despair :
Not Thunder pointed at his Head ;
The shatter'd World may strike him dead,
　　Not touch his Soul with Fear.
From this the *Grecian* Glory rose ;
By this the *Romans* aw'd their Foes :
　　Of this their Poets sing :
These were the Paths their Heroes trod ;
These Acts made *Hercules* a God,
　　And great *Nassau* a King.
Firm on the rolling Deck he stood,
Unmov'd, beheld the breaking Flood,
　　With black'ning Storms combin'd :
Virtue, he cry'd, will force his Way :
The Wind may, for a while, delay,
　　Nor alter our Design.
The Men whom selfish Hopes inflame,
Or Vanity allures to Fame,
　　May be to Fears betray'd :
But here, a Church for Succour flies,
Insulting Law expiring lies,
　　And loudly calls for Aid.

Yes

Yes, *Britons*, yes, with ardent Zeal
I come the wounded Heart to heal,
    The wounded Hand to bind:
See! Tools of arbitray Sway,
And Priests, like Locusts, scout away
    Before the *Western* Wind.
Law shall again her Force resume,
Religion clear'd from Clouds of *Rome*,
    With brighter Rays advance:
The *British* Fleet shall rule the Deep,
The *British* Youth, as rous'd from Sleep,
    Strike Terror into *France*.
Nor shall these Promises of Fate,
Be limited to my short Date,
    When I from Cares withdraw;
Still shall the *British* Scepter stand,
Shall flourish in a Female Hand,
    And to Mankind give Law.
She shall domestick Foes unite;
Monarchs beneath her Flags shall fight,
    Whole Armies drag her Chain:
She shall lost *Italy* restore,
Shall make th' Imperial Eagle soar,
    And give a King to *Spain*.
But know these Promises are given,
These great Rewards, imperial Heaven
    Does on these Terms decree;
That, strictly punishing Mens Faults,
You let their *Consciences and Thoughts*
    Rest absolutely free.
Let no false Politicks confine
In narrow Bounds your vast Design,
    To make Mankind unite;
Nor think it a sufficient Cause,
To punish Men by Penal Laws
    For not Believing right.
Rome, whose blind Zeal destroys Mankind;
Rome's Sons shall your Compassion find,

Who

Who ne'er Compaffion knew :
By nobler Actions theirs condemn ;
For what has been reproach'd in them,
    Can ne'er be prais'd in you.
Thefe Subject fuit not with the Lyre ;
Mufe to what Height doft thou afpire,
    Pretending to rehearfe
The Thoughts of God, and Godlike Kings ?
Ceafe, ceafe to leffen lofty Things,
    By mean ignoble Verfe.

***

Horace. Book IV. Ode V. *Imitated.*

Addreffed to His Grace the Duke of Marlborough,
inftead of Auguftus.

To whom it is dedicated in the Original.

Divis orte bonis, optime Romule.
Cuftos Gentis, &c.

I.

O Born ! when Heav'ns propitious deign'd to fmile,
    Thou beft and braveft Champion of our Ifle !
Too long haft thou been abfent from our Sight,
    Too long unhappy *Britons,* mourn
        Thy flow Return ;
And Senates wait to do their conqu'ring Gen'ral Right.

II.

Return, brave Prince, thofe radiant Beams reftore,
That grac'd thy Country, when thou grac'd its Shore ;
For like the Springs, when thy bright Afpect's feen,
    It on the People darts its Rays,
    And introduces Sun-fhine Days,
And all the Land does fmile, and all the Sky's ferene.

III.

As a fond Mother for her Son complains,
Whom the South-Wind on Foreign Coafts detains,
                                        Beyond

Beyond his wanted and his promis'd Time,
From his dear Home, and her more dear Embrace,
And will not from the Shore avert her Face !
    But upwards sends her Vows and Pray'r's,
    Expensive of her briny Tears,
In Hopes to see him reach his native Clime.
Thus urg'd by faithful Wishes and Desires,
Britain from *Germany* her *Marlborough* requires.

IV.

Safe by thy Presence Oxen plow the Fields,
And *Ceres* with Increase her Blessings yields ;
As every Project to our wish succeeds,
While by thy Influence at Land, and Sea
    From *Gallia's* Naval Threats is free,
And Virtue grows in Fashion from thy virtuous Deeds.

V.

To thee, and to thy chaste Examples due,
No Peer frequents the long-neglected Stew,
That Parents by their Childrens Looks are known,
    That Laws are put in Force,
    And Punishments come on of Course,
When obstinate offenders will those Laws disown.

VI.

Who fears the *French*, or who the grumbling *Scot,*
Or the dark Mischiefs false *Bavarians* Plot ?
Who values the *Hungarian* or the *Swede* ?
    If *Marlb'rough's* free from Harms,
    The World against us is in vain in Arms,
And in his Health alone *Britain's* from Danger freed.

VII.

Be thou but safe, we'll spend our Days,
And undisturb'd will Plants and Flower raise ;
Will lop the Sycamore, and prune the Vine,
    And to our own Freeholds will come,
Mindful of him that gifts us with a Home,
And toast our fam'd Defender's Health by which we dine.

VIII.

To thee our Wishes and our Cups go round,
With many Vows, and many Bumpers crown'd,   While

While we to Royal *Anna*'s join thy Name,
    With the same Rev'rence to thy Praise,
        As *Greece* antient Days,
Shew'd to their *Castor*'s or *Alcides*'s deathless Fame.
                        IX.
O matchless Prince ! for so the Muse requests,
Return, and lengthen our Thanksgiving Feasts ;
Extend them to an endless, Round of Years,
    Or make one Holiday of Time,
        'Till thou celestial Regions climb,
And leave us all disconsolate in Tears,
These are our Day-break Wishes, when athirst we wake,
And these our Sun-set Vows, when we full Bumpers take.

  Tibi summe Rheni Domiter, Parens Orbis,
  Pudice Princeps, gratias agunt urbes   Mart 1. 9.

THE

CABINET of LOVE.

——O passæ Genialia prælia Matres,
Virgineam intactæ Zonam tiscingit Sponæ,
Intrepidesque afflate animos, jam nuda Mariti
Membte Cupidineam fervent intrare Palæstram.
                    Quilket. Callip: Lib. 2.

The DISCOVERY.

TO *Sylvia*'s Room I (unsuspected) stole,
    Unseen by her, I crept into a Hole,
Where I could view the spacious Room all round,
Observe the Nymph, and not by her be found.

                                When

When firſt I enter'd, on the Bed ſhe lay,
Her Face half out, like *Sol* at Break of Day ;
And now, like him, ſhe thinks it Time to riſe ;
As he unclouds, ſo ſhe unveils her Eyes ;
Then by Degrees, ſhe rais'd herſelf upright,
Phœbus himſelf ne'er yet appear'd ſo bright ;
So clear ſhe ſeem'd, did not her ſable Hair
Eclipſe her Eyes, there'd be no looking there.
She naked ſtood, while I with Joy adore
The fineſt Shape I e'er had ſeen before ;
Her little, pretty, panting Bubbies were
As white as Snow, and as the Chryſtal clear.
I ſomething ſaw, which was but thinly hair'd,
It not too buſhy, nor too bald appear'd ;
The Charms of which, I'll from the Reader hide,
For t'was more lovely than I can deſcribe.
The Sight of which ſet all my Blood on Fire,
Made —— foam with over-much Deſire,
And ſwellin ſhew'd he wanted to be nigher.
Oh ! there I thought I could for ever dwell,
Partaking Bliſs beyond what Tongue can tell ;
The Sight would nouriſh me ten thouſand Years,
Give ſolid Joys, which are unmix'd with Fears.
I bleſs'd my Eyes, and would not change my Seat
For all the Pompous Riches of the Great.
She turn'd her round, than ſate upon the Bed ;
Her Lilly Hands pull'd ope her Maidenhead.
She ſtrove to view what I more plain could ſee,
Which rais'd my Paſſion to an Ecſtaſy,
The Sight alone ſoon made me ſhed my ——,
And ſpill that —— of which ſhe ſtood in Need.
Then from the Table ſhe her Garment took,
Where in her Pocket was a Bawdy Book ;
Which ſhe remov'd, and thence drew out a Tool,
Much like to that with which Men Women rule ;
She it apply'd where I'm aſham'd to tell,
And acted what I could have done as well.

Soon from her Womb a flimy Matter fprung ;
Poor —— ftarts, and thinks he fuffers wrong ;
And in Revenge, he now again lets fly,
And fpewing, fell down in an Agony.
With Tranfport he fome little Time lay dead ;
But foon reviving, rais'd his Coral Head.
She now leaves off, and lays the D——— by ;
Then with the Sheet, rubs her *Tu quoque* dry,
And whipes the M———e off her fnowy Thigh.
Thus fhe prepar'd to put her Veftments on,
Which fhade her Body, as a Cloud the Sun.
Some with fine Cloaths do make themfelves more bright,
But fhe fhines faireft in her natu'al Light.
And needs no Colour to fet off her Mein,
Who is all lovely, and of Beauty Queen.
As foon as dreft fhe from the Chamber went ,
And left me fighing in my Tenement :
I then crept out, and to the Bed I ran,
And kifs'd the Pillow that her Cheeks lay on.
I found the D———, which I brought away,
Whilft it was warm with the 'fore mention'd Play ;
And was refolv'd that he no more would prove
Poor —— Rival, who can only move
The Luft of Ladies, and not lay their Love.
'Tis I, faid ——, that muft quench the Fire,
The moft you do, ferves but to raife Defire, :
Thou lifeles, fapflefs, frozen, ftubborn Tool,
Doft think thou can'ft the Hearts of Women rule ?
No one that ever knew the Worth of me,
Will after take up with unjuicy thee.
Thus he infults this ta'en Prifoner,
Like fome ambitious Emperor,
Who has juft ended a fuccefsful War.
I thought it now was time to quit the Reom,
And pafs a Home my humble Captive's Doom.

DILDOIDES.

By Mr. Butler, *Author of* Hudibras.

*Occasioned by Burning a Hogshead of those Com-
modities at Stocks-Market, in the Year 1672.
pursuant to an Act of Parliament made for the
prohibiting of French Goods.*

SUCH a sad Tale prepare to hear,
As claims from either Sex a Tear.
Twelve *Dildoes* meant for the Support
Of aged Lechers of the Court,
Were lately burnt by impious Hand
Of trading Rascals of the Land,
Who envying their curious Frame,
Expos'd these *Priaps* to the Flame.
Oh! barbarous Times! when Deities
Are made themselves a Sacrifice!
Some were compos'd of shining Horns,
More precious than the Unicon's.
Some were of Wax, where ev'ry Vein,
And smallest Fibre, were made plain.
Some were for tender Virgins fit,
Some for the large salacious Slit
Of a rank Lady, tho' so torn,
She hardly feels when Child is born.

Dildo has Nose, but cannot smell,
No Stink can his great Courage quell;

At

At Sight of Plaifter he'll ne'er fail,
Nor faintly afk you what you ail;
Women muft have both Youth and Beauty,
Æ're——, damn'd Rogue, will do his Duty;
And then fometimes he will not ftand too,
Whate'er Gallant or Miftrefs can do.

But I too long have left my Heroes,
Who fell into worfe Hands than *Nero's*;
Twelve of them fhut up in a Box,
Martyrs as true as are in *Fox*,
Were feiz'd upon as Goods forbiden,
Deep, under lawful Traffick, hidden;
When Council grave, of deepeft Beard,
Were call'd for, out of City-Herd.
But fee the Fate of cruel Treachery,
Thofe Goats in Head, but not in Lechery,
Forgetting each his Wife and Daughter,
Condemn'd thefe *Dildoes* to the Slaughter.
Cuckolds with Rage were blinded fo,
They did not their Prefervers know.
One lefs fanatick than the reft,
Stood up, and thus himfelf addrefs'd:

Thefe *Dildoes* may do Harm, I know;
But pray what is it may not fo?
Plenty has often made Men proud,
And above Law advanc'd the Crowd:
Religion's Self has ruin'd Nations,
And caufed vaft Depopulations;
Yet no wife People e'er refus'd it,
'Caufe Knaves and Fools fometimes abus'd it.
Are you afraid, left merry Griggs
Will wear falfe——like Perriwigs;
And being but to fmall ones born,
Will great ones have of Wax and Horn.
Since even that promotes our Gain,
Methinks unjuftly we complain,

If

If Ladies rather chuse to handle
Our Wax in *Dildoe* than in Candle,
Much Good may't do 'em, so they pay for't,
And that the Merchant never stay for't :
For, Neighbours, is't not all one whether
In——or Shoes they wear our Leather?
Whether of Horn they make a Comb,
Or Inſtrument to chaſe the Womb,
Like you, I Monſieur *Dildoe* hate;
But the Invention let's tranſlate.
You treat 'em may like *Turks* and *Jews*,
But I'll have two for my own Uſe.
Priapus was a *Roman* Deity,
And much has been the World's Variety;
I am reſolv'd I'll none provoke,
From th' humble Garlick to the Oak.
He paus'd, another ſtrait ſtept in,
With limber——, and griſly Chin,
And thus did his Harangue begin.

For Soldiers, maim'd by Chance of War,
We artificial Limbs prepare :
Why then ſhould we bear ſo much Spite
To Lechers maim'd in am'rous Fight?
That what the *French* ſend for Relief,
We thus condemn as Witch or Thief?
By *Dildoe*, *Monſieur* ſure intends
For his *French* Pox to make amends;
Dildoe, without the leaſt Diſgrace,
May well ſupply the Lover's Place,
And make our elder Girls ne'er care for't,
Thought't were the Fortune to dance bare-foot.
Lechers, whom Clap or Drink diſable,
Might here have *Dildoes* to their Navel.
Did not a Lady of great Honour
Marry a Footman waiting on her;
When one of theſe timely apply'd,
Had eas'd her Luſt, and ſav'd her Pride,

Safely

Safely her Ladyſhip might have ſpent,
While ſuch Gallants in Pocket went.
Honour itſelf might uſe the Trade,
While——goes in Maſquerade.
Which of us able to prevent is
His Girl from lying with his 'Prentice,
Unleſs we other Means provide
For Nature to be ſatisfy'd?
And what more proper than this Engine,
Which would out-do 'em, ſhould three Men join:
I therefore hold it very fooliſh,
Things ſo convenient to aboliſh;
Which ſhould we burn, Men juſtly may
To that one Act the Ruin lay
Of all that throw themſelves away.

At this, all Parents Hearts began
To melt apace, and not a Man
In all the Aſſembly, but found
Theſe Reaſons ſolid were and found.
Poor Widows then with Voices ſhrill,
And ſhouts of Joy the Hall did fill;
For wicked P——have no Mind to her,
Who has no Money, nor no Jointure.

The one in Haſte broke thro' the Throng,
And cry'd, aloud, are we among,
Heathens or Devils, to let 'ſcape us
The Image of the God *Priapus?*
Green-ſickneſs Girls will ſtrait adore him,
And wicked fall down before him:
From him each ſuperſtitious Huſſy
Will Temples make of *Tuſſy Muſſy,*
Idolatry will fill the Land,
And all true——forget to ſtand.
Curſt be the Wretch, who found theſe Arts
Of loſing us the Womens Hearts;

For will they not henceforth refufe one,
When they have all that they had Ufe on?
Or how fhall I make one to pity me,
Who enjoys Man in his Epitome?
Befides what greater Deviation
From facred Rights of Propagation,
Than turning th' Action of the Pool
Whence we all come, to Ridicule?
The Man that would have Thunder made
With brazen Road, for Courfer made,
In my Mind did not half fo ill do,
As he that found this wicked *Dildo.*
Then let's with common Indignation,
Now caufe a fudden Conflagation
Of all the Inftruments of Lewdnefs;
And, Ladies, take it not for Rudenefs;
For never was fo bafe a Treachery
Contriv'd by Mortals againft Lechery.
Men would kind Husbands feem, and able,
With feigned Luft, and borrow'd Bawble.
Lovers themfelves would drefs their Paffion
In this fantaftick new *French* Fafhion;
And with falfe Heart and Member too,
Rich Widows for Convenience wooe.
But the wife City will take Care,
That Men fhall vend no fuch falfe Ware.

See now th' unftable vulgar Mind
Shook like a Leaf with ev'ry Wind;
No fooner had he fpoke, but all
With a great Rage for Faggots call:
The Reafons which before feem'd good,
Were now no longer underftood.
This laft Speech had the fatal Power
To bring the *Dildoes* lateft Hour.

Priapus

Priapus thus, in Box oppreft,
Burnt, like a *Phœnix* in her Neft;
But this fatal Diff'rence dies,
No *Dildoes* from his Afhes rife.

The DELIGHTS *of* VENUS.

Tranflated from Meurfius.

WHen Nature once, like *Nile*, the——o'erflows,
The clammy Womb, like *Egypt*, fruitful grows;
Octavia now began, juft in her Prime,
To ftain her Linnen with a Monthly Slime.
Juft at Sixteen her Breafts began to heave,
And into Snow-white Semi-Gloves to cleave.
On *Venus* Mount the Hair a Cov'ring made,
To hide Love's Altar with an envious Shade.
Grown ripe, her itching Fancy Pleafure feigns,
Yet fcarce knows what the Titulation means.
All Night fhe thinks on Man, both toils and fweats,
And dreaming——, and——upon the Sheets,
But never knew the more fubftantial Blifs,
And fcarce e'er touch'd a Man, but by a Kifs.
Her Virgin——ne'er knew the Joys of Love,
Beyond what D——, or her Finger gave.
Yet fain would fhe this private Secret know,
From whence and how the mutual Pleafures flow
To Man and Wife. Then from her Bed fhe rofe,
To *Tullia* went, and begg'd her to difclofe

H   The

The Grief she suffer'd on her Bridal Night;
The Charms, the Raptures, and the soft Delight,
That make the larger Amends for all the Pain
Which narrow——Virgins do suſtain.
Tullia conſents, and thus the Tale began.

Tull.] When I came reeking from the Bridal Bed,
Eas'd of that hateful Thing a Maidenhead;
Having juſt taſted Man, juſt newly——,
Finding the Pleaſure ſo ſublime, I cry'd,
And ſaid, How long have I ſupinely laid,
And dreamt, and languiſh'd in a lonely Bed?
Till this laſt bliſsful Night, I've liv'd in vain,
And ne'er enjoy'd that Godlike Creature, Man.
Had I but known the Bliſs, or had I gueſs'd
At the Delights with which I'm now poſſeſs'd,
I had not ſtaid for Marriage, that State-Trick,
But loſt my Reputation for a——.
Let not what I relate diſcourage you,
And all that happen'd, you ſhall truly know.
Callus the Bridegroom, and myſelf the Bride,
Dreſs'd and adorn'd in all the wanton Pride
That Art invents, Youth's Beauty to improve,
And adds freſh Fire to our impatient Love,
Were forc'd, altho' unwilling, to diſpenſe
With Kiſſing, and much more Impertinence.
But when our Friends and Wedding-Gueſts were gone,
And in the Scene of Love we left alone,
Naked I lay, claſp'd in my *Callus*'s Arms,
Dreading, yet longing for his ſweetning Charms;
Two burning Tapers ſpread around their Light,
And chas'd away the Darkneſs of the Night,
When *Callus* from my panting Boſom flew,
And with him from the Bed, the Bed-Cloaths drew.
I to conceal my naked Body try'd,
And what he wiſh'd to ſee, I ſtrove to hide,
But what I held, with Force he pull'd away,
'Till naked as a new born Babe I lay.

I bluſh'd

I blush'd,. but yet my Thoughts were pleas'd to find
Myself so laid, and him I lov'd, so kind,
Struggling I lay, expofed to his Eyes;
He view'd my Breaft, my Belly, and my Thighs,
And ev'ry Part that there adjacent lies.
No Part or Limb, his eager Eyes efcap'd,
Nay my plump B——ks too he faw and clafp'd.
He dally'd thus, thus rais'd the luftful Fire,
'Till Modefty was vanquifh'd by Defire.
I then look'd up, which yet I had not done,
And faw his Body naked as my own
I faw his —— with active Vigour ftrong,
Thick as my Arm, and, 'Faith, almoft as long.
Of cruel Smart I knew I fhould not fail,
Becaufe his——fo large, my —— fo fmall.
He foon perceiv'd my Blufhing and Surprife,
And ftrait my Hand unto his —— did feize;
Which bigger grew, and did more ftiffly ftand,
Feeling the Warmth of my enliv'ning Hand.
Thus far I 've told you of the pleafing Sight;
You know that —— our darling Favourite.
    It is defin'd, a hollow bonelefs Part
Of better Ufe, and nobler than the Heart ;
With Mouth, but without Eyes; it has a Head,
Soft as the Lips, and as the Cherry red ;
The——hang dangling in their hairy——,
From whence proceed the Spring of tickling Floods.
Good —— fhould be both thick as well as tall,
Your F—— D—— are a Size to fmall.
At firft they're hardly in our —— contain'd ;
For Maidenheads are by much Labour gain'd ;
But Men, well furnifh'd with ftout——, are wont
To force their Paffage thro' a bleeding——.
Man's unefteem'd, a hated Monfter made,
When his —— fhort, and can't for Favour plead.
Women do not the Man, but—— wed ;
For Marriage Joys are center'd in the Bed.

Now

Now *Callus* ftrok'd and kifs'd my Milk-white Breaft;
He fell, and faw the Beauties of the reft;
Stroking my Belly down, he did defcend
To the lov'd Place where all his Joys muft end.
He feiz'd my ——, and gently pull'd the Hair;
At that I trembled; there began my Fear.
My foft and yielding Thighs he open fore'd;
And quite into my —— his Finger thruft;
With which he grop'd, and fearch'd my —— all round,
And of a Maid the certain Tokens found.
Then wide as could be ftretch'd, my Thighs he fpread, ⎫
Under my B——ks too a Pillow laid, ⎬
And told me then the faireft Mark was made. ⎭
Then proftrate threw himfelf upon my Breaft,
That groan'd, with fuch unufual Weight oppreft.
My ——plump Lips his Finger drew afide,
And then to enter, but in vain he try'd:
His Body nimbly up and down he mov'd,
Againft my —— his ftiff T—— ftood.
Sharp was the Pain I fuffer'd, yet I bore't,
Refolving not to interrupt the Sport;
When fuddenly I felt the trickling ——
O'erflow my ——, my Belly, and the Bed.
I faw his ——, when *Callus* from me rofe, ⎫
Limber and weak, hang down his fnotty Nofe; ⎬
For when they ——, their Stiffnefs then they lofe. ⎭
But foon my *Callus* fix'd his Launce upright,
Rai'd by my Hand, again prepar'd to fight;
Tho' then within my —— he could not ——, ⎫
Oft times he fwore the Error he would mend, ⎬
And the warm Juice thro' ev'ry Paffage fend. ⎭
About my —— I felt a burning Pain,
Yet long'd with more Succefs to try again.
Callus once more new mounted, to begin,
Gave me his ——, and begg'd I'd put it in.
At firft againft fuch Impudence I rail'd;
But he with moving Arguments prevail'd:

He

He kifs'd and pray'd and would not be deny'd,
And faid —— blind, and needs muft have a Guide.
Where there's no Path, no Track, he runs aftray;
But in a beaten Road can find his Way.
I put it in, and made the Paffage ftretch,
Whilft he pufh'd on, t'enlarge the narrow Breach,
His —— bore forward with fuch Strength and Pow'r,
That 'would have made a—, had there been none before.
When half was in, and but one half remain'd,
I figh'd aloud, and of the Smart complain'd.
As he pufh'd on, the Pain I fharper found,
And drew his Weapon from my bleeding Wound.
Callus is vex'd to lofe his half-won Prize,
And fpews his juicy —— upon my Thighs.
My Hand upon my mangled —— I laid,
To feel the monftrous Wound his —— had made, }
And found my Blood had all befmear'd the Bed. }
Too late I did repent my curfed Fate,
And thus exclaim'd againft a marry'd State.

Are thefe the tempting Joys to wedlock join'd?
Are thefe the Joys that damn half Woman-kind?
Will the God *Hymen* nothing elfe fuffice,
But bleeding Virgins for a Sacrifice?
Men reap the Pleafure, Women all the Pain;
Our Grief's their Sport, they laugh when we complain.
But that a Hufband now muft be obey'd,
I'd always —— myfelf, and die a Maid.
But *Callus* laugh'd, and at my Sorrow fmil'd,
And with a Kifs would fain be reconcil'd;
My deareft Duck, my charming Fair, he cry'd,
(Whilft I in Sighs and Groans aione reply'd.)

Call.] Doft like a Child, for trivial Smart repine? }
In Time our Bodies we with Eafe fhall join; }
Then muft I drudge, while all the Pleafure's thine. }
Virgins can ne'er reap Wounds in *Venus*'s Wars,
But the Blood flows from honourable Scars,
Like the I fuffer, and like thee I bleed;
View my fore —— his tender wounded Head.

When

When, *Tullia*, this prolific Seed you spill'd,
An Infant, e'er begot or born, you kill'd.
Had half this —— within your —— been laid,
'Twould thee a Mother, me a Father made.
Wipe off those Tears, and as a Wife comply;
We'll —— again, and a new Method try.

   Tull:] I knew my Folly justly was reprov'd,
And blush'd, but yet my kind reprover lov'd,
Then submissive did for Pardon look,
And hugg'd him to my Bosom as I spoke.
Forgive the Weakness of a tender Maid,
And still what you Command shall be obey'd.
what Faults my Ignorance commits, forgive,
And I'll no more 'gainst your Endeavours strive.
My nice affected Modesty's subdu'd;
And what you bid, I'll do, tho' ne'er so lewd:
Still will I be consenting to thy Will,
And now get up, my Love, and take your Fill;
If you will try once more, I will comply,
Tho' I to —— do a Martyr die.

   When with a sporting Fondness this I said,
My Hand upon his —— I boldly laid.

   Callus reply'd; *Tullia*, my Soul, my Life!
How dull, how ignorant's a maiden Wife?
Should I return thee to thy Mother's Arms,
E'er fully I've enjoy'd thy Virgin Charms,
She'd call me Bungler, if there's nothing done,
And think me most unfit to be her Son.
Pleasure, when got with Pain, augments our Joys;
But when its got with Ease, too soon it cloys,
Thy kind Assurance premises Success,
Which should I not obtain, you'd love me less.
Untimely Modesty deserveth Blame;
Then since thou art a Novice at the Game,
Yield to my Wish, and do as I advise;
Experiance in this has made me wise.
Then from the Window he an Ointment brought,
Which his too hasty Passion had forgot.

His —— fmelt fweet with what was rubb'd upon't,
Aud feem'd as fitting for my Mouth as ——
As foon as this was done he made me rife,
And place myfelf upon my Hands and Thighs.
My Head down ftooping on the Bed did lie.
But my round B——ks lifted were on high,
Juft like a Cannon plac'd againft the Sky.
My bloody Smock he then turn'd up behind,
As if to —— me he had defign'd :
Then with his fweet and flipp'ry —— drew near,
And vig'roufly he charg'd me in the Rear.
His——, as foon as to my——apply'd,
Up to the Hilt into my——did flide,
He——, and afk'd me if my——was fore ?
Or his——hurt me as it did before ?

I anfwer'd, No, my Dear ; on, do not ceafe ;
But, oh ! do thus, do thus as long as e'er you pleafe.
This Stroke did fully anfwer our Intent,
For at one Inftant both together ——.
Juft as we——, I cry'd, I faint, I die,
And fell down in a blifsful Ecftafy.
Kind *Callus* then drew out his ——, and faid,
There, pretty Fool, you've loft your Maidenhead.

Of all the Joys that to delight are wont,
There's none fo fweet as——in a——.
Each rapt'rous Senfe is fo divinely blefs'd,
As can't by wifeft Mortals be exprefs'd.
I did my Fears and rafh Repentance blame,
And all my former Follies did difclaim :
Tho' all my Body were one bleeding Wound,
Yet ftill the Pleafure is too cheaply found,
For——and——fo mutually do love,
They'll all Obftructions to their Blifs remove :
(When Appetite provokes) the good old Caufe,
A——is then our Liberty and Laws ;
Then if all——down to Hell were hurl'd,
That lufcious darling Sin would damh the World.

Now

H 4

Now *Callus* had his rampant Fury laid,
And limber——hung down his dangling Head.
Since made a *perfect Woman*, ——and I
Arriv'd at such Familiarity.
But languishing poor ——could do no more;
'Tho' not for want of Will, but want of Pow'r.

But *Callus* swore, by all Love's mighty Gods,
He'd reinforce the Vigour of his——.

Then with Confections and a willing Mind,
Once more——was to——inclin'd.
I *Callus* then betwixt my Thighs receiv'd,
And nimbly up and down my B——ks heav'd.
Callus observing well the gamesome Play,
Within—— Lips his standing——did lay,
Then with a lusty Thrust——spew'd
A show'r of——, and all my Womb bedew'd;
I too let fly, and did so much abound
In——, I had almost poor——drown'd.

Weary with Toil, and spent, while *Callus* slept,
I from the Bed into the Chamber stept,
Hoping I should not be by *Callus* miss'd,
I set the Piss Pot to my——and piss'd;
But the salt Water, whilst 'twas trickling down,
Caus'd a sharp Pain I ne'er before had known;
So whilst I sigh'd, and my poor——bewail'd,
And 'gainst the too large——that made it, rail'd,
Callus awak'd; I blush'd, he laugh'd aloud,
To see upon my Thighs such Streams of Blood.
So to conclude, *Callus* no Time did lose,
But——me nine Times well before I rose.

Now, boldly put in Practice what you hear,
And don't the Loss of Reputation fear,
But a good——'fore all Things else prefer.

And since the wanton Tale has rais'd desire,
Go——yourself, and quench the lustful Fire.

Thus *Tullia* did her luscious Story end,
And with new Raptures fill her am'rous Friend.

The

The Fires which she before had long conceal'd,
Now rag'd aloft, and would not be repell'd.
She curs'd herself, that so much Time she'ad spent,
And ne'er knew what delicious——meant.
Tho' she was was to be marry'd the next Day,
She thought 'twas much too long for her to stay ;
And thus to *Tullia* quickly she reply'd,
Have I, dull I, to sixteen Years arriv'd,
And ne'er the Pleasure known of being—— ?
How many glorious Days have I pass'd by,
And ne'er yet tasted this ecstatick Joy ?
'Till now a perfect Ideot I've liv'd,
And seem as from a Lethargy reviv'd.
'Tis true, I've felt before, soft, gentle Fires,
Pin'd with strange Wishes, and unknown Desires.
Oft have I wonder'd why my Blood should rise,
My Spirits flash, and sparkle in my Eyes,
When Man has only kiss'd me by Surprise.
Something it fill'd me with, I can't relate,
And made me languish for I know not what.
But prithee, dearest *Tullia*, now go on,
And finish what you have so well begun ;
Instruct me well in this mysterious Art,
And hide not from me the minutest Part,
The Tale you've told, has raised a furious Flame ;
Is there no Way you can its Fury tame ?
I cannot 'till To-morrow, cannot stay ;
Contrive before, this Lechery to lay,
My Finger I don't like, for that's a foolish Way.
Tullia reply'd, my dear *Octavia*, you,
That I can teach, shall ev'ry Secret know.
Come this Way, I've a pretty Engine here,
Which us'd to ease the Torments of the Fair ;
And next those Joys which *charming Man* can give,
This best a Woman's Passion can relieve.
This D——'tis, with which I oft was wont
T'assivage the raging of my lustful——:

For

H 5

For wher——f vell, and glow with ftrong Defire,
'Tis only——can quench the luftful Fire ;
And when that's wanting, ——muft fupply,
The Place of——upon Neceffity.
Then on your Back lie down upon the Bed,
And lift your Petticoats above your Head ;
I'll fhew you a new Piece of Lechery,
Fer I'll the Man, you fhall the Woman be.
Your thin tranfparent Smock, my dear, remove,
That laft blefs'd Cover to the Scene of Love,
What's this I fee ! you fill me with Surprife,
Your charming Beauties dazzle quite my Eyes !
Gods ! what a Leg is here ! what lovely Thighs !
A Belly too, as polifh'd Iv'ry white,
And then a——would charm an Anchorite !
Oh ! now I wifh I were a Man indeed,
That I might gain thy pretty Maidenhead.
But fince, my Dear, I can't my Wifh obtain,
Let's now proceed t'inftruct you in the Game ;
That Game that brings the moft fubftantial Blifs;
F——of all Games the fweeteft is.
Ope wide your Legs, and throw them round my Back,
And clafp your fnowy Arms about my Neck.
Your B——ks then move nimbly up and down,
Whilft with my Hand I thruft the D——Home.
You'll fell the Titilation by and by ;
Have you no Pleafure yet, no tickling Joy ?
Oh ! yes, yes, now I faint, I die.
Octavia, now, quite fpent, to *Tullia* faid,
O ! what a foolifh ign'rant Thing's a Maid ?
I long impatiently 'till I am led
To that vaft Scene of Blifs, a Genial Bed.
If fimple——can fuch Joys produce,
What muft proceed from Man's prolifick Juice ?
Oh ! that muft pleafe one fure to fuch Excefs,
That no one can its Charms in Words exprefs.

'Tis

'Tis true, my *Tullia*, you have made me wife,
And drawn this Cloud of Ign'rance from my Eyes.
But, Faith, 'tis well I ſhall To-morrow wed,
Or elſe I'm ſure I never could have ſtaid,
But muſt have thrown away that Toy a Maidenhead.
Tullia, then ſmilling, to her Pupil cry'd,
I'm glad I've made you fit to be a Bride ;
Therefore I hope, that when you're in the Act,
You will upon the Pains I've took reflect,
And ſay, To *Tullia* 'tis this Bliſs I owe;
For ſhe to me did firſt the Secrets ſhow,
How 'tis the Pleaſure does from Man to Woman flow.
She taught me firſt the Raptures which proceed
From the Injection of Man's gen'rous——
But now let us, with needful Sleep, awhile
Refreſh our Limbs, tir'd with the pleaſing Toil.
In grateful Slumbers paſs the Night away,
In expectation of the coming Day ;
Which in thy richeſt Pride and Glory dreſs'd,
Shall give thee to the Youth to be poſſeſs'd.
And reap thoſe Joys which cannot be expreſs'd.

Lord ROCHESTER *against his* WHORE-PIPE.

WAS ever Mortal Man lik me,
Continually in Jeopardy,
And always, filly P——, by thee!
  'Tis ftrange you fhould be ftill fo ftout!
Have you forgot the double Clout,
That lately fwath'd your dropping Snout?
  But why fhould I at that admire,
When Ulcers, fill'd with liquid Fire,
Could not from——make thee retire?
  But in thefe hot and rigid Pains,
When Venom runs through all thy Veins,
(The Product of thy tainted Reins)
  Then, even then, thou didft effay
To lead my tim'rous Flefh aftray,
Still pufhing, though you made no Way.
  There's not a Petticoat goes by,
But from my Cod-piece out you fly,
Not to be held 'twixt Hand and Thigh.
  I never felt a foft white Hand,
But *Hector* like you ftrutting ftand,
As if the World you would command.
  Then muft I never reft, 'till fhe
Chafe and fqueeze out my Lechery,
Which is the very Strength of me.
  For all thefe crying Sins of thine,
The fuff'ring Part is always mine,
'Tis I am cramm'd with *Turpentine*.

For my Sake and your own, beware,
Remember that you Mortal are,
And liable to Scald and Scar.

But if audaciously you still
Will——be against my Will,
Know, thus thy Leachery I'll kill.

Cakes of Ice shall wall thee in,
'Till thou appear'st nought else but Skin,
Not like a——, but Chitterlin.

If what I've said will nothing do,
But sniveling——you still pursue,
Loving in Filth and Stench to stew,

My Sentence I'll in Action put,
Which shall so tame thee, not to rut,
That thou shalt rivel like a Gut.

For know, in Snow I'd rather lie,
Than still in *Ætna's* Flames to fry;
Thus——I'd tame thy Lechery.

The Mock SONG.

I Love as well as others do;
   I'm young, not yet deform'd;
My tender Heart, sincere and true,
   Deserves not to be scorn'd.
Why, PHILLIS, then. why will you lie
   With forty Lovers more?
Can I (said she) with Nature vie?
   Alas! I am, alas! I am a Whore.

Were all my Body larded o'er
   With Darts of Love so thick,

That

That you might find in ev'ry Pore
  A well hung ftanding——;
Whilft yet my Eyes alone were free,
  My Heart would never doubt,
In am'rous Rage and Ecftafy
  To wifh thofe Eyes, to wifh thofe Eyes——out.

An INTERLUDE.

Actus I. Scena I.

The Scene, A *Bed-Chamber.*

Enter Tarfandes *and* Swiranthe.

Tarf. FOR ftanding——we kind Nature thank,
  And yet adore thofe——that make 'em lank.
Unhappy Mortals! whofe fublimeft Joy
Preys on itfelf, and does itfelf deftroy.
  Swi. Do not thy——, Nature beft Gift, defpife;
That Girl that made it fall, will make it rife;
Tho' it awhile the am'rous Combat fhun,
And feems from mine into thy Belly run,
Yet 'twill return more vig'rous and more fierce
Than flaming Drunkard, when he's dy'd in *Tierce*;
It but retires, as lofing Gamefters do,
'Till they have rais'd a Stock to play a-new.

Tarf.

Tarf. What Pleafure has a Gamefter, if he knows,
Whene'er he plays, that he muft always lofe?

Swi. What——lofes, 'twere a Pain to keep;
We fay not, that our Nights are loft in Sleep;
What Pleafures we in thofe fôft Wars employ,
We do not wafte, but to the full enjoy.

[*Ex. Tarfander:*

Enter C E L I A.

Cel. Madam, Methinks thofe fleepy Eyes declare,
Too lately you have eas'd a Lover's Care;
I fear you have with Intereft repaid
Thofe eager Thrufts which at your——he made.

Swi. With Force united, my foft Heart he ftorm'd,
Like Age he doated, but like Youth perform'd.
She that alone her Lover can withftand,
Is more than *Woman,* or he lefs than *Man.*

[*Exeunt*

✿✿✿
✿✿

A Pane:

A Panegyrick *upon* CUNDUMS.

O All ye NYMPHS, in lawlefs-Love's Difport
    Affiduous! whofe ever open Arms
Both Day and Night ftand ready to receive.
The fierce Affaults of *Britain*'s am'rous Sons!
Whether with *Golden-Watch* or ftiff *Brocade*
You fhine in Play-houfe or the Drawing-Room
Whores thrice Magnificent! Delight of KINGS,
And *Lords* of goolieft Note; or in mean Stuffs
Ply ev'ry Evening near St. *Clement*'s Pile *,
Or Church of fam'd St. *Dunftan* †, or in Lane,
Or Alley's dark Recefs, or open Street,
Known by white Apron, bart'ring Love with Cft,
Or ftroling Lawyer's Clerk at cheapeft Rate;
Whether of ‡ NEEDHAM's or of ‖ JORDAN's Train,
Hear, and Attend: In CUNDUM's mighty Praife
I fing, for fure 'tis worthy of a Song §.
VENUS affift my Lays, Thou who perfid'ft
In City-Ball or Courtly-Mafquerade,
Goddefs fupream! fole Authrefs of our Loves
Pure and impure! whofe Province 'tis to rule
Not only o'er the chafter Marriage-Bed,
But filthieft Stews, and Houfes of kept Dames!

                         ‡ *To*

---

  * *St.* Clement's *Church in the* Strand.
  † *St.* Dunftan's *Church in* Fleet-ftreet.
  ‡ ‖ *Two. noted Bawds.*
  § Carmina digna Dea, certe eft Dea Carmina digna.
                       OVID.

‡ *To thee I call, and with a friendly Voice,*
Cundum I sing, by Cundum now secure
Boldly the willing Maid, by Fear awhile
Kept virtuous, owns thy Pow'r, and tastes thy Joys
Tumultuous; Joys untasted but for Them.
Unknown big Belly, and the squawling Brat,
Best Guard of Modesty! She Riots now
Thy Vot'ry, in the Fulness of thy Bliss.
" § Happy the Man, who in his Pocket keeps,
" Whether with Green or Scarlet Ribband bound,
" A well made Cundum——He, nor dreads the Ills
" Of *Shankers* or *Cordee*, or *Buboes* Dire!"
Thrice Happy He——(for when in lew'd Embrace
Of Transport-feigning Whore, Creature obscene!
The cold insipid Purchase of a Crown!
Bless'd Chance! Sight seldom seen! and mostly given
By Templar, or Oxonian——Best Support
Of *Drury*, and her starv'd Inhabitants;)
With Cundum arm'd he wages am'rous Fight
Fearless, secure; nor Thought of future Pains
Resembling Prick of Pins and Needle's Point,
E'er checks his Rapture, or disturbs his Joys;
So *AJAX*, *Grecian* Chief, with Seven-fold Shield,
Enormous! brav'd the *Trojan's* fiercest Rage;
While the hot daring Youth, whose giddy Lust
Or Taste too exquisite, in Danger's Spite
Resolves upon *Fruition*, unimpair'd
By intervening Armour, Cundum Hight!
Scarce three Days past, bewails the dear-bought Bliss.
For now tormenting sore with scalding Heat
Of Urine, dread fore-runner of a Clap!
With Eye repentant, he surveys his Shirt
Diversify'd with Spots of yellow Hue,

Sad

---

‡ To thee I call, but with no friendly Voice.
Devil *in* Milton.
§ Allusion *to the* Splendid Shilling.

Sad Symptom of ten thousand Woes to come!
Now no Relief, but from the Surgeon's Hand,
Or Pill-prescribing *Leach** , tremendous Sight
To Youth diseas'd! In Garret high he moans
His wretched Fate, where vex'd with nauseous *Draughts*
And more afflicting *Bolus*, he in Pangs
Unfelt before, curses the dire Result
Of lawless Revelling; from Morn to Eve
By never-ceasing keen *Emeticks* urg'd;
Nor slights he now his Grannum's Sage Advice:
Nor feels he only but in Megrim'd Head,
Head fraught with Horror---Child of Sallow Spleen,
Millions of idle Whims and Fancies dance
Alternate, and perplex his labouring Mind.
What er'st he has been told of sad Mischance
Either in *Pox* or *Clap*, of falling Nose,
Scrap'd Shins, and *Buboes*' Pains, of vile Effect!
All feels the Youth, or fancies that he feels,
Nay, be it but a *Gleet*, or gentlest *Clap*,
His ill-foreboding Fears deny him Rest,
And fancied Poxes vex his tortur'd Bones;
Too late convinc'd of CUNDUM's Sov'reign Use.
Hail, *Manes* of Love-propagating Pimp!
Long since deceas'd, and long by me ador'd;
From whose prolific Brain, by lucky Hit,
Or Inspiration from all gracious Heaven,
First sprang the mighty Secret; Secret to guard
From Poison virulent of unsound Dame.
Hail, happy *Albion*, in whose fruitful Land
The wondrous † Pimp arose, from whose strange Skill
In inmost Nature, thou hast reap'd more Fame,
More solid Glory, than from NEWTON's Toil;
NEWTON who next is *England's* noblest Boast:
If aught I can presage, as *Smyrna* once,

                                 Chios

---

* *An old Word for* Doctor.
† *Colonel* CUNDUM *who invented them; call'd so,
from his Name*.

Chios and *Colophon*, and *Rhodian*-Isle,
Famous for vast *Colos*; and *Argos* fair
And *Salamis*, well known for *Grecian* Fight
With mighty X E R X E S; and the Source of Arts,
High *Athens!* long contended for the Praise
Of H O M E R's Birth Place, blind, egregious Bard !
In after Times so shall with warm Dispute
Europa's rival Cities proudly strive,
Ambitious each of being deem'd the Seat
Where C U N D U M A N U S first drew vital Air.
Too cruel Fate——Partial to human Race——
To us Propitious——But O hard Decree !
Why, why so long in Darksome Womb of Night
Dwelt the profound Arcanum, late reveal'd;
Say I not rather why ye Niggard Stars,
Are not your Blessings given unpall'd, with Ill,
And Love, your greatest Blessing, free from Curse,
Curse of Disease! How many gallant Youths
Havy fallen by the Iron Hand of Death
Untimely, immature; As if, to Love,
Your everlasting Purpose, were a Crime.
But O ye Youths born under happier Stars,
Britannia's chiefest Hope ! upon whose Cheeks
Gay Health sits smiling, and whose nervous Limbs
Sweet Ease, her Offspring fair ! invigorates
Unbrac'd as yet by foul Contagion,
Fav'rites of Fortune ! let th' unhappy Lot
Of others, teach you timely to beware;
That when replete with Love, and spurr'd by Lust,
You seek the *Fair-One* in her Cobweb Haunts,
Or when allur'd by Touch of passing Wench,
Or caught by Simile insidious of the Nymph
Who in Green-Box, at Play-house nightly flaunts,
And fondly call Thee to Love's luscious Feast,
Be cautious, stay awhile, 'till fitly arm'd
With CUNDUM Shield, at * *Rummer* best supply'd,

Or

---

* *Two famous Taverns of Intrigue near* Covent-Garden.

Or never-failing § *Rose*; so may you thrum
Th' exstatic Harlot, and each joyous Night
Crown with fresh Raptures; 'till at last unhurt,
And sated with the Banquet, you retire.

By me forewarn'd thus may you ever tread
Love's pleasing Paths in blest Security.

---

§ *Two famous Taverns of Intrigue near* Covent-Garden.

❀❀❀❀❀❀❀❀❀❀❀❀❀❀❀❀❀❀❀❀❀❀

The Happy Life *of a* Country Parson.

By Dr. S W I F T.

Parson, these things in thy possessing
  Are better than the Bishop's blessing.
A *Wife* that makes conserves; a *Steed*
That carries double when there's need:
October, store, and best *Virginia*,
Tythe-Pig, and mortuary *Guinea*:
Gazettes sent *gratis* down, and frank'd,
For which thy Patron's weekly thank'd:
A large *Concordance*, bound long since:
Sermons to *Charles* the First, when Prince;
A *Chronicle* of ancient standing;
A *Chrysostom* to smooth thy band in.
The *Polyglott*——*three parts*,——my text,
Howbeit——*likewise*——*now to my next*,
Lo here the *Septuagint*——and *Paul*,
To *seem the whole*,——the *close of all*.

He

He that has thefe, may pafs his life,
Drink with the 'Squire and kifs his wife;
On *Sundays* preach, and eat his fill;
And faft on *Fridays*——if he will;
Toaft Church and Queen, explain the News,
Talk with Church-Wardens about the Pews,
Pray heartily for fome new Gift,
And fhake his head at Doctor S——t.

On a LADY *finging* to her Lute.

By Mr. WALLER.

FAir Charmer ceafe, nor make your voice's prize
 A heart refign'd the conqueft of your eyes:
Well might, alas! that threatned veffel fail,
Which winds and lightning both at once affail.
We were too bleft with thefe inchanting lays,
Which muft be heav'nly when an Angel plays:
But killing charms your lover's death contrive,
Left heav'nly mufic fhou'd be heard alive.
Orpheus cou'd charm the trees, but thus a tree,
Taught by your hand, can charm no lefs than he;
A poet made the filent wood purfue,
This vocal wood had drawn the Poet too.

On

❀❀❀❀❀❀❀❀❀❀❀❀❀❀❀❀❀
❀❀❀❀❀❀❀❀❀❀❀❀❀❀❀❀❀

On SILENCE.

By *Lord* Rocheſter.

I.

SIlence! coeval with Eternity;
   Thou wert, e'er Nature's ſelf began to be,
'Twas one vaſt Nothing, all, and all ſlept faſt in thee.

II.

Thine was the ſway, e'er heav'n was form'd, on earth,
E'er fruitful Thought conceiv'd creation's birth,
Or midwife Word gave aid, and ſpoke the infant forth.

III.

Then various elements, againſt thee join'd,
In one more various animal combin'd,
And fram'd the clam'rous race of buſy Human kind.

IV.

The tongue mov'd gently firſt, and ſpeech was low,
'Till wrangling Science taught it noiſe and ſhow,
And wicked Wit aroſe, thy moſt abuſive foe.

V.

But rebel Wit deſerts thee oft' in vain;
Loſt in the maze of words he turns again,
And ſeeks a ſurer ſtate, and courts thy gentle reign.

VI.

Afflicted Senſe thou kindly doſt ſet free,
Oppreſs'd with argumental tyranny,
And routed Reaſon finds a ſafe retreat in thee.

VII.

VII.

With thee in private modeſt Dulneſs lies,
   And in thy boſom lurks in Thought's diſguiſe;
Thou varniſher of Fools, and cheat of all the Wiſe!

VIII.

Yet thy indulgence is by both confeſt;
   Folly by thee lies ſleeping in the breaſt,
And 'tis in thee at laſt that Wiſdom ſeeks for reſt.

IX.

Silence, the knave's repute, the whore's good name,
   The only honour of the wiſhing dame;
The very want of tongue makes thee a kind of Fame.

X.

But could'ſt thou ſeize ſome tongues that now are free,
   How Church and State ſhould be oblig'd to thee?
At Senate, and at Bar, how welcome would'ſt thou be?

XI.

Yet ſpeech ev'n there, ſubmiſſively withdraws
   From rights of ſubjects, and the poor man's cauſe:
Then pompous Silence reigns, and ſtills the noiſy Laws.

XII.

Paſt ſervices of friends, good deeds of foes,
   What Fav'rites gain, and what the Nation owes,
Fly the forgetful world, and in thy arms repoſe.

XIII.

The country wit, religion of the town,
   The courtier's learning, policy o'th' gown,
Are beſt by thee expreſs'd; and ſhine in thee alone.

IV.

The parſon's cant, the lawyer's ſophiſtry,
   Lord's quibble, critic's jeſt; all end in thee,
All reſt in peace at laſt, and ſleep eternally.

F I N I S.